"OMG! Erin's book is chock-full of an abundance of healthy recipes you're going to love incorporating into your life! Sticky Asian Cauliflower Wings, Kickin' Black Pepper Pork Stir-Fry, and Salmon Quinoa Cakes.... SIGN ME UP!"

—Gaby Dalkin, author of
What's Gaby Cooking: Eat What You Want

"Fans of the *Well Plated* blog appreciate Erin's warm, encouraging voice and foolproof, comforting-yet-lightened-up recipes. *The Well Plated Cookbook* is Erin's most thoughtful and thorough recipe collection yet. She ensures that you're never left with a random half-cup of leftover beans and guides you to adjust the recipes to suit your season or pantry. *The Well Plated Cookbook* will become an indispensable resource in your kitchen."

—Kathryne Taylor, author of *Love Real Food*

"Packed to the brim with wholesome recipes and invaluable kitchen tips, *The Well Plated Cookbook* is an essential resource for anyone who wants to put quick, healthy meals on the table and enjoy every bite."

—Jeanine Donofrio, author of *Love and Lemons Every Day*

"This is everyday cooking at its most delicious. Erin's healthy tweaks of classic comfort foods transform them into guilt-free dishes, while her savvy Storage Tips and Market Swaps make this a great cookbook for beginners, as well as seasoned cooks."

—Tracy, Dana, Lori, and Corky Pollan,
New York Times bestselling authors of *Mostly Plants*

THE well plated
COOKBOOK

Avery
an imprint of Penguin Random House
New York

THE well plated COOKBOOK

Fast, Healthy Recipes You'll Want to Eat

ERIN CLARKE

Photography by Becky Hardin

AVERY

an imprint of Penguin Random House LLC
penguinrandomhouse.com

Most Avery books are available at special quantity discounts for bulk
purchase for sales promotions, premiums, fund-raising, and educational
needs. Special books or book excerpts also can be created to fit specific
needs. For details, write SpecialMarkets@penguinrandomhouse.com.

Library of Congress Cataloging-in-Publication Data

Names: Clarke, Erin, author.
Title: The well plated cookbook : fast, healthy recipes you'll want to eat / Erin
Clarke.
Description: New York : Avery, an imprint of Penguin Random House, 2020.
| Includes index.
Identifiers: LCCN 2020001745 (print) | LCCN 2020001746 (ebook) |
ISBN 9780525541165 (hardcover) | ISBN 9780525541172 (ebook)
Subjects: LCSH: Cooking (Natural foods) | LCGFT: Cookbooks.
Classification: LCC TX741 .C5825 2020 (print) | LCC TX741 (ebook) |
DDC 641.3/02—dc23
LC record available at https://lccn.loc.gov/2020001745
LC ebook record available at https://lccn.loc.gov/2020001746
p.   cm.

Printed in Canada
5th Printing

Book design by Ashley Tucker

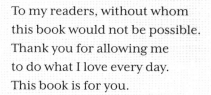

To my readers, without whom
this book would not be possible.
Thank you for allowing me
to do what I love every day.
This book is for you.

Contents

INTRODUCTION

My love affair with food began with a bowl of sweetened whipped cream. Early in my babyhood, my grammy discovered that a few spoonfuls would instantly quiet my fussing—until she stopped feeding me, at which point the tears would flow anew. As soon as I was old enough to hold a mixer, she taught me how to whip cream into soft peaks. From there, I graduated to layering it atop homemade shortcake, and finally to folding it gently into the most perfect, airy chocolate mousse. On the other side of the family, my grandma was busy showing me how to prod and poke at billowy, yeasty dough to determine the moment when it was ready to be shaped into the most ethereal homemade cinnamon rolls. By the time I headed to college, I was a seasoned baker with a deep love of breakfast goodies and desserts.

While my baking skills made me highly sought after in college study groups, once I graduated and began living on my own, I quickly discovered that a diet of scones and snickerdoodles was not as sustainable as I wished. In an effort to "eat healthy" (and to lose a few of the cookie pounds that had settled around my middle), I turned to what I assumed were the pillars of a balanced diet: plain chicken breasts, salads with the dressing ordered on the side, and as little fat as possible. Instead of being a part of the meal that I celebrated, dessert became something I avoided. I lost weight, but I wasn't happy. When a friend commented that I was too thin, I knew something had to change.

I took a hard, honest look at my post-graduate pantry, fridge, and freezer and didn't like what I saw. It was essentially a bizarre collection of premade diet meals and grocery-store discount-bin items. I had single-serving microwave lunches, brightly branded card-board boxes flashing promises of "health," and cans of this-and-that I'd bought on clearance then haphazardly tossed into my cart without any tangible idea of what I'd do with them. Healthy pantry staples and fresh, and even frozen, produce were noticeably absent.

I knew I could do better. I slowly taught myself to ignore the "lessons" I'd learned from magazines and slogans printed on shiny wrappers about which foods were "good" and which were "bad." I stopped purchasing premade lunches and instant oatmeal packets and filled my pantry with basics like brown rice, beans, and spices. I visited farmers markets, checked out cookbooks from the library, and called Grandma and Grammy to ask for their recipes. I realized that in my frenzy to cut the fat, I missed the foods of my childhood, the special recipes that had led me to fall in love with food in the first place.

These days I've found the happy in-between.

Instead of focusing on calories and fat, I've learned to build my meals around a collection of trusted, wholesome ingredients that leave me feeling nourished, inside and out. Rather than avoid my childhood favorites, I'm wild about creating balanced versions of classic comfort foods that swap in more nutritious ingredients. From macaroni and cheese (page 186) to that original chocolate mousse (page 300), these modern makeovers taste every bit as satisfying and scrumptious as their originals and offer bonus servings of vegetables, healthy fats, and whole grains.

Years of long work hours, student loan payments, and the constant effort of growing my blog have also taught me that maintaining a wholesome diet over the long-term requires more than a well-stocked pantry or even a stellar collection of recipes. Even in the best of scenarios, there are nights (and weeks) when meal planning simply does not happen and the refrigerator has more empty shelves than full ones.

This book is for the easy weeks and for the hard ones too. I know that families are busy, budgets are a reality, and kids often don't want to eat their vegetables. That's why, along with a crowd-pleasing collection of lightened-up family favorites like Buffalo Chicken Burgers (page 212) and a slam-dunk Caprese Chicken Skillet (page 133) that you'll make again and again, I've filled this book with clever cooking resources, rapid-fire meals, and flexible techniques for when you have little to no time to cook at all. With busy-day features like 4 Unboring Ways to Use Shredded Chicken (page 154), 4 Things to Do with a Can of Chickpeas (page 162), and Stuffed Sweet Potatoes (5 Ways!) (page 199), you'll be able to enjoy healthy meals on even the most hectic days.

This is a book of nutritious food and useful tips for real life—no gimmicks, hard-to-find ingredients, or *Iron Chef*–level kitchen skills required. I'll never ask you to buy an ingredient you'll use only once, spend hours fussing over a recipe, or trek across town looking for an obscure specialty item.

If there is anything I've learned about maintaining a healthy diet over the long haul, it's that in order to be sustainable, it needs to be practical. That's why you'll find many ingredients repeated and streamlined throughout the book. This is intentional, because I want you to always have what you need in your pantry and not spend money when it isn't necessary. I've even put careful thought into the ingredient amounts so that the recipes avoid awkward, partially-empty containers whenever possible (half-used can of beans, I'm looking at you).

In addition to useful Pro Tips to help you cook the recipes with confidence and success, I've also included ideas to adapt the recipes to different ingredients, called Market Swaps. You can master a single technique, then change it up to suit the season, personal preferences, or whatever leftover vegetables you have lurking in your refrigerator. Once you cook a recipe, I want you to enjoy the maximum reward for your efforts, especially the leftovers! I've given suggestions for storing and reheating leftovers, as well as complete spin-off recipes called Leftover Love that use them.

All of these recipes are special to me because they are not only nourishing and delicious, but at one point or another, I enjoyed them with someone I loved. I hope the stories that I've included alongside the recipes will inspire you to invite others into your kitchen (or take your kitchen on the road, potluck style) to create a well-fed community of your own.

My goal is to share the ways I've learned to cook faster, fresher meals that still feel special. I hope to take some of the mystery and stress away from healthy eating. Most of all, I hope to give you a big, juicy, double-napkin bite of the flavors and ingredients that make this world such a deliciously captivating place to live.

THE FIVES:
TIPS FOR BETTER COOKING
AND HEALTHY LIVING

Volumes have been written about the best ways to better our eating habits, organize our kitchens, and enhance our culinary prowess. As much as I might like, I don't have time to read them all, and I suspect you might not either. Instead of giving you an encyclopedia, here are a few short, simple ways to improve your cooking and add more nutritious foods to your diet.

—

5 Instant Ways to Be a Better Cook:
Easy, Immediate Ways to Improve Your Cooking

1. Toast your nuts. Nuts are one of my favorite ingredients in both cooking and baking. They add texture, warmth, and complexity to almost any dish, but they are also somewhat expensive and high in (good) fat. Make them count! Toasting nuts prior to adding them to a dish richly intensifies their flavor and enhances their crispness. Apply this technique to nuts used for salads, muffins, and quick breads, or try sprinkling a handful over your breakfast cereal for a filling, tasty boost. The only time you shouldn't toast nuts is if they will bake in the oven as part of a coating or a topping (such as on a fruit crisp), as the oven will do the toasting for you while the recipe bakes.

2. Shred your cheese directly from the block. Instead of buying preshredded cheese, spend an extra two minutes shredding your own. I promise it will be worth your time. The texture and flavor of freshly shredded cheese is noticeably superior, especially when melted. Preshredded cheese is often coated with an unappetizing starch-like substance to keep it from clumping, which in addition to being an unnecessary additive, keeps the cheese from reaching its full gooey potential. As a bonus, block cheese is usually less expensive than preshredded. To save even more time, shred entire blocks at once with the grater blade of a food processor, use what you need right away, then refrigerate the rest for use later on.

3. Taste as you go. It's no fun to arrive at the end of a recipe and realize that you should have added more of X at step 2, or Y at step 3.

Taste your food the entire time you cook it to ensure the dish is coming out as it should. (Provided it is safe of course! No sampling the raw chicken, please.) If you are just beginning to cook, this practice is harder because you might not yet know what a dish "should" taste like at any given moment, but persevere! Tasting along the way will help you learn how flavors evolve and tune you in to your own preferences.

4. **Read the recipe.** All the way through. Before you begin cooking. This may be painfully obvious, but I must state it. Reading the recipe from start to finish *before* you begin will prepare you for steps that come in quick succession, alert you to portions that need to be completed in advance (some recipes require overnight resting, for example), and prevent mistakes like forgotten ingredients or missed steps.

5. **Trust your instincts (and taste buds).** Now that I've lectured you to carefully study your recipes, I'm going to remind you that you are still in charge of your meal, and you know your own kitchen and palate best. I'm unfamiliar with the tricky spots in your oven, and the brand of ingredients you use may differ from mine in taste and performance. I can and do, however, provide clear guidance as to what your food should look and smell like along the way.

Recipes are the map and you, the cook, are the driver. Don't be afraid to do a U-turn—or to break the speed limit. Love cinnamon? Add an extra pinch to your Gingerbread Cookie Overnight Oats (page 35). Think those Chocolate-Covered Strawberry Brownies (page 279) smell done? Walk over to the oven and check on them, even if the buzzer hasn't yet sounded. Trust yourself and your intuition, and your taste buds will reward you.

———

5 Healthy Swaps to Make Right Now:
Improve Your Diet Without Adding a Minute to Your Prep Time or Altering the Menu

1. **Use whole wheat pasta in place of regular "white" pasta.** Whole grains are higher in fiber and protein than their white counterparts, so they will keep you full and happy for longer.

2. **Swap in nonfat plain Greek yogurt for sour cream.** High in protein, plain Greek yogurt offers the same tang and creamy mouthfeel as sour cream, without the added fat. Use the same amount of Greek yogurt in baking recipes that call for sour cream or spoon a big dollop over your favorite hearty soups, chilis, and Mexican-inspired dishes.

3. **Trade in white rice for whole grain options.** Instead of serving your stir-fry, soup, or curry with cooked white rice, try a whole grain option. Brown rice is the most direct exchange, but other options, such as farro and quinoa, can add another dimension of texture and a twist in flavor to your meal. Be sure to take note of cooking times and instructions and plan ahead, as whole grains often take longer to cook than their white counterparts.

4. **Replace vegetable oil with unsweetened applesauce or mashed banana.** Trading vegetable oil for unsweetened applesauce is one of the oldest and best healthy-baking tricks. In almost any quick bread, cake, or muffin recipe, you can swap half of the vegetable oil with the same amount of unsweetened applesauce with no noticeable difference in taste or texture. Mashed ripe banana is another excellent, though lesser-used option. Not only does it keep baked goods incredibly soft and tender, but when you make recipes with mashed banana, such as Chocolate Chip Coconut Banana Bread Pudding (page 287), you can add less sugar, since ripe bananas have a sweetness of their own. For a change of pace, try replacing half of the oil or even butter with the same amount of mashed ripe banana in your next quick bread or muffin recipe. You will taste the banana, so be sure that it's a recipe such as a chocolate muffin or berry quick bread that will benefit from the burst of fruity flavor.

Important note: While this swap works well for quick breads and oil-based cakes, it is not the best option for cookies and other recipes where the butter and sugar are creamed together. In those recipes, the butter is also used for texture. Don't worry—this book still has plenty of healthy dessert options for you!

5. Skip the meat (sometimes). Go meatless for dinner at least once a week. You're likely to consume more fruits and vegetables and less saturated fats this way, plus eating less meat has been shown to be kinder to your body and to the environment too. When dishes are as tasty and filling as my Portobello Philly Melts (page 204) and Slow Cooker Golden Coconut Lentil Soup (page 238), no one will wonder where the meat went.

—

5 Ways to Add More Fruits and Veggies to Your Diet:
Squeezing in Five Servings a Day Is Easier Than You Think

1. Fruit first. Give your day a healthy start by having a generous serving of fruit every morning with breakfast (and make sure you are eating breakfast too!). Tip: If you place the fruit on the bottom of your bowl *before* topping it with cereal or yogurt, you are more likely to use a larger portion of fruit.

2. Sneak in some spinach. Making a batch of pasta or a stir-fry? Add a 10-ounce package of thawed and well-drained chopped frozen spinach or stir in several generous handfuls of fresh spinach towards the end. Its mild flavor is nearly imperceptible, and you'll incorporate another vegetable serving into your day without hassle or complaint.

3. Rely on roasted vegetables. Before dinner, spend 10 minutes prepping a pan of roasted vegetables, slip them into the oven, and then forget about them until you are ready to eat. The oven does all the work to make them richly caramelized and borderline addictive, and they are endlessly customizable too (see Every-Night Roasted Vegetables, page 262).

4. Make bulk smoothies. Smoothies are one of the most efficient ways to maximize your fruit and vegetable intake, but some mornings the blender feels like too much of an effort, especially for a single serving. Instead, make one big smoothie batch, then pour it into ice cube trays to make "smoothie cubes."

Whenever you need a healthy breakfast or snack, pop as many cubes as you like into your to-go mug. They take about an hour to thaw, making them ideal for bringing to the office, gym, or on long afternoons running errands.

5. Swap in fruits and veggies at snack time. Think about the times of day when you are most likely to snack, and place a bowl of fruit or vegetables within easy reach, whether it's at your desk while you work or on the counter as you cook dinner. That bunch of grapes or bag of baby carrots isn't going to do you any good if it stays in the fridge—put it in your line of sight and munch away.

—

5 Kitchen Tools I Can't Live Without:
Forget the Fussy Gadgets—These Five Are a Cook's Best Friend

1. Dutch Oven. If our house ever catches fire, I'm ditching my wallet, laptop, and baby pictures and saving the Dutch oven instead. Of all the pieces of cookware I own, my 6-quart enamel Dutch oven is the one I consider the most essential. No matter if I'm making a pot of Cozy Roasted Parsnip Apple Soup (page 231), stirring a velvety sauce for Ultimate Creamy Mac and Cheese (page 186), or browning and braising chicken thighs for Raymonde's Moroccan Lemon Chicken (page 152), my Dutch oven is my weapon of choice. It cooks evenly, moves seamlessly from stove top to oven to table, and is a breeze to clean too.

2. Parchment Paper. Whether I'm roasting vegetables or baking cookies, I almost always line my baking sheets with parchment paper. It prevents sticking, quickens cleanup, and I find that baked goods like cookies brown more evenly when I use parchment paper. You can purchase large, tear-off-style rolls, but I use it so often I order precut sheets, which are readily available online. The extra minutes I save sizing and tearing the roll (and then fighting the poorly torn paper from curling back up on me) are worth it.

3. Fish Spatula. Don't let the name fool you—this long, flexible spatula's uses extend far beyond seafood. Use it to lift a particularly gooey batch of Double Trouble Fudge Cookies (page 270) from the baking sheet, flip a pan of roasted veggies, and top your Sweets 'n' Beets Hash with Avocado (page 23) with a sunny, runny egg. The fish spatula saves the day, every day.

4. Cheese Grater. I'm ferociously committed to shredding my own cheese, and you should be too (see 5 Instant Ways to Be a Better Cook, page 11). Having an easy-to-use and even easier-to-clean grater makes the task instantly attainable. I prefer plane-style graters over box graters. They're faster to wash and make shredding cheese directly over a steaming plate of pasta or crisp salad effortless.

5. One Really Good Chef's Knife. This will be your truest kitchen companion. Treat it with respect, and the two of you will chop many onions, herbs, and bars of chocolate together for years to come.

MY PANTRY STAPLES

Successful cooking begins with what's inside your pantry and behind your refrigerator door. Below are the ingredients you'll always find in my kitchen. Some, like pure maple syrup and kosher salt, are critical to ensure that the recipes you make from this book turn out properly. Others are items I keep on hand to ensure I can pull together a quick, healthy meal on even the busiest of days . . . or bake a fresh batch of The Very Best Oatmeal Chocolate Chip Cookies (page 273) whenever a craving strikes!

Kosher Salt: You will notice that all of my recipes call for kosher salt versus table salt. I find that table salt has a metallic, chemical taste that simply does not belong in food, while kosher salt has a soft, pleasant taste that brings food to life. Also, since the grains of kosher salt are larger, it's easier to control the amount you use. Kosher salt is widely available and sold right beside the table salt, so it is an easy adjustment to make.

Please note that if you decide to use table salt for these recipes, you will need to use less, to keep your food from being too salty, since table salt is ground more finely.

Extra Virgin Olive Oil: This is perhaps the single most used ingredient in my kitchen, aside from kosher salt. I stock two types: a less expensive brand for high-temperature roasting and sautéing, when flavor nuances will be lost to the heat, and a higher-quality, fruity oil for times when I use it as a garnish or in recipes in which it can be tasted and appreciated, like salad dressings.

Be sure to store your olive oils, along with your whole grains, baking flours, nuts, nut butters, and seeds, in a dark, cool place to keep them from going rancid.

Coconut Oil: Melted, cooled coconut oil is an excellent substitute for butter in baking recipes to make them dairy free. I also like to use it in place of canola oil in select baking recipes because I find its flavor to be richer. Fear not—the coconut flavor is incredibly mild when used in the amounts featured in this book. It's a dream for creating the shiniest chocolate coatings and drizzles too. Stir a bit in with your melted chocolate, then use it to make candied pretzels and chocolate-dipped fruit, and to add extra pizzazz to Chocolate-Covered Strawberry Brownies (page 279). Look for coconut oil that is solid at room temperature. I use virgin, unrefined coconut oil.

Plain Greek Yogurt: Oh how I adore this ingredient! Creamy, rich, and high in protein, plain Greek yogurt is one of my most trusted healthy cooking and baking weapons and a go-to snack. The recipes in this book call for nonfat plain Greek yogurt. For snacking, I recommend sticking with plain Greek and sweetening it yourself with honey, maple syrup, or fruit. Flavored yogurts are often packed with sugars and artificial sweeteners. For more about using Greek yogurt in healthy cooking and baking, see 5 Healthy Swaps to Make Right Now (page 12).

Pure Vanilla Extract: Vanilla extract is one of the single most important ingredients in healthy baking, so don't settle for imitation. It gives recipes richness and sweetness without sugar and enhances the flavors of the other ingredients too. Your investment will be rewarded.

Pure Maple Syrup: Pure maple syrup is a wonderful way to sweeten recipes more naturally. Unlike imitation maple syrup, which is made almost exclusively of high-fructose corn syrup and won't react properly in recipes, pure maple syrup is filled with magnificent flavor and offers vitamins and nutrients. I know real maple syrup is a pricier addition to your grocery cart, but as with pure vanilla extract, I promise it is worth it.

Coconut Sugar: With a light caramel-y flavor similar to brown sugar, coconut sugar is minimally processed and even offers vitamins and minerals. You'll find it in the baking aisle or health food section of most major grocery stores.

White Whole Wheat Flour: This is my #1 flour for all baking and the one you will find used almost exclusively throughout this book. It's 100% whole grain and has all the health benefits of regular whole wheat flour but is milled from a finer, lighter variety of wheat that makes it taste mild, like regular all-purpose flour. A variety of brands now offer white whole wheat flour. You can find it in the baking aisle or health food aisle at most grocery stores.

Dark Chocolate: In addition to being one of the great pleasures in life, dark chocolate is high in antioxidants, and some studies go as far as to say it can help lower blood pressure and improve brain function. Dark chocolate is also lower in sugar and more intense in flavor than milk or other sweet chocolates, so you can use less and still feel satisfied. Packages labeled "dark" can vary anywhere from 50% to 99% cocoa solids, which is a wildly large range of sugar content and flavor. For the recipes in this book, I recommend chocolate that is between 58% and 72% dark, depending upon your flavor preference. The higher the percentage, the more intense and the less sweet the chocolate will taste.

Nuts: A handful of nuts can instantly transform even the simplest of recipes. I always have a jar of toasted almonds, walnuts, and pecans on hand for sprinkling over my oatmeal, bowls of breakfast cereal, salads, and even pasta. They make meals more filling and more delicious. For max flavor benefit, be sure that you toast your nuts first (see 5 Instant Ways to Be a Better Cook, page 11).

Nut Butters: Generally, you can find two types of nut butters at the grocery store—the shelf-stable kind, which does not need to be stirred or refrigerated after opening, and the natural or "drippy" kind, which separates at room temperature. You'll also find a third sort that is labeled "natural" yet magically does not need to be refrigerated or stirred. It's confusing!

Your best bet is to look at the ingredients. Truly natural nut butters should contain only ground nuts and salt and will usually separate at room temperature. These nut butters are my favorite for spreading on toast and snacking. Unfortunately, they can be unpredictable in baking. For baking recipes, I prefer to use the natural nut butters that are stable at room temperature. While they do still have some additives (usually palm oil and a bit of molasses), they are a better choice than standard shelf-stable options. Never buy reduced fat nut butters, which typically replace the missing fat with a larger amount of sugar, corn syrup, and other additives.

Whole Grains: Open my pantry and you will find a sundry collection of whole grains. Farro, quinoa, and long grain brown rice are my three favorites. Farro is a delightfully nutty, hearty strain of wheat; quinoa is a quick-cooking, protein- and amino-acid-rich seed; and brown rice is similar to white, with added whole grain benefits. All are higher in protein and fiber than their white counterparts and are delicious added to salads and soups or paired with stir-fries. Make too much? Cooked grains freeze well for later use. You can find farro and quinoa near the rice at most grocery stores; some stores will group it in a special health food aisle too.

Reduced Sodium Canned Beans: One of the greatest bang-for-your-buck healthy ingredients in creation, canned beans—especially white beans such as chickpeas, great Northern, and cannellini, and black beans—are high in protein, fiber, and antioxidants. Add them to pastas, salads, and even scrambled eggs for an instant and inexpensive nutritional boost. Rinse the beans in a mesh sieve under cold water prior to using them to ensure your meals do not become overly salty.

Good-Quality Jarred Tomato Pasta Sauce: While I strive to use minimally processed ingredients whenever I can, I also recognize the value of select store-bought shortcuts. I keep a few jars of tomato-based pasta sauce handy for throwing together quick vegetable pastas during the week, such as Quick Chickpea Pasta (page 163), and I also use it as a timesaver in more comprehensive recipes, such as Better-than-a-Restaurant Baked Cauliflower Parmesan (page 170). Look for sauces that are made from ingredients you can pronounce, are low in sugar, and offer oodles of flavor (roasted garlic is my go-to). Avoid premade creamy sauces like Alfredo or vodka sauce, which are unnecessarily high in added fats. Sprinkle extra Parmesan over your tomato pasta instead.

HOW TO
Use This Book

Throughout this book, you'll find many helpful tips in sidebars and notes alongside the recipes. These tips include everything from the best way to store, reheat, and even repurpose leftovers, to swaps you can make to suit the ingredients you have on hand, to simple Next Level additions that will add new, unexpected dimensions of flavor.

Don't miss the handy **Resources** at the back of the book. **Helpful Recipe Lists** (page 308) groups the recipes into useful categories, such as One-Pan Meals. Last, the **Suggested Menus** (page 311) gives you the perfect mix of dishes to suit a wide range of occasions, from a Birthday Bash, to Game Day, to Last-Minute Dinner Guests.

Whole Wheat Blueberry
Banana Bread, page 42

Good Morning, Sunshine!

Fruit and Honey Scones · Sweets 'n' Beets Hash with Avocado

Ridiculously Addictive Maple Quinoa Granola

Freezer Breakfast Sandwiches (4 Ways!)

Simple, Tasty · Mushroom Bacon Swiss · Garden Veggie · Denver-Style

Cheesy Southwest Breakfast Casserole

The Creamiest Overnight Oats (6 Ways!)

Simple, Perfect · Power PB&J · Lemon Blueberry Crunch

Gingerbread Cookie · Caramel Coconut · Double-Chocolate Mocha

Superhero Smoothie · Cherry Berry Protein Smoothie

Whole Wheat Blueberry Banana Bread · Sunshine Bread

Clean Out the Pantry No-Bake Granola Bars

Lemon Chia Muffins · Every Day Apple-Cinnamon Pancakes

———•————————•———

19

When I was growing up, my father made Saturday morning breakfast an occasion to celebrate. Some of my most cherished memories are of standing beside him on those slow mornings, watching as he carefully folded whipped egg whites into the waffle batter or referenced the crusty pancake page of our cookbook for the umpteenth time, its batter-splattered pages revealing how often he cooked them for his daughters. He never used a mix, and now that I'm the one doing the cooking, I want to keep his quiet dedication alive.

My dad died unexpectedly when I was nineteen, and I miss him every day. Not surprisingly, a time I feel closest to him is when I am cooking weekend breakfast. Whether I'm doling out generous portions of Cheesy Southwest Breakfast Casserole (page 32) for brunch with friends, baking a loaf of Whole Wheat Blueberry Banana Bread (page 42) for my husband, Ben, and myself, or channeling my dad's pancake prowess via Every Day Apple-Cinnamon Pancakes (page 55), making breakfast for someone I love takes me right back to the years when he did the same for my sisters and me.

Since not every day can be Saturday, in addition to the leisurely, PJs-all-day breakfast recipes like my dad used to make, I've included plenty of quick and easy recipes, such as Cherry Berry Protein Smoothie (page 41), and make-ahead options, like Freezer Breakfast Sandwiches (page 28) and The Creamiest Overnight Oats (page 35), to keep you powered all week long.

Fruit and Honey Scones

ACTIVE TIME: 30 minutes · **TOTAL TIME:** 45 minutes · **YIELD:** 12 scones

Whenever I move to a new city, which has been four times in ten years, I have certain matters of Very Important Business to which I immediately attend. At the top of my list? Finding the best scones. Yes, I will eventually need to make a few friends and select my go-to grocery store, but who wants to do any of that on an empty stomach? Scones are the solution. Being armed with this piece of insider information makes the city feel immediately more like home.

Tender and flaky, with craggy tops and melt-in-your-mouth soft centers, these fruit-and-honey-studded scones are inspired by the best scones I've had in any city I've called home, Lazy Jane's Cafe in Madison, Wisconsin. Light and fluffy, these scones can be adapted to any fresh fruit that is in season, and are made from wholesome ingredients. In a pinch, you can omit the fruit entirely and enjoy the honey flavor on its own, or try replacing the fresh fruit with your favorite combination of chopped dried fruit, nuts, or chocolate chips.

6 tablespoons unsalted butter, cold

2 cups white whole wheat flour

1 tablespoon baking powder

⅛ teaspoon baking soda

1 teaspoon ground cinnamon

½ teaspoon kosher salt

¼ cup honey

2 large eggs, cold

¼ cup nonfat plain Greek yogurt, cold

1 teaspoon pure vanilla extract

1 cup fresh fruit of choice, diced into ¼-inch pieces if large

Milk or cream, for brushing

1. Place a rack in the center of your oven and preheat the oven to 375 degrees F. Line a baking sheet with parchment paper or a silicone baking mat. Cut the butter into a small dice and place it in the freezer while you prepare the other ingredients.

2. In a large bowl, whisk together the flour, baking powder, baking soda, cinnamon, and salt. In a separate bowl, whisk together the honey, eggs, Greek yogurt, and vanilla extract until well blended.

3. Remove the butter pieces from the freezer and scatter them over the flour mixture. With a pastry blender or your fingers, work the butter into the flour until the mixture is dry and crumbly and the largest pieces of butter are the size of small peas. Add the fruit (if it's very juicy, blot the excess moisture away with a paper towel first) and with a rubber spatula, gently fold it in.

4. Pour the wet ingredients into the bowl with the dry ingredients. By hand with a wooden spoon or rubber spatula, stir very gently, just until they are combined. The dough will be shaggy and crumbly but should still feel moist to the touch and hold together when lightly pressed. If the dough is crumbly and not holding together, knead it in the bowl a few times, until it comes together and creates a soft dough.

recipe continues

5. Divide the dough in half, then turn the first half out onto a lightly floured work surface. Pat it into a flat, even disk that is 1 inch thick. The disk will be about 5 inches in diameter. With a knife or bench scraper, cut the disk into 6 even wedges. Gently pull the wedges apart and arrange them on the prepared baking sheet, leaving about 1½ inches of space between each. Repeat with the second half of the dough. Lightly brush the tops of the scones with the milk.

6. Bake for 15 to 17 minutes, until the scones are light golden brown, feel dry to the touch, and a toothpick inserted into the center of a scone comes out clean. Transfer immediately to a cooling rack. Enjoy warm.

MAKE-AHEAD & STORAGE TIPS:
Unbaked scones freeze like a dream. Shape and slice the dough into wedges as directed in step 5, then arrange the wedges on the parchment-lined baking sheet. Place the baking sheet in the freezer until the wedges harden, then individually wrap the wedges in plastic and freeze in a ziptop bag. When ready to bake, unwrap the scones and bake directly from frozen, increasing the baking time by a few minutes as needed.

Baked scones are best enjoyed the day they are made but can be individually wrapped and stored at room temperature for 2 days or frozen for up to 1 month. Let thaw overnight in the refrigerator. To reheat, place the scones on a baking sheet and warm in a 350-degree-F oven for 8 to 10 minutes.

NEXT LEVEL:
For a twist, try these delicious flavors and combinations:

- Blueberries + the zest of 1 small lemon (about ¾ teaspoon zest)
- Raspberries + ¼ teaspoon pure almond extract
- Dried cherries + dark chocolate chips

PRO TIP:
Scones can also be made with frozen fruit. Choose a fruit that does not need to be cut into smaller pieces prior to baking, such as blueberries or raspberries, or chop larger fruit, such as peaches or strawberries, before freezing. Add the frozen fruit to the batter (no need to thaw), breaking apart any pieces that have stuck together.

Sweets 'n' Beets Hash with Avocado

ACTIVE TIME: 50 minutes · **TOTAL TIME:** 1 hour 5 minutes · **YIELD:** Serves 4

I assumed that marriage would involve a lot of compromise. What I didn't realize was that most of it would involve the thermostat. In a his/hers battle for indoor climate control, I crank up the heat during the day, while Ben shuts it off at night. By the time we wake up, the house feels like an icebox. A rib-sticking breakfast is in immediate order.

Hash is a quintessential warm-you-up recipe that (unlike the thermostat) receives universal household approval. In this version, sweet potatoes stand in for humdrum standard white potatoes. The beets give the hash a ruby, jewellike appearance that pops beside the vibrant green avocados and makes this dish a bit of a show-off. The play of textures between the wonderful crispy bits that stick to the bottom and sides of the skillet along with the creaminess of the avocados and eggs makes for a particularly satisfying eating experience. A splash of bright balsamic vinegar rounds the flavors and brings every ingredient to life.

This hash leans heavy on the veggies, and reheated leftovers topped with freshly fried eggs make for an exceptionally quick, flavorful meal. I'm as likely to make this hash for Ben and myself during the week as I am for an eager group at weekend brunch.

1½ tablespoons extra virgin olive oil

2 medium-large sweet potatoes (about 1½ pounds), peeled and cut into ⅓-inch dice (about 4½ cups)

2 medium beets (about ⅔ pound), peeled and cut into ¼-inch dice (about 2 cups)

1 teaspoon kosher salt

¼ teaspoon ground black pepper

¼ cup water

1 small yellow onion, cut into ¼-inch dice (about 1 cup)

1 tablespoon balsamic vinegar

¼ teaspoon red pepper flakes, plus additional to taste

4 large eggs

2 medium avocados, sliced

---

1. In a large, high-sided, and heavy-bottomed skillet or Dutch oven with a tight-fitting lid, heat the oil over medium-high heat, swirling the oil to coat the pan. Once hot, add the sweet potatoes, beets, salt, and black pepper. Stir to combine and let cook until the vegetables are barely beginning to soften, about 4 minutes.

2. Carefully add the water (stand back, as it will splash), cover the pan, and reduce the heat to medium low. Let cook until the vegetables become slightly more tender but still maintain a good amount of chew, 5 to 7 minutes, stirring once halfway through. Uncover, increase the heat to medium high, and add the onion. Continue cooking, stirring occasionally, until the vegetables are fork tender and most of the liquid has cooked off, 9 to 11 additional minutes.

3. Add the vinegar and red pepper flakes. Let cook 1 minute. Taste and add additional salt, black pepper, or red pepper flakes as desired.

recipe continues

4. Reduce the heat to medium low. Make 4 wide wells in the hash. Crack 1 egg into a small bowl or liquid measuring cup and carefully pour it into a well. Repeat with the remaining eggs. Cover the pan and let cook until the whites are set and the yolks are as runny or firm as you like, 5 to 7 minutes for a lightly runny yolk, checking every few minutes to ensure the eggs do not overcook.

5. Scoop the hash onto plates, ensuring each serving receives a generous amount of veggies, an egg, and any delicious, crispy bits that have collected on the bottom of the skillet. Top with the avocados. Enjoy immediately, with additional seasoning to taste.

STORAGE TIPS:
Store leftover vegetables in the refrigerator for up to 4 days. Reheat gently in a lightly oiled skillet and top with a freshly poached or fried egg and avocado.

NEXT LEVEL:
• For an extra serving of greens, just before forming the wells for the eggs, stir in a few handfuls of roughly chopped spinach or arugula until it wilts, about 1 minute.

• Begin the recipe by cooking 4 strips of roughly diced bacon in the skillet over medium-low heat until crisp and the fat has cooked out, 12 to 15 minutes. With a slotted spoon, remove the bacon to a paper towel–lined plate. Pat the bacon dry and set aside. Discard all but 1½ tablespoons of the pan drippings. Omit the olive oil and cook the sweet potatoes and beets in the drippings instead. Sprinkle the cooked bacon over the finished hash.

LEFTOVER LOVE:
Sweets 'n' Beets Burritos: Scramble leftover vegetables with eggs, and sprinkle with shredded Havarti, fontina, mozzarella, or similar melty cheese. Serve hot, wrapped inside a warmed whole wheat tortilla with avocado.

Ridiculously Addictive Maple Quinoa Granola

ACTIVE TIME: 20 minutes · **TOTAL TIME:** 1 hour 15 minutes · **YIELD:** 5½ cups

Premade granola, along with overpriced fleece vests and sporty hiking sandals, fits into that chichi retail category of expensive items that make me *feel* wholesome and hip without actually being so. I used to buy pricey bags of it in an effort to be "healthy." The truth is most store-bought granola is laden with added sugars and unnecessary oils.

Making granola yourself is fabulously rewarding. It's simple, money-saving, and gives you control of the ingredients. As this maple quinoa granola proves, it's also *addictive*. This recipe has a blend of tasty textures from the different grains and mix-ins. The quinoa gives it a pleasant crunch, the coconut makes it warm and toasty, and a touch of molasses adds depth and richness. The first time I baked up a pan, I felt like I was conquering the health universe. I couldn't believe how easy it was and how much better it tasted than store-bought granola. You will find yourself making up excuses to pop into the kitchen to "check" on the leftovers again and again.

2⅓ cups old-fashioned oats

½ cup uncooked quinoa

1 cup raw nuts (a mix of whole almonds and pecan halves is my favorite)

½ cup unsweetened shredded coconut

¼ cup chia seeds

2 teaspoons ground cinnamon

½ teaspoon kosher salt

⅓ cup pure maple syrup

3 tablespoons melted coconut oil or canola oil

3 tablespoons unsulphured molasses (not blackstrap)

2 teaspoons pure vanilla extract

1 large egg white

¾ cup mix-ins of choice: chocolate chips, dried fruit (such as cranberries, apricots, cherries, raisins, or figs), chopped if larger than a nickel

1. Place a rack in the center of your oven and preheat to 300 degrees F. Line a large rimmed baking sheet with parchment paper.

2. In a large bowl, stir together the oats, quinoa, nuts, coconut, chia seeds, cinnamon, and salt with a rubber spatula until combined. Pour in the maple syrup, oil, molasses, and vanilla. Stir to coat, until the dry ingredients are evenly moistened.

3. In a small bowl, briskly whisk the egg white with a fork or small whisk until it is foamy. Add it to the granola mixture and stir, doing your best to evenly incorporate the egg white throughout.

4. Carefully pour the granola onto the prepared baking sheet and spread into a single layer, pressing it down with the back of the spatula. Bake for 20 minutes, then remove the granola from the oven. With a large, flexible spatula, carefully flip large sections of the granola over, doing your best to keep them intact. With the back of the spatula, press the granola back into a single layer. Rotate the pan 180 degrees, return it to the oven, then bake for an additional 15 to 20 minutes, until the granola is golden brown, feels almost dry to the touch, and smells irresistible. It will continue to crisp as it cools.

5. Place the baking sheet on a cooling rack. Let the granola cool completely on the sheet (no cheating!), then carefully stir in the mix-ins, breaking up the granola as you do. Enjoy with milk, yogurt, overnight oats (page 35), over ice cream or frozen yogurt, or on its own by the handful.

STORAGE TIPS:
Store the granola in an airtight container at room temperature for 2 weeks or freeze in a ziptop bag for up to 2 months.

MARKET SWAPS:
This granola is filled with tasty possibility. Use any blend of nuts, seeds, chocolate (of course!), and dried fruits that you like. A few of my favorite combinations:

- Almonds and dried blueberries, plus ¼ teaspoon pure almond extract added in with the vanilla extract

- Chocolate chips and dried cherries

- Pistachios and diced dried apricots

- Pepitas and dried cranberries

Freezer Breakfast Sandwiches
(4 Ways!)

ACTIVE TIME: 30 minutes · **TOTAL TIME:** 2 hours

YIELD: 6 sandwiches (plus enough leftover egg scraps to make 3 additional sandwiches or to snack on)

Every fall, Ben and I drive back to our alma mater for a home football game. On the way, we spend a night with his grandparents, then hit the road early to make it to campus before the tailgating begins. Our first pitstop: a certain establishment known for its golden arches and fries. My go-to order: the English muffin breakfast sandwich.

These Freezer Breakfast Sandwiches are the way-better homemade equivalent of that fast-food fave. Making them yourself means that you can control the ingredients and customize them: I've included three of my favorite twists, but feel free to use the base recipe to create your own. These sandwiches are designed to be frozen and reheated fully assembled, so you can enjoy drive-through convenience without the line. Your body and budget will thank you too!

SIMPLE, TASTY BREAKFAST SANDWICH MASTER RECIPE:

10 large eggs

⅔ cup nonfat milk

½ cup nonfat plain Greek yogurt

½ teaspoon kosher salt

½ teaspoon ground black pepper

2 to 3 dashes hot sauce

6 whole wheat English muffins, split

6 thin cheese slices, such as cheddar, Monterey Jack, pepper Jack, or Swiss

6 slices cooked meat (ham, bacon, Canadian bacon, chicken or turkey breakfast sausage patties), optional

VARIATION 1:
Mushroom Bacon Swiss, add:

2 teaspoons extra virgin olive oil

8 ounces sliced cremini (baby bella) mushrooms (about 2½ cups)

VARIATION 2:
Garden Veggie, add:

2 teaspoons extra virgin olive oil

1 cup shredded carrots (about 5 ounces or 2 medium)

3 cups baby spinach (about 3 ounces)

VARIATION 3:
Denver-Style, add:

1 tablespoon extra virgin olive oil

1 small yellow onion, cut into ¼-inch dice (about 1 cup)

1 medium red bell pepper, cut into ¼-inch dice (about 1 cup)

1 medium green bell pepper, cut into ¼-inch dice (about 1 cup)

Simple, Tasty Breakfast Sandwich Master Recipe:

1. Place racks in the upper and lower thirds of your oven and preheat the oven to 375 degrees F. Lightly coat a 9×13-inch baking dish with nonstick spray. Line a large baking sheet with parchment paper.

2. In a large bowl, whisk together the eggs, milk, Greek yogurt, salt, pepper, and hot sauce until combined and mostly smooth. The yogurt may have a few small lumps. Carefully pour the mixture into the prepared baking

recipe continues

dish. Bake in the lower third of the oven for 25 to 30 minutes, until puffed at the edges and a thin, sharp knife inserted into the center comes out clean. The eggs will puff up in the oven, then settle as they cool. Place the pan on a cooling rack and let cool completely.

3. While the eggs cool, arrange the English muffin halves split-sides up on the prepared baking sheet. Place in the upper third of the oven and toast until the English muffins are lightly golden, about 5 minutes. Watch carefully so that they do not burn. If serving the sandwiches immediately, leave the oven heated.

4. With a long, flexible spatula, gently lift the eggs out of the pan and onto a cutting board in one big piece. With a biscuit cutter or drinking glass that is roughly the diameter of your English muffins, cut the eggs into 6 rounds. Save the scraps for snacking, or (if you aren't too particular about the appearance of your filling) piece them together to form

additional sandwiches. If you prefer not to have any scraps and don't mind some extra egg edges peeking out of your English muffins, use a knife to cut the eggs into 6 large rectangles instead.

5. Assemble the sandwiches: Top the bottom half of each English muffin with an egg round, slice of cheese, and slice of meat. To enjoy immediately, place the sandwiches open-faced (without their tops) in the oven for a few minutes, until the cheese is melted, then add the muffin top prior to serving.

6. To freeze: Fully assemble each sandwich and let cool completely, if it is not already. Wrap the whole sandwich in a square of aluminum foil and label with the flavor and date. Place the sandwiches in a ziptop bag. Freeze for up to 2 months.

7. To reheat from frozen: Unwrap a sandwich and place on a paper towel–lined plate (the towel will help absorb some of the moisture).

Garden Veggie

Denver-Style

Mushroom Bacon Swiss

Microwave on medium power for 2 to 4 minutes, depending upon your microwave, until the cheese is melted and the egg is warmed through.

For Mushroom Bacon Swiss:

Begin the recipe by heating the oil in a medium nonstick skillet over medium-high heat. Add the mushrooms and sauté until they are softened and have given up their liquid, 6 to 8 minutes. Set aside to cool. Prepare the master recipe, folding the sautéed mushrooms into the beaten eggs in step 2. Continue with the master recipe as directed. Use Swiss for the cheese and bacon for the meat.

For Garden Veggie:

Begin the recipe by heating the oil in a medium nonstick skillet over medium heat. Add the carrots and sauté until softened, about 4 minutes. Stir in the spinach a few handfuls at a time until it wilts, 1 to 2 minutes. Set aside to cool. Prepare the master recipe, folding the sautéed vegetables into the beaten eggs in step 2. Continue with the master recipe as directed. Use any cheese you enjoy (cheddar and Havarti are my favorites for this version).

For Denver-Style:

Begin the recipe by heating the oil in a medium nonstick skillet over medium heat. Add the onion and red and green bell peppers. Sauté until the vegetables are softened, 7 to 8 minutes. Set aside to cool. Prepare the master recipe, folding the sautéed vegetables into the beaten eggs in step 2. Continue with the master recipe as directed, extending the baking time by a few additional minutes as needed. Use cheddar for the cheese, and ham or Canadian bacon for the meat.

PRO TIP:
If you'd like to make the sandwiches with bacon, you can bake the bacon in the upper third of the oven while the eggs bake in the lower third: Line a rimmed baking sheet with foil, place a cooling rack on top, and lightly coat the rack with nonstick spray. Arrange the bacon on the sheet in a single layer. Bake until it is as crispy as you like, 15 to 20 minutes, depending upon the thickness of your bacon. Carefully transfer the bacon to a paper towel–lined plate and gently pat dry. The more crowded oven may extend the baking time of your eggs, so keep an eye on them and add time as needed.

NEXT LEVEL:
These sandwiches are also delicious with a tablespoon or two of fresh herbs folded into the beaten eggs. I especially love chives with the simple version, thyme with the mushroom bacon Swiss, and dill with the garden veggie version.

Cheesy Southwest Breakfast Casserole

ACTIVE TIME: 40 minutes · **TOTAL TIME:** 8 hours · **YIELD:** 8 servings

I'm not sure when I'll grow too old to expect that my mother will feed me when I'm home for the holidays, but it hasn't happened yet. Every Christmas, my sisters and I, our spouses, and my nieces squeeze into my mom's three-bedroom house and eagerly await her breakfast spread. The menu is designed to feed a hungry hoard and always includes some version of an overnight breakfast casserole. My mom has made dozens over the years, and this recipe is inspired by our favorites. With a Southwest spin, it layers chili-and-cumin-spiced ground turkey, colorful bell peppers, generous handfuls of melty Monterey Jack cheese, and corn tortillas. Assemble the evening before so the tortillas soften overnight—they'll give the casserole a rich, creamy texture reminiscent of an extra-cheesy, super-stuffed tamale. It's devastingly tasty, memorable, and a guaranteed crowd-pleaser. Don't be surprised if your weekend guests request it two mornings in a row.

For the Casserole:

10 large eggs

1 cup nonfat milk

1 cup prepared salsa, plus additional for serving

1½ teaspoons extra virgin olive oil

1 small yellow onion, cut into ¼-inch dice (about 1 cup)

1 pound 93% lean ground turkey

1 medium red bell pepper, cut into ¼-inch dice (about 1 cup)

1 medium green bell pepper, cut into ¼-inch dice (about 1 cup)

2 teaspoons garlic powder

2 teaspoons chili powder

2 teaspoons smoked paprika

1 teaspoon kosher salt

1 teaspoon ground cumin

10 (6-inch) corn tortillas, cut into quarters

2 cups shredded Monterey Jack cheese (about 8 ounces)

For Serving:

Sliced avocado, nonfat plain Greek yogurt, chopped fresh cilantro

Green Enchilada Sauce (page 176), optional

1. Lightly coat a 9×13-inch baking dish with nonstick spray. In a large bowl, whisk together the eggs, milk, and salsa. Set aside.

2. Heat the oil in a large nonstick skillet over medium-high heat. Add the onion and cook until beginning to soften, about 3 minutes. Add the turkey, red and green bell peppers, garlic powder, chili powder, smoked paprika, salt, and cumin. Brown the meat, breaking it into small pieces with a wooden spoon or sturdy spatula, until it is cooked through and no longer pink, about 6 minutes. Remove from the heat.

3. Spoon a heaping 1 cup of the meat mixture into the prepared baking dish and scatter it into an even layer (the bottom of the dish will not be completely covered). Top with half of the tortilla quarters, overlapping the pieces slightly if needed. Next, add half of the remaining meat mixture and one-third of the cheese, spreading each into an even layer. Layer on the remaining tortillas, remaining meat mixture, and the next third of the cheese. Gently pour the egg mixture over the top. Reserve the final one-third portion of the

recipe continues

cheese in the refrigerator for baking. Cover the dish tightly with plastic wrap and refrigerate for at least 6 hours or overnight.

4. When ready to bake: Remove the casserole from the refrigerator and let it stand at room temperature while you preheat the oven. Place a rack in the center of your oven and preheat the oven to 350 degrees F. Tear off a piece of aluminum foil large enough to cover the baking dish and lightly coat one side with nonstick spray. Remove the plastic from the dish, then cover the dish with the sprayed foil, sprayed-side down.

5. Bake the casserole, covered, for 40 minutes. Remove from the oven, uncover, and sprinkle with the reserved cheese. Return to the oven and continue baking, uncovered, until the center of the casserole is set and the cheese is melted, about 20 additional minutes. Let stand 5 minutes. Slice and serve hot with avocado, Greek yogurt, cilantro, enchilada sauce, and additonal salsa as desired.

MAKE-AHEAD & STORAGE TIPS:
Brown the meat and veggies and store in the refrigerator up to 1 day in advance of assembling the casserole.

Refrigerate leftovers for up to 4 days or freeze for up to 3 months. Reheat in a 350-degree-F oven, either from the refrigerator or directly from frozen (no need to thaw first). Cover with foil, then bake until heated through, 20 to 30 minutes (if refrigerated) or 45 minutes (if frozen). Except if freezing in a glass dish (such as Pyrex), the cold dish may shatter if placed directly into a hot oven. To avoid this, you can either thaw the casserole in the refrigerator overnight or let the dish warm up at room temperature first (the dish can be cool but not cold).

For speedier reheating, warm individual servings in the microwave.

The Creamiest Overnight Oats (6 Ways!)

ACTIVE TIME: 10 minutes · **TOTAL TIME:** 8 hours · **YIELD:** 2 servings (easily multiplied)

In keeping with the rest of my life, I came upon the trend of overnight oats approximately two years after it became popular. I've been making up for lost time ever since! Not a week goes by that I don't thank myself for spending a few minutes one evening stirring up a big, multi-serving batch. Overnight oats last all week in the refrigerator, so you can wake up each morning to a homemade, nourishing breakfast that's ready to serve or can be taken with you on the road.

Think of overnight oats as a playground for your breakfast creations. I've given you my favorite master recipe, with fiber-rich chia seeds that plump overnight and make the oats even more thick and filling, plus yummy vanilla extract and maple syrup. I also included five delectable spin-offs. We're as likely to eat a jar of these dreamy oats on a lazy Sunday as to grab them in a hurry on a Monday morning. The Caramel Coconut is an ideal treat for the weekend, the Gingerbread Cookie hits the spot in the cooler months, and I'll happily devour the Double-Chocolate Mocha year-round. Try them all, and you're sure to find a favorite to suit every season and mood.

SIMPLE, PERFECT OVERNIGHT OATS MASTER RECIPE:

⅔ cup old-fashioned oats

1 cup unsweetened almond milk, plus additional to taste

⅓ cup nonfat plain Greek yogurt, plus additional to taste

1 tablespoon chia seeds

2 teaspoons pure maple syrup

½ teaspoon pure vanilla extract

¼ teaspoon ground cinnamon

⅛ teaspoon kosher salt

Toppings of choice: fresh or dried fruit (chopped if large), toasted nuts, chocolate chips, granola, almond butter, or peanut butter

VARIATION 1:
Power PB&J, add:

2 tablespoons creamy peanut butter

2 tablespoons no-sugar-added strawberry jam

1 cup chopped diced fresh strawberries

VARIATION 2:
Lemon Blueberry Crunch, add:

¾ teaspoon lemon zest (from 1 small lemon)

⅔ cup fresh blueberries

4 tablespoons Ridiculously Addictive Maple Quinoa Granola (page 26) or other prepared granola

VARIATION 3:
Gingerbread Cookie, add:

Additional 1½ teaspoons pure maple syrup

Additional ¼ teaspoon ground cinnamon

¼ teaspoon ground ginger

Tiny pinch ground cloves

2 tablespoons dried cranberries

VARIATION 4:
Caramel Coconut, add:

3 Medjool dates, pitted and finely chopped

1 tablespoon creamy almond butter

3 tablespoons toasted unsweetened shredded coconut

VARIATION 5:
Double-Chocolate Mocha, add:

Additional 1½ teaspoons pure maple syrup

2 tablespoons unsweetened cocoa powder

2 teaspoons instant espresso powder

1 tablespoon mini chocolate chips

recipe continues

Simple, Perfect Overnight Oats
Master Recipe:

1. The night before: In a mixing bowl, stir together the oats, almond milk, Greek yogurt, chia seeds, maple syrup, vanilla, cinnamon, and salt. Spoon the mixture into two 8-ounce or larger mason jars or airtight containers, dividing it evenly. For easier transfer, place the oats in a liquid measuring cup with a spout, then slowly pour them into the jars. Add your desired toppings. Do not stir again. If you will be adding berries or other bulky toppings, use jars that are 12 ounces or larger. If you'd like to add fruit that is especially juicy, such as strawberries or peaches, or a topping that tastes best when it is crisp, such as granola, wait to add it until the day you plan to eat the oats. Place in the refrigerator for at least 6 hours or overnight.

2. The next morning (or up to 4 days later): Uncover the oats and stir. Add a little more Greek yogurt if you prefer a thicker consistency, or almond milk for a thinner consistency. Enjoy immediately, right from the jar, or transfer to a serving bowl, adding any extra mix-ins or toppings you like.

For Power PB&J:

Stir the peanut butter in with the other ingredients in step 1, then divide between the jars. Top each serving with 1 tablespoon jam. Do not stir again. Just before serving, swirl in the jam and top each serving with ½ cup strawberries.

For Lemon Blueberry Crunch:

Stir the lemon zest in with the other ingredients in step 1, then divide between the jars. Top each serving with ⅓ cup fresh blueberries. Do not stir again until you are ready to serve. Just before serving, top each serving with 2 tablespoons granola.

For Gingerbread Cookie:

Stir the additional maple syrup, additional cinnamon, ginger, and cloves in with the other ingredients in step 1, then divide between the jars. If you will be enjoying within 1 day, top each serving with 1 tablespoon dried cranberries. Do not stir again until you are ready to serve. If you will be enjoying the oats at a later date, wait to top with the cranberries until the night before or morning of.

For Caramel Coconut:

Stir the dates and almond butter in with the other ingredients in step 1, then divide between the jars. If you will be enjoying within 1 day, top each serving with 1½ tablespoons coconut. Do not stir again until you are ready to serve. If you will be enjoying the oats at a later date, wait to top with the coconut until the night before or morning of.

For Double-Chocolate Mocha:

Stir the additional maple syrup, cocoa powder, and espresso powder in with the other ingredients in step 1, then divide between the jars. If you will be enjoying within 1 day, top each serving with ½ tablespoon mini chocolate chips. Do not stir again until you are ready to serve. If you will be enjoying the oats at a later date, wait to top with the chocolate chips until the night before or morning of.

Superhero Smoothie

ACTIVE TIME: 10 minutes · **TOTAL TIME:** 10 minutes · **YIELD:** One 12-ounce smoothie (without ice)

I have an alter ego. She does yoga at sunrise, eats a healthy breakfast every morning, and folds the laundry immediately after it exits the dryer. Essentially, she is a superhero. Since in real life I wear my yoga pants everywhere except yoga class, I've found an alternative: the Superhero Smoothie. No matter how busy a day I'm facing, starting it with this powerhouse smoothie gives me the boost I need to save the world—or at least fold the laundry.

If you've been shy about green smoothies before, this one will be your gateway. The tropical flavors of the pineapple and banana make it sweet and fruity and the peanut butter is creamy and satisfying. Once everything is blended together, the kale is undetectable. It's a power-packed drink that will leave you feeling super all day long.

2 cups stemmed and roughly chopped curly or lacinato (dinosaur) kale (about 2 stems curly or 4 stems lacinato)

¾ cup unsweetened almond milk, plus additional to taste

1 medium banana (about 8 ounces), cut into slices and frozen (about a generous ½ cup sliced)

½ cup frozen pineapple chunks

1 tablespoon creamy peanut butter

Ice (optional)

Place the ingredients in your blender in the following order: kale, almond milk, banana, pineapple, and peanut butter. Blend until smooth. For a thicker smoothie, add a few ice cubes. For a thinner smoothie, splash in additional almond milk. Sip and take on your day!

MAKE-AHEAD & STORAGE TIPS:
Leftover smoothie (or the second half of a double batch) can be refrigerated in a mason jar or similar container with a tight-fitting lid (the less air in the jar, the better) for up to 1 day. Stir before sipping.

PRO TIP:
This smoothie works best in a high-powered blender. If you don't have a high-powered blender, blend the kale and almond milk together first, then add the remaining ingredients and blend again.

Cherry Berry Protein Smoothie

ACTIVE TIME: 5 minutes · **TOTAL TIME:** 5 minutes · **YIELD:** One 12-ounce smoothie (without ice)

Shortly after college, I entered a serious smoothie phase. On any given day, I could create a rainbow of smoothies that would be the envy of a high-end California gym. I eventually burned out my blender, but fortunately, I discovered this dreamy recipe before the blender met its smoky demise. With Greek yogurt and chia seeds, this blend is sweet, creamy, and reminds me of an old-fashioned milkshake. It's naturally high in protein and will keep you full all morning. Years (and a replacement blender) later, it is still one of my favorites for breakfast or a post-workout reward.

¼ cup unsweetened almond milk, plus additional to taste

1 cup loosely packed baby spinach (about 1 handful)

½ cup nonfat plain Greek yogurt

¾ cup frozen pitted sweet cherries

½ cup frozen blueberries

1 tablespoon creamy almond butter

1 tablespoon chia seeds

¼ teaspoon pure vanilla extract

Ice (optional)

Place the ingredients in a blender in the following order: almond milk, spinach, Greek yogurt, cherries, blueberries, almond butter, chia seeds, and vanilla extract. Puree until smooth. If you'd like a thicker smoothie, add a few ice cubes and blend again. For a thinner smoothie, add a splash of additional almond milk. Enjoy immediately or transfer to a jar with a tight-fitting lid and refrigerate for up to 4 hours.

PRO TIP:
Because this smoothie is thick, for the easiest blending and smoothest results, I recommend a high-powered blender. If you do not have a high-powered blender, start by blending the almond milk, spinach, and yogurt. Once smooth, blend in the cherries. Finally, add the remaining ingredients and blend again. You can also add a splash of extra almond milk or water to help the smoothie combine. If it ends up thinner than you'd like, add a small handful of ice or extra frozen fruit at the end.

NEXT LEVEL:

• For an extra protein punch, add ½ to 1 full scoop of chocolate or vanilla protein powder.

• *Even More Chocolate:* Add chocolate protein powder and 1 to 2 teaspoons unsweetened cocoa powder (a little goes a long way).

Whole Wheat Blueberry Banana Bread

ACTIVE TIME: 20 minutes · **TOTAL TIME:** 1 hour 40 minutes
YIELD: One 4½×8½-inch loaf (8 to 10 slices)

Some women collect shoes. I collect banana bread recipes (Okay, FINE . . . I collect shoes too). This banana bread is the breakfast equivalent of your trustiest, most broken-in pair of boots, your simultaneously cute and comfortable heels, and your go-anywhere classy black flats all rolled into one. It's a true staple that you'll find yourself reaching for again and again.

Of the dozens (hundreds?) of loaves of banana bread I've baked, this Whole Wheat Blueberry Banana Bread is my soul (or should I say *sole*) mate. It's moist and tender with just the right amount of banana flavor. It also happens to be whole grain, naturally sweetened with maple syrup, and swaps most of the oil for Greek yogurt. By the time you are on your third slice, you'll wish you had doubled the recipe. How's that for a perfect fit?

½ cup raw walnut halves

2 tablespoons coconut oil

1½ cups mashed overripe bananas (about 3 extra large or 4 small-medium)

1 large egg, at room temperature

½ cup pure maple syrup or honey

¼ cup nonfat plain Greek yogurt, at room temperature

1½ teaspoons pure vanilla extract

1 teaspoon baking soda

¼ teaspoon ground cinnamon

¼ teaspoon kosher salt

1½ cups white whole wheat flour

1 cup blueberries, divided

1. Place a rack in the center of your oven and preheat the oven to 350 degrees F. Spread the walnuts on an ungreased baking sheet. Place in the oven and toast until the walnuts smell fragrant and are crisp, 8 to 10 minutes. Watch very carefully towards the end of the baking time to ensure they do not burn. Transfer to a cutting board. Let cool a few minutes, then roughly chop and set aside. Leave the oven heated.

2. In a small microwave-safe bowl, microwave the coconut oil for 15 seconds. Continue to microwave in 15-second bursts, just until melted. Set aside and let cool to room temperature. (Alternatively, you can melt the coconut oil in a small saucepan over medium heat.) Lightly coat a 4½×8½-inch loaf pan with nonstick spray.

3. In a large bowl, whisk the bananas with the egg. Whisk in the maple syrup and yogurt until well combined. Last, whisk in the vanilla extract and melted coconut oil. If the coconut oil resolidifies, microwave in 10-second bursts, just until it liquifies. If you do not have a microwave or your bowl is not microwave safe, warm the bowl over a saucepan of simmering water on the stove over medium heat.

4. Sprinkle the baking soda, cinnamon, and salt as evenly over the top as you can. With a rubber spatula or wooden spoon, stir to combine. Sprinkle the flour evenly over the top, then gently and patiently stir it in, just until the flour disappears. The batter will be lumpy and shaggy.

recipe continues

5. Add the toasted walnuts and ¾ cup of the blueberries to the bowl. Gently fold to combine.

6. Scrape the mixture into the prepared pan and smooth the top. Sprinkle the remaining ¼ cup blueberries over the top. Bake for 35 minutes, then check the color of the bread. If it is browning too quickly at the corners, loosely tent the pan with aluminum foil. Continue baking for 25 to 35 additional minutes, until a small, thin knife inserted into the center comes out without any wet batter clinging to it (repeat the test once or twice to be sure it's completely baked). If you aren't sure, you can also insert an instant-read thermometer into the bread's center. Once it registers 200 degrees F, the bread is done. Place the pan on a cooling rack and let the bread cool in the pan for 15 minutes. Remove the bread from the pan and transfer to the rack to finish cooling completely.

STORAGE TIPS:

Store the bread in an airtight container lined with paper towels for up to 2 days at room temperature; 5 days in the refrigerator; or freeze, tightly wrapped, for up to 3 months. I also love to wrap and freeze individual slices, then thaw them one at a time for a quick, healthy homemade breakfast treat. To reheat, let the frozen bread thaw overnight in the refrigerator then reheat gently in the microwave or wrap in foil and warm in a 350-degree-F oven.

NEXT LEVEL:

Bourbon Banana Bread: If you are feeling sassy, omit the blueberries (or swap them for 1 cup of dark chocolate chips) and add 1 tablespoon bourbon along with the vanilla extract.

MARKET SWAPS:

Feel free to swap the blueberries for the same amount of raspberries (fold them into the batter very gently) or your other favorite banana bread mix-ins. Chocolate chips are a well-documented favorite around here, as are dried fruits such as chopped apricots, golden raisins, and cherries, and nuts like pistachios and pecans.

This recipe also works well with frozen blueberries. Add the frozen blueberries to the batter directly without thawing, breaking apart any that have stuck together, then bake as directed. Frozen berries are likely to streak the bread with blue, but your bread will still taste marvelous.

TO MAKE MUFFINS:

Lightly coat a standard 12-cup muffin tin with nonstick spray. Divide the batter among the 12 muffin wells. (I like to use a large scoop for this to make sure the muffins are the same size and bake evenly, and I find this method helps them rise more fully too.) Bake at 375 degrees F for 18 to 22 minutes, until the tops are golden and spring back lightly when touched and a toothpick inserted into the center of a muffin comes out clean. Let cool in the pan for 5 minutes, then gently transfer to a cooling rack to cool completely.

Sunshine Bread

ACTIVE TIME: 30 minutes · **TOTAL TIME:** 1 hour 40 minutes
YIELD: One 4½×8½-inch loaf (8 to 10 slices)

I am unbearably chipper in the morning (well, after a cup of coffee anyway!). The day feels fresh and brimming with contagious possibility. Whether or not you share my AM enthusiasm, you can't help but smile when you take a bite of this bread. Brightly flavored with orange and ginger, this marvelous loaf is an all-around mood booster.

Pineapple and shredded carrots are the secret ingredients that make this bread ultramoist and sweet, without excess sugar or oil. This bread is also whole wheat and generously packed with wholesome ingredients like plump golden raisins and sunflower seeds, so while your first slice might be enough to keep you full, you can feel perfectly justified reaching for your second.

⅓ cup coconut oil

1¾ cups white whole wheat flour

1½ teaspoons baking powder

½ teaspoon baking soda

1½ teaspoons ground cinnamon

1 teaspoon ground ginger

½ teaspoon kosher salt

2 cups peeled and shredded carrots (about 10 ounces or 4 medium)

½ cup golden raisins

¼ cup dry-roasted, unsalted sunflower seeds

2 large eggs, at room temperature

½ cup honey

1½ teaspoons pure vanilla extract

Zest of 2 medium oranges (about 2 tablespoons)

¼ cup freshly squeezed orange juice (from about half of 1 of the oranges above)

1 (8-ounce) can crushed pineapple in 100% juice

1. Place a rack in the center of your oven and preheat the oven to 325 degrees F. Lightly coat a 4½×8½-inch loaf pan with nonstick spray. Set aside.

2. In a medium microwave-safe bowl, microwave the coconut oil for 30 seconds. Continue to microwave in 15-second bursts, just until melted. (Alternatively, you can melt the coconut oil in a medium bowl set over a saucepan of simmering water on the stove over medium heat.) Set aside and let cool to room temperature.

3. In a large bowl, whisk together the flour, baking powder, baking soda, cinnamon, ginger, and salt. Fold in the carrots, golden raisins, and sunflower seeds until evenly incorporated.

4. To the bowl with the coconut oil, add the eggs, honey, vanilla, orange zest, and orange juice. Whisk until smoothly combined. If the coconut oil resolidifies, microwave in 10-second bursts, just until it liquifies. If you do not have a microwave or your bowl is not microwave safe, warm the bowl over a saucepan of simmering water on the stove over medium heat.

5. Drain off as much excess liquid from the pineapple as possible, then whisk it into the wet ingredients.

6. Make a well in the center of the dry ingredients, then pour the wet ingredients into the center. By hand with a spatula

recipe continues

or wooden spoon, stir gently, folding the ingredients together just until combined and the flour disappears. The batter will be thick and shaggy.

7. Scrape the batter into the prepared pan and smooth the top. Bake for 30 minutes, then loosely tent the bread with aluminum foil to keep it from turning too brown (this is the honey caramelizing in the oven). Continue baking for 35 to 45 additional minutes, until a thin, sharp knife inserted into the very center comes out clean (repeat the test once or twice to ensure the bread is thoroughly baked and no batter clings). The moisture content of your carrots and pineapple will affect the baking time, so check the bread several minutes early and don't be afraid to let it bake longer if needed. If you aren't sure, you can also insert an instant-read thermometer into the bread's center. Once it registers 200 degrees F, the bread is done.

8. Place the pan on a cooling rack and let cool for 5 minutes. Run a knife along the edges of the bread to loosen it from the pan if needed, then gently remove the loaf from the pan and let cool on the rack completely. Use a large, sharp knife to cut into thick slices. Taste the sunshine!

STORAGE TIPS:

Store the bread in an airtight container lined with paper towels at room temperature for 2 days, in the refrigerator for 4 days, or freeze, tightly wrapped, for up to 3 months. Let thaw overnight in the refrigerator.

For quick grab-and-go breakfasts, I like to wrap and freeze individual slices. I pull one out of the freezer the night before, then in the morning, a fresh, homemade breakfast awaits.

PRO TIP:

Make the most of your citrus: Zesting citrus releases flavor-packed oils. To make sure those precious oils don't go to waste, zest the orange directly into your mixing bowl instead of onto a cutting board, where the oils can be lost.

MARKET SWAPS:

- For a nutty twist, swap the sunflower seeds for ⅓ cup chopped toasted walnuts or pecans.
- For a tropical twist, replace the sunflower seeds with ⅓ cup unsweetened shredded coconut.
- Though carrot is my favorite, you can also make this bread with grated apple, zucchini, or even a combination. If using grated zucchini, prior to adding it to the batter, squeeze it between several layers of paper towels to remove as much excess moisture as possible. Whichever option you choose, do not omit the pineapple. It's necessary for both moisture and sweetness.

Clean Out the Pantry
No-Bake Granola Bars

ACTIVE TIME: 25 minutes · **TOTAL TIME:** 2 hours 45 minutes

YIELD: One 8×8-inch pan (about 12 bars)

Meet my favorite way to tidy up the odd bits of nuts, dried fruit, and seeds that love to collect in the back of my pantry. With little beyond peanut butter, honey, and a wooden spoon, you can turn the hodgepodge in your cupboard into this filling, nutrient-rich breakfast and snack that will have you hooked at first bite. I've included my favorite blend of ingredients below, but feel free to swap them out for the same amount of your own pantry scraps. If the dough seems too sticky, a few more tablespoons of oats will do the trick. Too dry? A small spoonful of nut butter will fix it right up. I recommend storing these in the refrigerator. On-the-record reason: They will soften at room temperature because they do not contain preservatives like store-bought bars and are no-bake. Off-the-record reason: Without the additional barrier of the refrigerator door separating the bars and me, I'd polish off the pan before lunch.

1¼ cups old-fashioned oats, plus additional as needed

⅓ cup chopped mixed raw nuts and seeds of choice, such as almonds, pecans, sunflower seeds, or pepitas

¼ cup chia seeds

¼ cup uncooked quinoa

¼ cup ground flaxseed meal

½ cup honey

½ cup creamy peanut butter or nut butter of choice, plus additional as needed

1 teaspoon pure vanilla extract

½ teaspoon ground cinnamon

¼ teaspoon kosher salt

¼ cup mixed dried cranberries, dried cherries, or other dried fruit of choice, chopped if larger than a nickel

¼ cup dark chocolate chips

1. Place a rack in the center of your oven and preheat the oven to 350 degrees F. Spread the oats, mixed nuts and seeds, chia seeds, quinoa, and flaxseed onto a large, ungreased rimmed baking sheet. Bake until slightly toasted and fragrant, 8 to 10 minutes. Transfer to a large mixing bowl. Turn the oven off.

2. Line an 8×8-inch baking pan with parchment paper, leaving a few inches of overhang on two opposite sides like handles. Generously coat with nonstick spray. Set aside.

3. In a microwave-safe bowl or small saucepan, combine the honey and peanut butter. If microwaving, microwave on high for 30 seconds, then stir. Continue heating in

15-second bursts, stirring until the mixture is thin and smoothly combined. If using a saucepan, warm gently over medium heat and stir. Do not let the mixture boil. Remove from the heat. Stir in the vanilla extract, cinnamon, and salt. Let cool for 10 minutes.

4. Pour the peanut butter mixture over the top of the oat mixture. Add the dried fruit and chocolate chips, then stir until the ingredients are evenly moistened. At this point, judge the consistency of the dough. Depending upon your mix-ins and your brand of nut butter, you may need more liquid or more dry ingredients. The dough should be soft and moldable, and it should hold together when

recipe continues

pressed and not be overly sticky or crumbly. If it seems too wet, add a few more oats. If it's too dry, add a little more nut butter and/or honey.

5. Scoop the mixture into the parchment-lined baking pan. With a spatula or your fingers, press it into an even layer. If the mixture sticks to your fingers, place a sheet of plastic wrap over the top to act as a barrier, then press on the plastic wrap's surface instead.

6. Place the pan in the refrigerator to set for at least 2 hours or overnight. Once fully chilled, lift the mixture from the pan using the parchment "handles" and place on a cutting board. With a very sharp knife, slice into bars of desired size. Enjoy immediately or store in the refrigerator or freezer for later.

STORAGE TIPS:
Refrigerate leftovers for up to 1 week or freeze for up to 3 months.

I like to wrap and freeze individual bars, then pull them out of the freezer on demand.

Lemon Chia Muffins

ACTIVE TIME: 20 minutes · **TOTAL TIME:** 35 minutes · **YIELD:** 12 muffins

These Lemon Chia Muffins are light and springy, pleasantly plump, and make me want to settle into a porch swing with a cup of tea. Protein- and fiber-rich chia seeds stand in for traditional poppy seeds, the lemon glaze gives the muffins a happy burst of sweetness and citrus, and almond extract adds a memorable touch. I love these bright, filling muffins as much for breakfast as I do for a healthy snack. They don't take long to whip up, are appropriate for both peaceful moments alone and for rushing from one errand to the next, and are equal parts nourishing and delectable.

For the Muffins:

4 tablespoons unsalted butter

1 cup white whole wheat flour

1 cup all-purpose flour

1 teaspoon baking powder

¼ teaspoon baking soda

½ teaspoon kosher salt

½ cup honey

⅔ cup nonfat plain Greek yogurt, at room temperature

2 large eggs, at room temperature

2 teaspoons lemon zest (from about 2 medium lemons)

¼ cup freshly squeezed lemon juice (from about 1 of the lemons above)

1 teaspoon pure vanilla extract

⅛ teaspoon pure almond extract

2 tablespoons chia seeds

For the Lemon Glaze:

½ cup powdered sugar, plus additional to taste

1 tablespoon freshly squeezed lemon juice, plus additional to taste

1. Place a rack in the center of your oven and preheat the oven to 350 degrees F. Lightly coat a standard 12-cup muffin pan with nonstick spray.

2. Cut the butter into a few pieces and place in a medium microwave-safe bowl. Heat in the microwave for 30 seconds, then continue heating in 15-second bursts, just until it melts. Set aside to cool. (Alternatively, you can melt the butter in a heatproof bowl placed over a large saucepan of simmering water.)

3. In a large mixing bowl, whisk together the white whole wheat flour, all-purpose flour, baking powder, baking soda, and salt.

4. To the bowl with the butter, add the honey and whisk to combine. Add the Greek yogurt, eggs, lemon zest, lemon juice, vanilla extract, and almond extract and whisk until smooth. If the butter resolidifies, microwave in 10-second bursts, just until it liquifies. If you do not have a microwave or your bowl is not microwave safe, warm the bowl over a saucepan of simmering water on the stove over medium heat.

5. Make a well in the center of the dry ingredients. Pour the wet ingredients into the well, then with a wooden spoon or spatula, gently stir to combine, stopping as soon as the flour disappears. Fold in the chia seeds. The batter will be thick.

recipe continues

6. Scoop the batter into the 12 muffin wells, dividing evenly (they will be about three-fourths of the way full). Bake for 18 to 22 minutes, until barely golden, a toothpick inserted into the center of a muffin comes out clean, and the tops spring back lightly when touched. Set the pan on a cooling rack and let the muffins cool in the pan for 5 minutes. With a dull knife, gently loosen the muffins, then carefully transfer them to the rack to finish cooling completely.

7. While the muffins cool, prepare the glaze: Whisk together the powdered sugar and lemon juice. If you desire a thinner glaze, add more lemon juice 1 teaspoon at a time; for a thicker glaze, add additional powdered sugar. Drizzle over the cooled muffins.

STORAGE TIPS:
Store muffins in an airtight container lined with paper towels at room temperature for up to 3 days, or tightly wrap each muffin in plastic, transfer to a ziptop bag, and freeze for up to 3 months. Let thaw overnight in the refrigerator.

PRO TIP:
This recipe yields enough glaze for a light drizzle, which for me is the perfect amount of sweetness. If you'd like a more generous glaze, combine ¾ cup powdered sugar, 1 tablespoon lemon juice, and 1 to 2 teaspoons milk.

NEXT LEVEL:
For super-duper-lemony muffins, add ½ teaspoon pure lemon extract when you add the other extracts.

MARKET SWAPS:
Try this recipe with orange zest and orange juice in place of the lemon.

Every Day Apple-Cinnamon Pancakes

ACTIVE TIME: 45 minutes · **TOTAL TIME:** 45 minutes · **YIELD:** Twelve 4-inch pancakes

I grew up in a pancake house. Well, it was a pancake house, a waffle house, and a bacon house, but pancakes were the reigning favorite. More than any other breakfast dish, they fill my heart with tender memories of weekend mornings spent cooking with my dad.

These apple-and-cinnamon-studded pancakes taste weekend special, but the easy-going batter, which is made entirely in the blender, is simple enough for a productive weekday. Little kitchen helpers can assist with the cooking, and you'll have fewer dishes to wash in the end.

In place of flour, these pancakes use oats, which lend a warm, homey flavor that is such a natural pairing with the apple, you'll wonder why you haven't been making pancakes this way all along. It does take some patience to cook them, but I promise that your low-and-slow technique will be rewarded. These pancakes can also be easily frozen and reheated, so before you wash your blender, consider making an extra batch to stow away for a future morning. Every day is the right day for these sweet cinnamon pancakes!

---

2 tablespoons unsalted butter

¾ cup nonfat plain Greek yogurt

½ cup nonfat milk

1¾ cups old-fashioned oats

2 large eggs

2 tablespoons pure maple syrup

1 teaspoon pure vanilla extract

¾ teaspoon ground cinnamon

1 tablespoon baking powder

½ teaspoon kosher salt

1 cup shredded crisp-tart apple, such as Honeycrisp or Fuji (about 1 large or 2 small)

½ cup chopped toasted pecans or ⅓ cup dried cranberries (optional)

For serving: pure maple syrup, additional chopped pecans, peanut butter or almond butter, Warm Cinnamon Sautéed Apple Topping (see Next Level)

---

1. If you'd like to keep the pancakes warm between batches, place a rack in the center of your oven and preheat the oven to 200 degrees F.

2. In a small microwave-safe bowl, microwave the butter for 15 seconds. Continue to microwave in 15-second bursts, just until melted. Set aside and let cool to room temperature.

3. Place the Greek yogurt, milk, oats, eggs, maple syrup, vanilla, cinnamon, baking powder, salt, and melted, cooled butter in a blender. Blend until the batter is very smooth, stopping to scrape down the sides of the blender a few times. Depending upon your blender, this will take a few minutes. Continue blending until you don't see any remaining bits of oats, and the batter is creamy. Stop the blender, then stir in the apple and the pecans or cranberries, if using. Do not blend again.

4. Heat a large nonstick skillet or griddle over medium-low heat. Unless the manufacturer of your pan directs otherwise, lightly coat the surface of the pan with nonstick spray (some nonstick pans and griddles may not need it).

recipe continues

5. Once the skillet is heated, drop the batter by ¼ cupfuls into the pan and, with the flat bottom of your measuring cup or the back of a spoon, spread the pancakes to be ½ inch thick. Let cook slowly for 3 to 4 minutes on the first side, until the edges look dry and small bubbles appear on top. Gently flip (the underside should be golden) and continue cooking on the other side for 1 to 2 additional minutes, until golden. Adjust the heat as needed between batches. If your pancakes are turning golden before they are cooked through, reduce the heat of your skillet accordingly; if they don't seem to be cooking through at all and you've gone a few minutes over the cook time, increase the temperature a little. Repeat with the remaining batter.

6. Serve the pancakes immediately or place on a baking sheet and keep warm in the oven. Add your favorite toppings and enjoy.

STORAGE TIPS:

To freeze, lay the pancakes in a single layer on a parchment-lined baking sheet, then place in the freezer. Once the pancakes are frozen, transfer them to a ziptop bag and store for up to 2 months. (Do not put unfrozen pancakes in a ziptop bag without first freezing them flat or they will turn into a big pancake blob.) To reheat, lightly thaw the pancakes for about 30 seconds in the microwave, then pop them into the toaster for a lightly crisp exterior.

Leftover pancakes can be refrigerated for up to 2 days, then reheated in the toaster, in a nonstick skillet on the stove over medium-low heat, or warmed gently in the microwave.

NEXT LEVEL:

Warm Cinnamon Sautéed Apple Topping:
Heat a large cast-iron skillet or similar heavy-bottomed skillet over medium-low heat. Cut 2 large firm, sweet-crisp apples, such as Honeycrisp or Fuji, into ½-inch dice (leave the peels on; you will have about 3 cups of apples total). To the skillet, add 2 tablespoons unsalted butter. Once the butter has melted, add the apples, 1½ tablespoons packed light or dark brown sugar, ½ teaspoon ground cinnamon, and a good pinch of kosher salt. Let cook, stirring occasionally, until the apples are tender but not yet mushy and your kitchen smells like warm apple pie, about 8 minutes. Spoon generously over pancakes (and yogurt and ice cream and oatmeal and . . .). *Yield: About 1¾ cups.*

MARKET SWAPS:

Zucchini Bread Pancakes: Swap the apple for the same amount of shredded zucchini, pressing the zucchini until very dry with paper towels before adding it to the batter. Swap the pecans for walnuts and the dried cranberries for golden raisins.

Let's Party!

Girls' Night Sangria · Melon Margaritas

Warm Antipasti Dip

Caramelized Onion Bacon Dip

Honey Roasted Grape Crostini

Cocoa Loco Roasted Nuts · Cowboy Caviar

Taco Stuffed Mini Peppers

Sticky Asian Cauliflower Wings

Sweet Potato Pizza Bites

I enthusiastically embrace any excuse to throw a party. It's your half birthday? We need cake, Caramelized Onion Bacon Dip (page 68), and bubbly. Our favorite show is on? Watch-party with Girls' Night Sangria (page 60). You're having an exceptional hair day? Let's make Melon Margaritas (page 63) and Sweet Potato Pizza Bites (page 83) to show it off!

Parties often have the reputation of being fancy and fussy, but the most memorable ones I've hosted have been anything but. At the very first party I threw in our new home—a raucous Friendsgiving when nearly thirty adults squeezed into our living room—three of our guests had to sit on office chairs, four on the couch, and two on the stairs because we didn't have enough furniture. I served appetizers off of paper plates because half of the real plates were buried in moving boxes. My friends are still gabbing about how much fun they had. Don't wait for things to be perfect to have people over. The best parties are all about the company—and, of course, the food!

Once you bid perfection *adieu*, the pressure is lifted and a fantastic party is less complicated to host than you think. Here are a few tips to keep your stress level down, the fun level up, and ensure everyone (yourself included) has a fabulous time:

• Don't cook too much. Whether I'm hosting two or twenty, I have a primordial fear of running out of food. Combine that angst with a genuine desire to make and share so many of my favorite recipes, and before I know it, I'm stocked with enough groceries to cater a small wedding and I'm equally as stressed. My new rule: I cook no more than four things, two that I can prep the day before and two that I can prep the day of. I force myself to write down when each item needs to start cooking. I double-check that nothing will be fighting for space in the oven or on the stove. The rest, I buy or divvy up among my friends. Speaking of . . .

• Say yes. When your friends offer to bring a dish, take them up on it, especially if the party is large and you are feeling overwhelmed. Trust that the offer is sincere. Plus, when each member contributes to a meal, it gives the gathering an especially communal feel.

• Put the drinks where you want people to gather. Hoping to keep everyone in the kitchen? Arrange the drinks and glasses there (if your counterspace is tight, try setting up a small table). Want everyone OUT of the kitchen so you can do your *thang*? Move the drinks to the living room.

• Cut in half the list of things you plan to accomplish in the final hour before the party. The last sixty minutes before a party pass in a freak, fast-motion time warp. As someone who's greeted guests with a vacuum cleaner in one hand and an unapplied lipstick tube in the other, I can attest to the validity of this statement.

• Prepare for the friend who shows up ten minutes early. Related: Don't be that friend.

• Choose simple recipes that you know will be hits. Ahem, all of the recipes in this section!

This chapter is a collection of all-time party crowd-pleasers. You'll find recipes to suit any occasion, from Cinco de Mayo, to ladies' night, to game-watches, to whatever your favorite excuse to throw a party may be. I've also included plenty of make-ahead tips so you can get a head start, especially if you plan to cook multiple dishes. Pick a recipe, call a friend, and let the party begin!

Girls' Night Sangria

ACTIVE TIME: 10 minutes · **TOTAL TIME:** 6 hours 10 minutes, or overnight
YIELD: Serves 4 to 6 . . . or 2 (multiply the recipe to your heart's content and your party's thirst level)

Whoever said rosé wine is meant for summer only clearly has never attended my book club. Drop by one of our monthly "meetings" and you might mistake it for a wine tasting. The laughs are plentiful, the book is optional, and everyone stays up too late. It's one of my favorite nights of the month. Our beverage of choice? Rosé. No matter the season or what other bottles are on the table, the rosés are the first poured and polished off.

When I host book club, I like to make something a little extra special to start the party on a festive note, and this Girls' Night Sangria is a crowd favorite. It's fun and fruity but not overly sweet. With its flirty color and jewel-toned berries, this pink drink is ideal for both casual gatherings like girls' night and more formal occasions like bridal and wedding showers, Mother's Day, or an elevated brunch. Since sangria tastes best after resting several hours or even overnight, it's a busy hostess's BFF too.

---

1 (750-ml) bottle dry rosé wine

Juice of 1 small lemon (about 3 tablespoons)

Juice of 1 small lime (about 1½ tablespoons)

¼ cup Grand Marnier, or similar orange liqueur, such as Cointreau

¼ cup brandy

1½ cups quartered fresh strawberries

1 cup fresh raspberries

Ice, for serving

Additional strawberries and raspberries, for garnish (optional)

---

1. In a large pitcher, stir together the rosé, lemon juice, lime juice, Grand Marnier, and brandy. Gently stir in the strawberries and raspberries. Refrigerate for at least 6 hours, ideally overnight.

2. When ready to serve, fill glasses with ice. Pour the sangria over the ice, then spoon a portion of the soaked fruit from the pitcher into each glass. Garnish with additional fruit as desired. Cheers!

NEXT LEVEL:
To keep your sangria cold without watering it down, swap the ice cubes for frozen strawberries and raspberries.

Melon Margaritas

ACTIVE TIME: 15 minutes · **TOTAL TIME:** 15 minutes · **YIELD:** 1 to 6 drinks (5 ounces each)

You know that feeling when you order a fruit salad only to be disappointed by a disproportionately large amount of honeydew (six pieces of honeydew and only two grapes??). This recipe is honeydew's redemption!

It turns out that all honeydew needs to be craveable is tequila and lime. Pureed into a fresh juice and then shaken up, it makes the most utterly refreshing, unexpected margaritas. Every person I've watched taste them reacts the same way: They sip gingerly at first, then state with astonishment *but I don't like honeydew!* (usually several times), then rush to finish their drink and pour a second from the pitcher before it runs out.

This recipe works well with both in- and out-of-season honeydew, though I love it most at the peak of summer, when honeydew is at its juiciest and margaritas their most thirst quenching.

For the Honeydew Mix:

2½ cups 1-inch diced honeydew (about ½ of a small, 3-pound melon; see Next Level for a creative way to use the second melon half)

2 tablespoons light agave nectar or simple syrup (see Pro Tips)

¼ teaspoon kosher salt

For a Single Margarita:

Ice

¼ cup Honeydew Mix

2 ounces (¼ cup) silver/blanco tequila

1 ounce (2 tablespoons) freshly squeezed lime juice (about 1 medium lime)

For garnish: fresh lime slice, small slice of melon

For a Whole Pitcher (6 drinks):

1 batch (1½ cups) Honeydew Mix

12 ounces (1½ cups) silver/blanco tequila

6 ounces (¾ cup) freshly squeezed lime juice (about 6 medium limes)

Ice, for serving

For garnish: fresh lime slices, small slices of melon

1. Make the honeydew mix: Place the diced honeydew cubes in a blender and puree until very smooth. Let stand in the blender until the juice settles to the bottom and the foam rises to the top. The amount of foam will vary based on the season and from melon to melon. With a large spoon, skim off the foam and discard. Measure 1½ cups of the juice for making the margaritas (do this directly in your blender's pitcher if it has measurements printed on it). If your melon is particularly juicy, save any extra juice in a separate container and use for smoothies, sipping, or margarita refills.

2. Add the measured juice back to the blender if necessary. Add the agave and salt, then blend to combine.

3. For a single margarita (or up to 2): Fill a serving glass and cocktail shaker with ice. To the cocktail shaker, add the honeydew mix, tequila, and lime juice. Shake vigorously for 30 seconds, then strain into the prepared glass. Enjoy immediately, garnished with lime and melon slices as desired.

recipe continues

For a pitcher: If your honeydew mix is still fairly pulpy even after skimming the foam, strain it into a large pitcher. (If it isn't pulpy, you can pour it directly into a large pitcher, without straining.) Stir in the tequila and lime juice until well combined. Divide between ice-filled glasses, or refrigerate the pitcher until ready to serve, up to 6 hours. Immediately before serving, give the mixture an energetic stir. Garnish with limes and melon slices as desired and sip away.

PRO TIPS:

- While I love myself a salty margarita rim, I do not recommend salting the rim of the glasses for these particular margaritas, as the salt can overwhelm the delicate flavor of the honeydew. The ¼ teaspoon added to the melon mix is just the right amount. If you'd like to dress up your glasses, try rimming them with coarse sparkling sugar instead.

- *To make simple syrup:* Combine equal parts water and granulated sugar in a saucepan. Heat over medium, stirring occasionally, until the sugar dissolves. Let cool, then transfer to a small airtight container or jar and refrigerate until chilled, or for up to 3 weeks.

NEXT LEVEL:

- *For Minty Melon Margaritas* (best for individual margaritas): Add 10 fresh mint leaves to the cocktail shaker with the melon mix, tequila, and lime juice in step 3. Garnish with additional fresh mint leaves.

- *For Spicy Melon Margaritas* (best for individual margaritas): Add 1 thin, round slice of jalapeno to the cocktail shaker in step 3. Garnish with an extra jalapeno slice.

- *Melon Ice Cubes:* Use a melon baller to scrape out about 10 balls from the extra half honeydew you'll have after making a batch of honeydew mix. Place the balls in a large sealable plastic container, then freeze until hardened. Add to serving glasses in addition to (or in place of) the ice cubes.

MARKET SWAPS:

These margaritas are also delicious made with cantaloupe or watermelon in place of the honeydew. Cantaloupe juice will be foamy and need to be skimmed. If using watermelon, your juice may be extra pulpy. If it is, pour it through a mesh sieve, using a big spoon to squish the liquid through. Discard the pulp, then proceed with the recipe as directed.

Warm Antipasti Dip

ACTIVE TIME: 40 minutes · **TOTAL TIME:** 1 hour 10 minutes · **YIELD:** Serves 10 to 12 (about 5½ cups)

If the opportunity presents itself, I highly recommend marrying into an Italian family. My in-laws are from northern Italy, and thus our family gatherings are a delectable mashup of American and Italian favorites. Cream cheese–based dips sit proudly beside plates of Italian antipasti: cured meats, marinated artichokes swimming in olive oil, and Parmesan so sharp you can feel the crystals dissolve on your tongue. We wash it all down with glasses of prosecco and Manhattans and wonder why anyone would do it any other way.

This Warm Antipasti Dip is my tribute to our Italian-American hodgepodge. I lightened up its all-American cream cheese base with Greek yogurt, then loaded it with Italian-inspired mozzarella, garlic, spices, and classic antipasti favorites like artichokes, roasted peppers, olives, and salami. In the oven, the dip bubbles and the salami becomes tantalizingly crisp. This dip is equal parts fresh and indulgent, familiar and unexpected. *Buon appetito!*

---

1 whole grain baguette or similar crusty whole grain artisan bread (about 12 ounces), cut into ½-inch-thick slices

1 tablespoon extra virgin olive oil, divided

1 (8-ounce) package reduced fat cream cheese, at room temperature

¼ cup nonfat plain Greek yogurt

2 cloves garlic, minced (about 2 teaspoons)

1 teaspoon Italian seasoning

½ teaspoon red pepper flakes

⅛ teaspoon kosher salt

1 cup shredded part-skim mozzarella cheese (about 4 ounces)

1 (7.5-ounce) can or jar artichoke hearts, drained, roughly chopped into bite-sized pieces, and patted as dry as possible (about heaping ½ cup)

1 pint cherry tomatoes, halved (about 2 cups), divided

1 (12-ounce) jar roasted red bell peppers, drained, chopped into ¼-inch pieces, and patted as dry as possible (about 1 cup), divided

1 cup halved pitted Kalamata olives (about 6 ounces), divided

6 thin slices of deli salami, chopped into small pieces (about ½ cup or 1½ ounces)

¼ cup finely grated Parmesan cheese (about ¾ ounce)

¼ cup thinly sliced fresh basil leaves

---

1. Place a rack in the upper third of your oven and preheat the oven to 400 degrees F. Lightly coat an 8×8-inch baking dish or similar 2-quart casserole dish with nonstick spray and set aside.

2. Arrange the bread slices on a large rimmed baking sheet (you can leave it unlined or line it with parchment paper for easy cleanup). Brush ½ tablespoon of the oil over the first sides of the slices. Flip the slices over and brush the second sides with the remaining ½ tablespoon oil. Place in the oven and bake for 5 minutes. Remove the pan from the oven, flip the slices over, then return to the oven and continue baking until lightly toasted, 5 to 6 additional minutes. Set aside to cool. Reduce the oven temperature to 350 degrees F.

3. In the bowl of a standing mixer fitted with the paddle attachment or a medium mixing bowl, beat the cream cheese, Greek yogurt, garlic, Italian seasoning, red pepper flakes, and salt together on medium speed

recipe continues

until smooth and combined, about 1 minute. With a rubber spatula, fold in the mozzarella, artichoke hearts, three-quarters of the cherry tomatoes, half of the bell peppers, and half of the olives, reserving the rest to sprinkle on top. Spread the mixture evenly in the prepared baking dish.

4. Scatter the salami and remaining tomatoes, bell peppers, and olives evenly over the top. Sprinkle with the Parmesan. Bake 25 to 30 minutes, until bubbling and hot throughout. Sprinkle with the basil. Serve hot with the toasted bread slices.

MAKE-AHEAD & STORAGE TIPS:

Dip is best enjoyed the day it is made but can be stored in the refrigerator for up to 2 days.

Enjoy at room temperature or transfer to a small baking dish, cover the dish with foil, and rewarm on the center rack in a 250-degree-F oven for 15 minutes or until hot.

Caramelized Onion Bacon Dip

ACTIVE TIME: 45 minutes · **TOTAL TIME:** 1 hour

YIELD: Serves 8 (fewer if you have some serious dip enthusiasts; about 3½ cups)

I have yet to determine a social situation that wouldn't benefit from a bowl of this dreamy, extra-addictive dip. Office party? Slide the bowl on over to your boss and await a raise. Black-tie affair? Bacon knows no dress code. Game watch at your crush's place? Arrive with this dip. Leave with a date.

Caramelized onions are the heart of this winning appetizer's bold taste, giving it big flavor with less fat; Greek yogurt provides creaminess and protein without the heft of mayonnaise; and a few strategic strips of bacon make for an obsessive salty-sweetness that will have your guests hovering around the bowl.

6 strips thick-cut bacon

2 teaspoons extra virgin olive oil

2 large yellow onions, thinly sliced (about 6 cups)

¾ teaspoon kosher salt, divided

3 cloves garlic, minced (about 1 tablespoon)

2 tablespoons water

¾ teaspoon ground black pepper, divided

1 cup nonfat plain Greek yogurt, at room temperature

8 ounces reduced fat cream cheese, at room temperature

1½ teaspoons Worcestershire sauce

⅛ teaspoon cayenne pepper

For serving: chips (potato chips, pita chips, pretzels), fresh vegetables (carrots, thinly sliced bell peppers, cherry tomatoes), or crackers. Kettle-cooked potato chips and pretzels are the house favorites.

1. Place a rack in the center of your oven and preheat the oven to 400 degrees F. Line a large rimmed baking sheet with aluminum foil, then place a cooling rack on top. Lightly coat the rack with nonstick spray. Arrange the bacon slices in a single layer on the rack. Bake the bacon until crisp, 15 to 20 minutes, depending upon its thickness. Remove to a paper towel–lined plate and lightly pat dry. When cool enough to handle, chop or crumble into small pieces. Set aside. Reduce the oven temperature to 350 degrees F.

2. Meanwhile, heat the oil in a large, heavy-bottomed skillet over medium-low heat. Add the onions and ¼ teaspoon of the salt. Sauté until the onions are brown, soft, and deeply caramelized, about 25 minutes, stirring occasionally. Add the garlic, water, and ¼ teaspoon of the black pepper and cook just until the liquid evaporates, about 3 minutes. Remove from the heat, then scrape the mixture onto a cutting board. Let cool for 15 minutes, then coarsely chop.

3. While the onions cool, in the bowl of a stand mixer fitted with the paddle attachment or a large mixing bowl, beat together the Greek yogurt, cream cheese, Worcestershire, cayenne, and remaining ½ teaspoon salt and ½ teaspoon black pepper on medium speed

until smooth. By hand with a rubber spatula or wooden spoon, fold in the caramelized onions and bacon. Taste and add additional salt or black pepper as desired.

4. Scrape the dip into an ovensafe serving dish, such as a small casserole or gratin dish, and smooth the top. Bake for 10 to 15 minutes, until warmed through. Enjoy warm or at room temperature, with desired accompaniments, or refrigerate until ready to serve. You can rewarm the dip in the oven right before serving (best option), or simply set it out and let it come to room temperature (still a good option).

MAKE-AHEAD & STORAGE TIPS: Caramelized onions can be made and refrigerated up to 3 days in advance. Refrigerate leftovers for up to 4 days.

LEFTOVER LOVE:
• Spread onto a turkey or ham sandwich, butter the outsides of your bread, then toast the sandwich on both sides in a small skillet over medium-low heat until golden.

• Smear generously on a toasted everything, rye, or whole wheat bagel.

Honey Roasted Grape Crostini

ACTIVE TIME: 25 minutes · **TOTAL TIME:** 50 minutes · **YIELD:** 24 crostini (serves 6 to 8)

I'm not sure why the decorating gene—the one that inspires my mother to rearrange furniture at 5 a.m. and my two sisters to create quaint front porches that Martha Stewart would envy—skipped right over me, but I can't select a throw pillow without group texting all three of them for approval. Fortunately, when it comes to beautifying an appetizer spread, these Honey Roasted Grape Crostini do my work for me. Set down a tray of this stunning starter at your next party, and the party will instantly become more elegant. The best part? You don't need to be Martha to make them. There are only a few simple steps, and the results are spectacular.

Roasting the grapes in honey and olive oil concentrates their juices and gives them a jammy depth that is sublime when paired with tangy goat cheese. Savory fresh thyme balances the grapes' sweetness, and toasted walnuts give the crostini a pleasing crunch.

⅓ cup raw walnut halves

1 pound seedless red grapes, removed from their stems (about 2½ cups)

2 tablespoons extra virgin olive oil, divided

2 tablespoons honey

¼ teaspoon kosher salt

1 whole grain baguette (about 12 ounces), cut into twenty-four ½-inch-thick slices

4 ounces goat cheese, at room temperature

1 tablespoon chopped fresh thyme

1. Place racks in the upper and lower thirds of your oven and preheat the oven to 350 degrees F. Spread the walnuts in a single layer on an ungreased rimmed baking sheet. Bake on the upper rack until the nuts are toasted and fragrant, 8 to 10 minutes. Watch carefully towards the end of the baking time to ensure the nuts do not burn. Transfer to a cutting board. Let cool, then chop fairly finely and set aside. Increase the oven temperature to 400 degrees F.

2. Line a second, rimmed baking sheet with parchment paper. Place the grapes in the center of the baking sheet and drizzle with 1 tablespoon of the olive oil, the honey, and salt. Gently toss to coat, then spread into a single layer. Bake on the upper rack for 20 to 25 minutes, until the grapes are soft and beginning to shrivel and collapse. Let cool to room temperature.

3. While the grapes roast, arrange the baguette slices on a clean baking sheet, lined with parchment paper for easy cleanup if you like (feel free to brush off the baking sheet used for the walnuts and repurpose it here). Brush the first sides of the slices with ½ tablespoon of the olive oil. Flip the slices over and brush the second sides with the remaining ½ tablespoon oil. Place on the lower oven rack (it's fine for the bread and grapes to be in the oven at the same time) and bake for 5 minutes. Remove the pan from the oven, flip the bread slices over, then return to the oven and continue baking until lightly toasted, 5 to 6 additional minutes. Let cool.

4. Assemble the crostini: Spread each baguette slice with softened goat cheese and arrange a

recipe continues

few grapes on top, discarding any juices that have collected on the baking sheet (you will have about 4 grapes per crostini). Arrange on a serving plate, then sprinkle generously with the walnuts and thyme. Enjoy immediately.

MAKE-AHEAD TIPS:
Up to 1 day in advance: Toast and chop the walnuts, roast the grapes, and toast the baguette slices. Store each in a separate container. Refrigerate the grapes and store the walnuts and baguette slices at room temperature. When ready to serve, warm the grapes slightly in the microwave or on the stove until they are barely warm, or place on the counter and let come to room temperature. Assemble as directed.

MARKET SWAPS:
- *Roasted Strawberry Crostini:* Swap the grapes for 1 pound of stemmed, hulled strawberries, the walnuts for pecans, and the thyme for thinly sliced fresh basil.

- Not a fan of goat cheese? Swap in ricotta, cream cheese, mascarpone, or feta that's been whipped in the food processor until smooth and creamy.

Cocoa Loco Roasted Nuts

ACTIVE TIME: 15 minutes · **TOTAL TIME:** 2 hours 30 minutes · **YIELD:** Serves 10 to 12 (about 3 cups)

Everything you've heard about Hawaii—the pristine beaches, the technicolor sunsets, the double rainbows—it's true, all of it. I assumed I'd visit someday, and when one of my best friends moved to Kauai, I bumped it straight to the top of my bucket list. I expected that we would have a good time (I mean, *Hawaii!*), but I wasn't prepared for how swiftly and completely the island would steal my heart.

One of the best bites on Kauai was at Kauai Nut Roasters, an unassuming shop that offered tantalizing gourmet nuts in dozens of different flavors. After extensive sampling, I can attest that the coffee coconut is the best of the best. It took me more tries than I care to count to re-create those nuts—if you've been within three miles of my house, you've likely sampled a version of them—but it was absolutely worth the effort to bring this recipe home. The combination of coffee, cocoa powder, and coconut, along with the natural sweetness of maple syrup and deep toasting in the oven, makes these nuts a leap above the standard party snack. They are an elegant addition to cocktail parties and always appreciated as a thank-you to the hostess or as a holiday gift. Roasting up, then chowing down on a batch of these island-inspired nuts, is paradise.

½ cup unsweetened shredded coconut

1 cup raw whole almonds

1 cup raw walnut halves

1 cup raw pecan halves

1 large egg white

4 tablespoons pure maple syrup, divided

2 teaspoons pure vanilla extract

3 tablespoons finely ground coffee (the fresher and finer ground, the better)

1 tablespoon unsweetened cocoa powder

¼ teaspoon kosher salt

1. Place racks in the upper and lower thirds of your oven and preheat the oven to 300 degrees F. Spread the coconut into a single layer on an ungreased rimmed baking sheet and place it on the lower rack. Bake until the coconut is fragrant and beginning to turn golden, 7 to 10 minutes, tossing once halfway through. Set aside to cool.

2. Meanwhile, line a second rimmed baking sheet with parchment paper. Spread the nuts in a single layer on the baking sheet. Bake on the upper rack for 15 minutes. It is fine to have both the baking sheet with the nuts and the one with the coconut in the oven at the same time—set a timer, don't wander far from the oven, and watch carefully towards the end of each baking time to ensure they do not burn.

3. While the nuts bake, in a large mixing bowl, briskly whisk the egg white until foamy but not stiff. Whisk in 2 tablespoons of the maple syrup and the vanilla. In a separate small bowl, stir together the coffee, cocoa powder, and salt.

4. Once the nuts have baked 15 minutes, remove them from the oven and let cool 5 minutes. Transfer them to the mixing bowl with the egg white mixture. With a large

recipe continues

spoon, stir to combine. Sprinkle the coffee mixture over the top, then stir again to coat the nuts evenly. Pour the nuts back onto the same baking sheet and spread them into a single layer. Return the pan to the oven, placing it on the lower rack where you were previously toasting the coconut. Bake 10 additional minutes, or until the nuts are brown, crisp, and smell fantastically toasty. If you break a nut in half, its center should be a light tan.

5. While the nuts finish baking, place the toasted coconut in a food processor or blender. Pulse until coarsely chopped, about 8 pulses total (do not skip this step or the coconut will not stick to the nuts).

6. Once the nuts have finished baking, leave them on the baking sheet and drizzle the remaining 2 tablespoons maple syrup over the top. Sprinkle on the coconut. Toss to coat the nuts evenly (be careful; the pan will still be hot), then spread them back into a single layer. Let the nuts cool on the sheet for at least 2 hours, breaking them up once or twice throughout. The nuts will be sticky at first but will continue to set as they dry. Transfer to a serving bowl or storage container.

STORAGE TIPS:
Toasted nuts can be stored at room temperature for 2 weeks or frozen for 2 months.

Cowboy Caviar

ACTIVE TIME: 25 minutes · **TOTAL TIME:** 1 hour 25 minutes · **YIELD:** Serves 8 to 10 (about 8 cups)

Once you bring Cowboy Caviar to a party, it becomes nearly impossible to bring anything else. Show up without it and you may not receive a warm welcome. Don't take it personally. Fresh, zippy, and loaded with universally appealing Tex-Mex ingredients, this chunky dip can't help stealing attention.

Also known as bean salsa, Texas caviar, and "that one dip I couldn't stop eating," Cowboy Caviar is a confetti combination of pantry staples like black beans and corn and fresh ingredients like tomatoes and jalapeno. I load mine with extra veggies, then top it with big chunks of avocado. The result is creamy, hearty, and fabulously fresh.

The longer Cowboy Caviar sits, the better it tastes, so it's an ideal make-ahead party dish. In addition to being dynamite scooped with tortilla chips (how I serve it at parties), Cowboy Caviar is a useful thing to have in your refrigerator. Check out the Leftover Love section (opposite) for more tasty ways to use it.

For the Cowboy Caviar:

½ small red onion, finely chopped (about ½ cup)

1 (15-ounce) can reduced sodium black beans, rinsed and drained

1 (15-ounce) can reduced sodium black-eyed peas, rinsed and drained

1 cup corn kernels (frozen and thawed, canned and drained, or cut fresh from the cob)

1 medium red bell pepper, cut into ¼-inch dice (about 1 cup)

1 medium jalapeno, seeded and finely chopped (about 2 tablespoons)

2 large avocados, cut into a rough ⅓-inch dice (about 2½ cups)

1 pint cherry tomatoes, halved (about 2 cups)

Multi-grain tortilla chips, for serving

For the Dressing:

2 tablespoons plus 1 teaspoon red wine vinegar

2 tablespoons extra virgin olive oil

½ teaspoon honey

1 clove garlic, minced (about 1 teaspoon)

¾ teaspoon kosher salt

½ teaspoon ground black pepper

1. Make the cowboy caviar: Place the red onion in a small bowl and cover with cold water. Set aside while you prepare the other ingredients. This step keeps the onion's flavor but removes some of its lingering bite.

2. In a large bowl, stir together the black beans, black-eyed peas, corn, bell pepper, and jalapeno. Gently fold in the avocados and tomatoes.

3. In a small bowl or large liquid measuring cup, whisk together the dressing ingredients: the vinegar, oil, honey, garlic, salt, and pepper. Pour the dressing over the bean mixture.

4. Drain the red onion and add it to the bowl. Stir until completely combined. Taste and adjust the seasoning as desired. If time allows, refrigerate for 1 hour to allow the flavors to marry. Before serving, give the caviar several good stirs to reincorporate any dressing that has sunk to the bottom. Scoop generously with tortilla chips.

MAKE-AHEAD & STORAGE TIPS:

This recipe tastes even better as it sits, making it an ideal make-ahead option for a party. You can prep and refrigerate it up to 8 hours in advance. If making ahead, wait to add the avocados within 1 hour of serving so they don't turn brown.

Store leftovers in the refrigerator for 3 to 4 days.

LEFTOVER LOVE:

• *Cowboy Caviar Burritos:* In a large nonstick skillet, sauté 1 pound lean ground turkey. Season to taste with chili powder, cumin, garlic powder, salt, and pepper. Stir in the leftover Cowboy Caviar until warmed through. Sprinkle with cheese and wrap inside warmed whole wheat tortillas.

• Prepare and cook the chicken for Santa Fe Grilled Chicken Salad (page 91). Spoon Cowboy Caviar generously over the top of the grilled chicken and serve.

• Mix with greens and Zesty Ranch Dressing (page 90) for a simple, fresh green salad.

• Spoon inside Bibb lettuce for yummy Cowboy Caviar lettuce wraps.

MAKE-AHEAD & STORAGE TIPS:

Up to 1 day in advance: Prepare the peppers and filling through step 3. Let each cool completely, then mound the filling inside the pepper halves as directed in step 4 (do not sprinkle on the last 1¼ cups cheese until just before baking). Transfer the stuffed peppers to an airtight container and refrigerate. When ready to bake, let the peppers come to room temperature while you preheat the oven, then proceed with the recipe as directed.

Leftover stuffed peppers can be refrigerated up to 1 day. Rewarm in a 400-degree-F oven until heated through, about 5 minutes.

Taco Stuffed Mini Peppers

ACTIVE TIME: 40 minutes · **TOTAL TIME:** 1 hour

YIELD: 40 to 60 mini pepper halves (serves 10 to 12 as part of a large party spread; 4 to 6 if you have a group of hungry Tex-Mex food lovers; 2 if you are a member of my household)

You know that unspoken party rule not to take the last appetizer on the plate? That rule does not apply to Taco Stuffed Mini Peppers. Tender, sweet baby bell peppers stuffed with a cheesy, Southwest-spiced blend of ground turkey, pepper Jack cheese, and tomatoes, then baked until hot and bubbly, these little bites cause ordinarily well-behaved adults to drop all pretense of manners.

I originally envisioned this recipe as an ideal component of a fiesta-themed bash or game day, and they certainly work beautifully for either. Just between you and me, however, every time I make them, we end up devouring the entire pan, ruin our appetites for dinner, and skip straight ahead to dessert. We've yet to be upset about it. Whether you make a batch for a group of two or twelve, these primo peppers are guaranteed to vanish.

---

1 pound mini sweet peppers (20 to 30 peppers)

1 teaspoon kosher salt, divided

1 teaspoon extra virgin olive oil

1 pound 93% lean ground turkey

1 tablespoon chili powder

1 teaspoon ground cumin

½ teaspoon garlic powder

¼ teaspoon ground black pepper

1 (10-ounce) can diced tomatoes and green chiles in their juices

1½ cups shredded pepper Jack cheese (6 ounces; use Monterey Jack if you prefer the peppers more mild), divided

2 tablespoons finely chopped fresh cilantro

---

1. Place racks in the upper and lower thirds of your oven and preheat the oven to 375 degrees F. Line two large baking sheets with parchment paper. Cut the mini peppers in half lengthwise (leave the stems on). With the tip of a small spoon or your fingers, remove the seeds and membranes.

2. Place the halved peppers on the baking sheets, cut-sides up. Sprinkle with ½ teaspoon of the kosher salt. Bake 15 to 20 minutes, until the peppers are slightly tender but not mushy, switching the pans' positions on the upper and lower racks halfway through. Remove from the oven. Leave the oven heated.

3. While the peppers bake, in a large nonstick skillet, heat the oil over medium-high heat.

Add the turkey, chili powder, cumin, garlic powder, pepper, and remaining ½ teaspoon kosher salt. Brown the meat, breaking it apart into small pieces until it is cooked through, 4 to 5 minutes. Add the diced tomatoes and green chiles, increase the heat to high, and continue cooking until most of the liquid has cooked off, 4 to 5 additional minutes. Remove from the heat. Stir in ¼ cup of the cheese.

4. With a small spoon, mound the filling into the baked pepper halves. Sprinkle the remaining 1¼ cups cheese over the top. Return the pans to the oven and bake for 5 minutes, until the cheese is melted. Sprinkle with the fresh cilantro. Let cool slightly, then transfer to a serving plate. Serve hot or at room temperature.

Sticky Asian Cauliflower Wings

ACTIVE TIME: 40 minutes · **TOTAL TIME:** 55 minutes · **YIELD:** Serves 4 (about 3½ cups)

It's a nightmare to go out for wings with me. I'll insist I don't want any, only to slowly inch my way closer to your plate until you feel obligated to share. One will satisfy my craving, and your plate is safe until we go out for wings again.

These Sticky Asian Cauliflower Wings? STAND BACK! I can easily, gleefully devour an entire sheet pan. They have all the qualities that prompt you to crave wings in the first place—the lip-smacking sauce, the bold flavor, the "fried" exterior and tender interior—with none of the heaviness to slow you down.

Cauliflower might seem like an odd choice for a "wing," but its mild, firm florets work better than you imagine. To mimic the deep-fried flavor of classic wings, I toss the florets in a quick batter, roast them at a high temperature until soft and caramelized, then coat them with a sweet, spicy Asian-inspired sauce. As often as I make these wings for parties, I'm just as likely to make them only for myself. For a dynamite dinner, they're delicious mixed with rice, as a filling for lettuce wraps (make some extra sauce for drizzling over the top and add a sprinkle of shredded carrot), or the way I eat them most often: in true wing spirit, straight off the plate, with messy fingers.

For the Wings:

¾ cup white whole wheat flour

2 teaspoons garlic powder

¼ teaspoon kosher salt

¼ teaspoon ground black pepper

¾ cup water

1 medium head cauliflower (about 2½ pounds), cut into bite-sized "wing" florets (about 6 cups florets)

1 tablespoon toasted sesame seeds

For the Sauce:

¼ cup honey

3 tablespoons low sodium soy sauce

1 tablespoon minced fresh ginger

1 tablespoon rice vinegar

1½ teaspoons sambal oelek (fresh chili paste) or Sriracha

1. Place racks in the upper and lower thirds of your oven and preheat the oven to 425 degrees F. Line two large rimmed baking sheets with parchment paper.

2. Prepare the wings: In a large mixing bowl, whisk together the flour, garlic powder, salt, and pepper. Pour in the water, then mix until you have a smooth batter. Add the cauliflower and toss to evenly coat the florets.

3. Divide the florets between the two baking sheets. Shake off any excess batter as you

go and ensure the florets do not touch one another. Place the pans in the upper and lower thirds of the oven and bake for 15 minutes. Switch the pans' positions on the upper and lower racks, then continue baking for 10 additional minutes, or until the florets are hot, golden, and caramelized. Set aside and leave the oven heated.

4. While the cauliflower bakes, prepare the sauce: In a small saucepan, combine the

recipe continues

honey, soy sauce, ginger, vinegar, and sambal oelek. Bring to a simmer over medium-high heat and cook, stirring often, for 3 to 4 minutes, until the sauce is thickened and reduced by approximately half.

5. Carefully transfer the baked florets to a large mixing bowl. Pour the sauce over the top and toss to coat. Sprinkle in the sesame seeds and toss once more. Spread the wings back onto one of the baking sheets in a single layer (no need to change out the parchment paper). Return the pan to the upper third of the oven and bake for 5 additional minutes.

The wings will be lightly browned, soft, and sticky. Remove from the oven and transfer to a serving plate. Enjoy immediately.

STORAGE TIPS:
While the wings are best when fresh, they can be refrigerated for up to 3 days. To reheat: Preheat the oven to 400 degrees F. Line a baking sheet with foil and lightly coat the foil with nonstick spray. Arrange the wings in a single layer on top. Bake until hot, about 8 minutes.

Sweet Potato Pizza Bites

ACTIVE TIME: 50 minutes · **TOTAL TIME:** 1 hour · **YIELD:** About 28 bites (serves 6 to 8)

This appetizer is a reminder that the crowd favorite at any party is rarely the frilly pâtés or the hard-to-pronounce canapés. It's pizza. Plain. Simple. Pizza.

No matter how many different appetizers I make, these obsessively good, outrageously easy mini "pizzas" are the ones my friends eat first and stop talking about last. Roasted sweet potato slices form the "crust" of these appetizer-sized pizza bites. Sweet potatoes are high in vitamins and a tasty pairing with pizza sauce and cheese. Plus, they save the fuss of making from-scratch pizza dough, not to mention the larger fuss of shaping said pizza dough into tiny rounds.

In addition to its spot at the top of the party-food hit list, these sweet potato bites are nutritious enough to serve as a kid-friendly dinner, paired with a hearty green salad or side. Feel free to swap the bacon for any of your favorite pizza toppings, use only one of the two sauces the recipe suggests, or plate up a colorful mix.

---

4 strips thick-cut bacon

2 small-medium sweet potatoes (about 1 pound; look for long, narrow sweet potatoes, as these yield the most uniform pizza bites)

1½ tablespoons extra virgin olive oil, divided

½ teaspoon kosher salt

½ teaspoon ground black pepper

6 tablespoons Creamy Basil Pesto (page 100) or store-bought pesto, or marinara sauce (for a fun mix, top half of the pizzas with pesto and half with marinara)

⅔ cup shredded part-skim mozzarella cheese (about 2¾ ounces)

1 tablespoon finely chopped fresh chives

1½ tablespoons finely grated Parmesan cheese

---

1. Place a rack in the center of your oven and preheat the oven to 400 degrees F. Line a large rimmed baking sheet with aluminum foil, then place a cooling rack on top. Lightly coat the rack with nonstick spray. Arrange the bacon slices in a single layer on the rack. Bake the bacon until crisp, 15 to 20 minutes, depending upon its thickness. Remove to a paper towel–lined plate and lightly pat dry. When cool enough to handle, chop or crumble into small pieces. Set aside. Increase the oven temperature to 425 degrees F.

2. While the bacon cooks, scrub the sweet potatoes (no need to peel) and cut into ⅓-inch-thick coins. Line a second baking sheet with foil or parchment paper, then arrange the sweet potato slices in a single layer on top. Brush the first side of the slices with ½ tablespoon of the olive oil, flip them over, then brush the other side with the remaining 1 tablespoon oil. Sprinkle with the salt and pepper.

3. Bake the sweet potatoes for 15 to 20 minutes, until golden brown underneath. Remove from the oven, flip the slices over, then return to the oven and bake for an additional 5 to 8 minutes, until they are just tender but not so soft that they begin to fall apart. While the slices bake, prepare any remaining pizza toppings.

recipe continues

4. Assemble the pizzas: Top each sweet potato round with a small spoonful of pesto or marinara. Sprinkle the slices evenly with the mozzarella and crumbled bacon. Return the pan to the oven and bake for 3 to 5 additional minutes, until the cheese is melted and bubbly. Immediately sprinkle the chives and Parmesan over the top. Let the pizzas rest on the baking sheet for 2 minutes, then carefully transfer to a serving plate. Enjoy hot or at room temperature.

MAKE-AHEAD & STORAGE TIPS:
The bacon can be cooked and stored in the refrigerator up to 1 day in advance.

Untopped sweet potato rounds can be roasted 1 day in advance. Refrigerate in an airtight container, separating any layers with parchment paper or wax paper. When ready to assemble, rewarm the rounds on a parchment-lined baking sheet in a 425-degree-F oven. Once the slices are warm, add the sauce and toppings and bake as directed.

The pizza bites are best enjoyed the day they are made but can be refrigerated up to 1 day. To reheat: Preheat the oven to 400 degrees F. Line a baking sheet with foil or parchment paper and lightly coat it with nonstick spray. Place the pizza bites on the sheet and bake for 5 to 10 minutes, until hot.

Book Club Salad
(A Great, Green
Party Salad),
page 116

Seriously
Satisfying
Salads

Three Back-Pocket Salad Dressings

Go-to Citrus Dressing · Zippy Lemon Yogurt Dressing · Zesty Ranch Dressing

Santa Fe Grilled Chicken Salad

Maple Roasted Butternut Squash Salad with Arugula and Farro

Summer Celebration Orzo Salad with Chickpeas and Creamy Basil Pesto

Creamy Basil Pesto · **Balsamic Farro Salad with Edamame and Cranberries**

Modern Macaroni Salad · Picnic Slaw · Roasted Beets with Honey Orange Ricotta

Killer Kale Salad (3 Ways!)

Mexican Kale Salad · Mediterranean Kale Salad · Harvest Kale Salad

Shaved Brussels Sprouts Salad · Book Club Salad (A Great, Green Party Salad)

—————•————•

I am the person at the party who brings a salad. I'm also the person who brings dessert, so thankfully when the host opens the door and sees me holding a bowl of something suspiciously green, she tends to let me in anyway.

People often view salad as a food you have to or should eat. If you feel this way, you've settled, because salad can and should be a food that you *want* to eat. Every recipe in this chapter—from Summer Celebration Orzo Salad with Chickpeas and Creamy Basil Pesto (page 97), to Santa Fe Grilled Chicken Salad (page 91), to my autumn-love Maple Roasted Butternut Squash Salad with Arugula and Farro (page 95)—is categorically crave worthy, filling, and something you'll eat out of desire instead of obligation.

Most of the salads in this chapter can last for several days in the refrigerator, meaning you can make a big batch on Sunday, then enjoy portions for quick, nutritious meals throughout the week. I've also included plenty that taste fabulous at room temperature, so they're ideal for potlucks and dinner parties. By the end of this chapter, you'll be the person who brings the salad too!

3 Back-Pocket Salad Dressings

You will never ever regret making your own salad dressing from scratch. For whatever reason (ahem, laziness), I dread making it at first, but I persevere. A few short minutes later, my dressing is complete and I'm holding a jar of homemade sunshine.

In addition to being able to control the ingredients (and thus avoid the excess sugars, unnecessary fats, and preservatives found in many store-bought dressings), making dressing yourself is money saving and enormously satisfying. It's a moment of joy to sit down with a beautiful bowl of salad when you've prepared every element from start to finish.

Zesty Ranch
Dressing

Go-to Citrus
Dressing

Zippy Lemon
Yogurt Dressing

Go-to Citrus Dressing

ACTIVE TIME: 5 minutes · **TOTAL TIME:** 5 minutes · **YIELD:** About ⅓ cup

¼ cup freshly squeezed citrus juice of choice (from about 1 medium lemon, 2 medium limes, or ½ medium orange)

3 tablespoons extra virgin olive oil

1 teaspoon honey

½ teaspoon kosher salt

In a small mixing bowl or a large liquid measuring cup, whisk together all of the ingredients until combined: the juice, oil, honey, and salt. Alternatively, you can shake all of the ingredients together in a mason jar with a tight-fitting lid. Use immediately or refrigerate in an airtight jar for up to 1 week.

PRO TIP:
If you'd like to make a larger amount of dressing so that you have plenty of leftovers (or if you like your salad heavier on the dressing in general), feel free to multiply any of these recipes by as many times as you like.

Zippy Lemon Yogurt Dressing

ACTIVE TIME: 10 minutes · **TOTAL TIME:** 10 minutes · **YIELD:** About ¾ cup

½ cup nonfat plain Greek yogurt

Zest of 2 medium lemons (about 2 teaspoons)

¼ cup freshly squeezed lemon juice (from about 1 of the medium lemons above)

2 tablespoons extra virgin olive oil

2 teaspoons honey

1 large clove garlic, very finely minced or grated (about 1 teaspoon)

½ teaspoon kosher salt

¼ teaspoon ground black pepper

In a small mixing bowl or a large liquid measuring cup, whisk together all of the ingredients until combined: the Greek yogurt, lemon zest, lemon juice, oil, honey, garlic, salt, and pepper. Taste and adjust the seasoning as desired. Use immediately or refrigerate in an airtight jar for up to 1 week.

NEXT LEVEL:
- *The Herby:* Add a few tablespoons of chopped fresh parsley, mint, tarragon, dill (my favorite for spring), chives, or a combination.

- *The Frenchie:* Add 1 tablespoon Dijon mustard.

- *The Spicy:* Add a pinch (or as much as you dare) cayenne pepper.

Zesty Ranch Dressing

ACTIVE TIME: 10 minutes · **TOTAL TIME:** 10 minutes · **YIELD:** About 1¼ cups

1 cup nonfat plain Greek yogurt

2 tablespoons extra virgin olive oil

2 tablespoons nonfat milk, plus additional as needed

1 tablespoon freshly squeezed lemon juice

¾ teaspoon garlic powder

½ teaspoon onion powder

½ teaspoon chili powder

½ teaspoon dried dill weed

¼ teaspoon kosher salt

¼ teaspoon Worcestershire sauce

⅛ teaspoon cayenne pepper

In a medium mixing bowl or a large liquid measuring cup, whisk together all of the ingredients until combined: the Greek yogurt, oil, milk, lemon juice, garlic powder, onion powder, chili powder, dill weed, salt, Worcestershire, and cayenne. If you'd like a thinner dressing, add more milk, 1 teaspoon at a time, until your desired consistency is reached. Taste and adjust the seasoning as desired. Use immediately or refrigerate in an airtight jar for up to 1 week.

LEFTOVER LOVE:
This dressing also makes a phenomenal marinade for grilled chicken. Place the chicken in a ziptop bag (if making chicken breasts, I like to pound them to an even thickness first), then pour the dressing over the top. Close the bag, removing as much air as possible. "Squish" the bag so that the dressing coats the chicken on all sides. Place in a small baking dish and refrigerate for at least 2 hours or up to 1 day. Let the chicken stand at room temperature for 10 minutes, then grill, shaking off excess marinade first.

Santa Fe Grilled Chicken Salad

ACTIVE TIME: 50 minutes · **TOTAL TIME:** 1 hour 40 minutes · **YIELD:** Serves 3 or 4 as a main

When I visit my sisters in Kansas City, my favorite spot to have lunch is a gourmet salad shop called The Mixx. Each salad overflows with fresh ingredients, the combinations of toppings are creative and unique, and the portions are generous and satisfying. I always walk away feeling inspired (and FULL).

This chicken salad is a riff on one of my favorite menu items. It combines juicy grilled cilantro lime chicken, light and crunchy romaine, creamy avocados, and a star lineup of Southwest ingredients like black beans, corn, and jalapenos. The handful of crushed tortilla chips makes me feel like I'm pigging out at a taco bar, when what I'm actually doing is feeding myself a nourishing, well-balanced meal.

For the Cilantro Lime Chicken:

1 pound boneless, skinless chicken breasts or boneless, skinless chicken thighs, trimmed of excess fat

Zest of 2 medium limes (about 1½ teaspoons)

¼ cup freshly squeezed lime juice (from the same 2 limes)

2 tablespoons extra virgin olive oil

2 cloves garlic, minced (about 2 teaspoons)

2 teaspoons honey

½ teaspoon ground cumin

½ teaspoon kosher salt

¼ teaspoon ground black pepper

Canola oil, for grilling

For the Salad:

8 cups chopped romaine lettuce (about 2 romaine hearts)

1½ cups shredded carrots (about 8 ounces or 3 medium)

2 medium jalapenos, seeds and membranes removed, finely chopped (about ¼ cup)

1 (15-ounce) can reduced sodium black beans, rinsed and drained

1 (7-ounce) can Mexican-style corn, drained

1 cup chopped fresh cilantro

¼ teaspoon kosher salt

¾ cup Zesty Ranch Dressing (page 90), plus additional to taste

2 medium ripe avocados, diced (about 2 cups)

1 cup crushed tortilla chips or tortilla strips

1. Prepare the chicken breasts: Place the chicken on a cutting board, leaving some space between the pieces. Cover with a large piece of plastic wrap. With a mallet, lightly pound the meat to an even thickness so that each piece cooks evenly (if using chicken thighs, you can skip this step).

2. Place the chicken in a large ziptop bag. To the bag, add the lime zest, lime juice, oil, garlic, honey, cumin, salt, and pepper. Seal the bag, removing as much excess air as possible, then "squish" to combine the marinade ingredients and coat the chicken evenly. Lay the bag in a small baking dish. Refrigerate for at least 1 hour or up to 8 hours.

3. When ready to grill, remove the chicken from the refrigerator and let stand at room temperature for 10 minutes. Preheat an outdoor grill or indoor grill pan to medium high (425 to 450 degrees F). Lightly oil the grill. Grill the chicken until completely cooked through and the temperature on an instant-read thermometer reads 165 degrees F, 10 to 14 minutes for chicken breasts or 6 minutes for chicken thighs, flipping the chicken once

recipe continues

or twice throughout. The amount of time you need will vary based on the size and thickness of your chicken. Remove to a cutting board, cover, and let rest 5 minutes. Uncover the chicken and cut into bite-sized pieces.

4. Assemble the salad: Place the romaine in a large serving bowl. Top with the chicken, carrots, jalapenos, black beans, corn, cilantro, and salt. Spoon ¾ cup dressing over the top. Toss to combine. Add the avocados, then lightly toss again. Sprinkle with the tortilla chips and drizzle with your desired amount of additional dressing. Taste and season with additional salt or pepper as desired.

MAKE-AHEAD & STORAGE TIPS:
The grilled chicken can be stored in the refrigerator for up to 3 days.

The entire salad (dressed or undressed) can be refrigerated for up to 3 days. I like it even better on day two, once the flavors have gotten cozy. If you plan to enjoy it over multiple days, add the tortilla chips to individual servings as you go, to keep them from becoming soggy. The avocados will also turn brown as the salad sits, so if you prefer the bright green color, wait to add them to the salad as well.

LEFTOVER LOVE:
Double the chicken, then use the extra for additional meals throughout the week. Try it fajita-style with sautéed onions and peppers; layer it with cheese for quesadillas; top with Cowboy Caviar (page 76); or mix with rice, beans, cheese, and sautéed vegetables to create a burrito bowl.

Maple Roasted Butternut Squash Salad with Arugula and Farro

ACTIVE TIME: 30 minutes · **TOTAL TIME:** 50 minutes
YIELD: Serves 4 to 6 as a side or 2 or 3 as a main

This Maple Roasted Butternut Squash Salad is everything I could want or dream of in an autumn meal: caramelized sweet squash; tart, plump cranberries; hearty whole grains; and a zippy vinaigrette. Keep your pen beside your fork. You will want to write this salad a love letter after your first bite. Tip: Semi-pearled farro is the term to describe farro that has some (but not all) of the outer hull removed. It's the kind most commonly sold in the United States and can be found at most major grocery stores.

For the Salad:

½ cup raw walnut halves

¾ cup uncooked semi-pearled farro, rinsed and drained

1 small butternut squash (about 1½ pounds)

1 tablespoon extra virgin olive oil

1 tablespoon pure maple syrup

1¼ teaspoons kosher salt

¼ teaspoon ground black pepper

5 ounces baby arugula (about 5 cups)

½ cup dried cranberries

⅓ cup crumbled goat cheese (about 1 ⅓ ounces)

For the Maple Dijon Dressing:

3 tablespoons extra virgin olive oil

2 tablespoons apple cider vinegar

1 tablespoon pure maple syrup

2 teaspoons Dijon mustard

1 clove garlic, minced (about 1 teaspoon)

1 teaspoon kosher salt

¼ teaspoon ground black pepper

1. Make the salad: Place a rack in the center of your oven and preheat the oven to 350 degrees F. Spread the walnuts on an ungreased baking sheet. Place in the oven and toast until the walnuts smell fragrant and are crisp, 8 to 10 minutes. Set aside to cool. Increase the oven temperature to 400 degrees F.

2. Cook the farro according to the package instructions. Place in a large serving bowl.

3. While the farro cooks, roast the butternut squash: Peel the butternut squash and trim off the top and bottom ends. Cut the neck away from the round base, then stand the base up on its flat end and cut in half from top to bottom. Scoop out the seeds and discard. Cut the squash (both base and neck) into ¾-inch cubes (you should have about 4 cups of cubes). Place the cubes in the center of a large rimmed baking sheet. Drizzle with the oil and maple syrup and sprinkle with the salt and pepper. Toss to coat the cubes, then spread into an even layer. Bake for 20 to 25 minutes, until fork tender, turning the squash once halfway through.

4. While the squash bakes, prepare the dressing: In a small bowl or large liquid measuring cup, whisk together the dressing

recipe continues

ingredients: the oil, vinegar, maple syrup, mustard, garlic, salt, and pepper, until combined. (Alternatively, you can shake all of the dressing ingredients together in a mason jar with a tight-fitting lid.) While the farro is still warm, pour enough of the dressing over it to moisten it, then with a large spoon or spatula, stir to combine.

5. Assemble the salad: Transfer the squash and any juices that have collected on the pan to the bowl with the farro. Add the arugula and cranberries. Roughly chop the toasted walnuts, then add them as well. Toss to combine and pour a little more dressing over the top if the salad seems too dry. Sprinkle with the goat cheese. Enjoy warm or at room temperature, with extra dressing as desired.

STORAGE TIPS:

This salad is best enjoyed the day it is made, as the arugula wilts over time. If you'd like to enjoy it throughout the week, add the arugula only to the portion of the salad that you are serving immediately. Store the arugula and the butternut squash/farro mixture separately in the refrigerator for 3 to 4 days.

MARKET SWAP:

Not a fan of goat cheese? You can simply omit it or swap it for feta or a mild blue cheese such as gorgonzola.

Summer Celebration Orzo Salad with Chickpeas and Creamy Basil Pesto

ACTIVE TIME: 35 minutes · **TOTAL TIME:** 55 minutes

YIELD: Serves 10 to 12 as a side or 4 to 6 as a main

This vibrant, summery salad is a bite out of your best life. A blend of lively pesto, height-of-summer veggies like zucchini and tomatoes, nourishing chickpeas, peppery arugula, and comforting orzo pasta, it tastes of farmers market mornings, lingering summer afternoons, and backyard barbecues. It's fresh and bountiful and the sort of thing I'd pack for a picnic behind my hypothetical beach house in Malibu. Or the Hamptons. My salad fantasies are flexible like that.

This salad yields a generous amount, is filling, and keeps well. In addition to being ideal for actual, nonhypothetical potlucks from coast to coast, it makes for quick, packable lunches and is a tasty side for grilled chicken, fish, or burgers. Don't skip the shower of feta on top. It adds a creamy, salty element that will leave this recipe lingering in your memory long after you've finished your plate.

3 medium zucchini, yellow summer squash, or a mix (about 1 pound)

3 ears of corn (about 2½ pounds), husks and silks removed

1 tablespoon extra virgin olive oil

½ teaspoon kosher salt

¼ teaspoon ground black pepper

8 ounces dry whole wheat orzo

¾ cup Creamy Basil Pesto (page 100), plus additional to taste

1 pint cherry or grape tomatoes, halved (about 2 cups)

1 (15-ounce) can reduced sodium chickpeas, rinsed and drained

3 cups lightly packed baby arugula (about 3 ounces)

¾ cup crumbled feta (about 4 ounces), divided

3 tablespoons freshly squeezed lemon juice (from about 1 small lemon)

1. Option 1, cook the zucchini and corn on the grill: Preheat an outdoor grill or indoor grill pan to medium heat. Trim off the ends of the zucchini and halve lengthwise. Place on a large plate or sheet pan with the corn (leave the corn on the cob). Drizzle the vegetables with the oil and season with the salt and pepper, then rub to coat them evenly. Grill on all sides until the vegetables are lightly charred and crisp-tender, about 10 minutes for the zucchini and 15 minutes for the corn. Transfer to a cutting board and let cool. Once cool enough to handle, stand the corn on one end and carefully cut away the kernels. Coarsely chop the zucchini into ¼- to ½-inch pieces. Set aside.

Option 2, cook the zucchini and corn in the oven: Place racks in the center and upper third of your oven (about 6 inches from the top) and preheat the oven to 425 degrees F. Line a large baking sheet with parchment paper. Trim the ends off of the zucchini and cut into a ¼-inch dice. Place the zucchini in the center of the baking sheet. Drizzle with the olive oil and sprinkle with the salt and pepper. Spread into a single layer and bake on the center rack for 10 minutes. While the zucchini bakes, stand the corn on one end and carefully cut away the kernels. Once the zucchini has

recipe continues

baked 10 minutes, remove the baking sheet from the oven and carefully stir in the corn kernels. Return the pan to the center rack and bake for an additional 15 minutes, or until the vegetables are tender, stirring once halfway through. Move the sheet pan to the upper rack and switch the oven to broil. Broil until the corn is browned and lightly crisp, 2 to 3 minutes. Watch carefully towards the end of the broiling time so that the vegetables do not burn. Remove from the oven and set aside.

2. While the vegetables grill or bake, cook the orzo to al dente, according to the package instructions. Drain, then add to a large mixing bowl. Immediately stir in the pesto while the orzo is still warm.

3. To the bowl with the orzo, add the tomatoes, chickpeas, arugula, ½ cup of the feta, the lemon juice, and the cooked corn and zucchini. Stir gently to combine. Taste and adjust the salt and pepper as desired and add a little more pesto if you'd like the salad to be creamier or have a stronger pesto flavor. Sprinkle the remaining ¼ cup feta over the top. Enjoy immediately or press a sheet of plastic wrap against the top to protect the pesto from air and refrigerate.

STORAGE TIPS:
Refrigerate leftovers in an airtight container with a sheet of plastic wrap pressed over the top for up to 3 days. I find this salad most enjoyable at room temperature, so remove it from the refrigerator at least 15 minutes prior to serving.

MARKET SWAPS:
Not a fan of feta? Swap it for part-skim mozzarella, cut into a ¼-inch dice, or mini mozzarella pearls. Since feta is saltier than mozzarella, you may want to season the salad with a bit of extra salt to balance its flavor.

Creamy Basil Pesto

ACTIVE TIME: 15 minutes · **TOTAL TIME:** 15 minutes · **YIELD:** Generous 2¼ cups

At no time do I feel more consumer savvy than when I'm walking home from the farmers market in the summer, my bag stuffed to the brim with fresh basil (take that, you tiny grocery store packets!). Every year, I use my bounty to make a great big batch of this vibrant pesto. Unlike the oily pestos you might be accustomed to seeing in a jar, this one is thick and creamy thanks to the Greek yogurt. It's ideal as a quick pasta sauce, spread for sandwiches (try combining it with mozzarella and tomato for the most magical grilled cheese), a dip for grilled chicken or shrimp skewers, and even a marinade. What pesto we don't devour immediately, I freeze in individual containers. On a dark and chilly winter day, I'll pull one out for dinner and let the pesto's sun-soaked flavor revive my weary spirit and remind me that summer will come again.

½ cup raw walnuts

4 cloves garlic, peeled and left whole

2 cups loosely packed fresh basil leaves

½ teaspoon kosher salt

½ teaspoon ground black pepper

¾ cup extra virgin olive oil

½ cup finely grated Parmesan cheese (about 1½ ounces)

1 (10-ounce) package frozen chopped spinach, thawed

2 tablespoons freshly squeezed lemon juice (about ½ medium lemon)

⅔ cup plain nonfat Greek yogurt

1. Place the walnuts and garlic in the bowl of a food processor fitted with a steel blade. Blend for 10 seconds.

2. Add the basil, salt, and pepper. With the processor running, slowly pour in the oil through the feed tube. Puree until smooth, 45 seconds to 1 minute. Add the Parmesan and puree for 1 minute, stopping to scrape down the bowl as needed.

3. Place the spinach in a mesh sieve or small colander and squeeze out as much water as possible. Place a double layer of paper towels on top and press it further so that the spinach is as dry as possible. Add the dried spinach to the food processor, then add the lemon juice. Puree until smoothly blended, 1 to 2 minutes. Add the Greek yogurt and continue blending, until the pesto is smooth, creamy, and the most gorgeous green color, about 1 minute more. Use immediately or store for later use (see Storage Tips on facing page).

STORAGE TIPS:

Air steals the freshness of pesto, so avoid as much contact with it as possible when storing. Place the pesto in an airtight container, then press a sheet of plastic directly over its surface before closing the lid. Refrigerate for 3 days or freeze for 3 months or longer. I once discovered a container of pesto that was at least 5 months old in our freezer and it was still quite delicious.

LEFTOVER LOVE—MY FAVORITE WAYS TO USE CREAMY BASIL PESTO:

- As a sandwich spread (especially on grilled cheese, page 222).

- On homemade pizzas.

- As a sauce with grilled or roasted vegetables, especially cherry tomatoes, eggplant, and bell peppers.

- As a dip with grilled chicken or shrimp.

- Mixed with cooked pasta.

- Summer Celebration Orzo Salad (page 97).

- Thinned with a bit of extra virgin olive oil and lemon juice, then tossed with mixed greens for a simple, flavorful salad.

- As a fresh and tasty marinade for grilled meat, seafood, or veggies.

Balsamic Farro Salad
with Edamame and Cranberries

ACTIVE TIME: 15 minutes · **TOTAL TIME:** 45 minutes · **YIELD:** Serves 4 to 6 as a side or 2 as a main

In my fantasy life, my refrigerator is neatly stocked with uniform containers, each filled with a beautiful, wholesome dish like the ones behind the glass counter at fancy gourmet grocery stores. In my real life, my refrigerator resembles a chaotic rummage sale. The lids don't match, jars of condiments are scattered throughout, and apples roll freely about the produce drawer.

Fortunately, the extent to which my storage containers match one another has no bearing on the deliciousness they contain. Never is that more true than when I have this Balsamic Farro Salad prepped and waiting for me. Nutty farro tossed with a bright balsamic dressing, creamy feta, chewy cranberries, and filling edamame is a triumph of taste and texture. Don't let the short ingredient list fool you. Every forkful zings with flavor.

For the Salad:

½ cup uncooked semi-pearled farro, rinsed and drained

1½ cups frozen shelled edamame, thawed

3 green onions, finely chopped (about ½ cup)

⅔ cup dried cranberries

⅔ cup crumbled feta (about 3⅓ ounces)

For the Dressing:

2 tablespoons extra virgin olive oil

2 tablespoons balsamic vinegar

½ teaspoon kosher salt

¼ teaspoon ground black pepper

1. Prepare the salad: Cook the farro according to the package instructions. Transfer it to a large serving bowl.

2. While the farro cooks, prepare the dressing: In a small bowl or large liquid measuring cup, whisk together the oil, vinegar, salt, and pepper. Immediately pour over the farro while it is still warm. Toss to combine.

3. To the farro, add the edamame, green onions, and cranberries. Toss to combine, then sprinkle the feta over the top. Stir gently, just until the feta is incorporated. Taste and season with additional salt and pepper as desired. Enjoy immediately or refrigerate until ready to serve.

MAKE-AHEAD & STORAGE TIPS:
This is a fantastic party salad, as it tastes marvelous at room temperature and its flavor improves as it sits. Make it 1 day in advance for a gathering, and store leftovers in the refrigerator for up to 3 days.

LEFTOVER LOVE:
I love this salad as a bright, filling side with simply grilled chicken or fish or mixed with spinach or arugula for a hearty green salad. If you'd like to use it for a green salad, make extra dressing, then reserve some to drizzle over the top once you've added the greens.

Modern Macaroni Salad

ACTIVE TIME: 35 minutes · **TOTAL TIME:** 1 hour 35 minutes
YIELD: Serves 8 to 10 as a side or 3 or 4 as a main

"Salad" is a loose term here in the Midwest. If your aunt Gertrude tells you she's bringing a salad to the family reunion, she could be referring to any number of items, including but not limited to Jell-O salad (filled with crushed pineapple and topped with a blend of cream cheese and Miracle Whip); fluff salad (cream cheese blended with Cool Whip, instant pudding mix, and mini marshmallows); Asian salad (uncooked ramen noodles, canned mandarin oranges, canola oil, and sugar); or macaroni salad. She is probably not referring to vegetables.

This updated version of macaroni salad is my modern twist. It swaps the suspect sugary, mayo-based dressing for a lighter, multi-dimensional blend of Greek yogurt, honey, and ranch dressing-ish spices. Whole wheat pasta noodles stand in for the standard white, and an array of colorful veggies provide much needed freshness and crunch.

It's a potluck superstar, but it also makes a family-friendly dinner. Its creamy texture, familiar ranch profile, and kid-friendly veggie assortment appeal to little ones yet it is dynamic enough to please parents too.

For the Pasta Salad:

8 ounces dry whole wheat elbow macaroni or similar small whole wheat pasta, such as small shells (about 2 cups)

2 medium carrots, peeled and shredded (about 5 ounces or 1 cup)

1 pint cherry or grape tomatoes, halved (about 2 cups)

1 medium yellow bell pepper, cut into ¼-inch dice (about 1 cup)

1 cup peas, fresh, or frozen and thawed

4 ounces cheddar cheese, cut into ¼-inch cubes (about ¾ cup)

2 tablespoons chopped fresh dill

For the Dressing:

¼ cup nonfat plain Greek yogurt

1 tablespoon extra virgin olive oil

1 tablespoon Dijon mustard

1 teaspoon white vinegar

1 teaspoon honey

1½ teaspoons kosher salt

1 teaspoon garlic powder

1 teaspoon onion powder

½ teaspoon ground black pepper

1. Make the salad: Cook the pasta until al dente, according to the package instructions. Drain in a colander and rinse under cold water. Shake the colander to toss the pasta and remove additional water. Let sit in the colander for 5 minutes, tossing occasionally. You want the pasta to be as dry as possible.

2. Meanwhile, make the dressing: In a small bowl or large liquid measuring cup, whisk together the Greek yogurt, oil, mustard, vinegar, honey, salt, garlic powder, onion powder, and pepper.

3. Transfer the drained pasta to a large serving bowl. Add the carrots, tomatoes, bell pepper, peas, and cheese. Pour the dressing over the top, then mix until evenly coated. Taste and season with additional salt or pepper as desired. Stir in the dill. Refrigerate for 1 hour prior to serving to allow the flavors to marry. Serve chilled or at room temperature.

MAKE-AHEAD & STORAGE TIPS:
This salad can be prepared and refrigerated up to 1 day
in advance, and leftovers stored for up to 3 days. If you
plan to serve it the next day, reserve about a third of the
dressing and stir it in just before serving.

Picnic Slaw

ACTIVE TIME: 15 minutes · **TOTAL TIME:** 2 hours 15 minutes · **YIELD:** Serves 6 to 8 as a side

I am a professional picnicker. Whether it's an outdoor summer concert, informal barbecue in the park, or just a nice night to sit outside and watch the sun set, you best believe I will be there with my checkered blanket, wine, and an extra-large container of this picnic slaw.

Colorful, crisp, and dressed with a lively, lemony spiced dressing, this pairs-with-anything, travel-friendly recipe is my go-to picnic or potluck side. Unlike bland, goopy, mayo-based coleslaws, this recipe can sit at room temperature without becoming soggy or watery. Chewy golden raisins and toasty pepitas give it the right balance of sweetness and surprise pops of texture, while a generous handful of cilantro provides the welcome freshness of a cool summer breeze. The bonus healthy twist here is swapping the traditional shredded cabbage for broccoli slaw, which also includes thinly shredded broccoli stalks. Broccoli slaw is mild in flavor and conveniently available in the produce section beside the regular bagged coleslaw mixes.

For the Slaw:

1 (12-ounce) package broccoli slaw (about 4 cups; see Pro Tip to make your own)

2 cups shredded carrots (about 10 ounces or 4 medium)

2 green onions, thinly sliced (about ¼ cup)

1 cup chopped fresh cilantro

¾ cup dry-roasted, unsalted pepitas

⅓ cup golden raisins

For the Dressing:

3 tablespoons extra virgin olive oil

3 tablespoons freshly squeezed lemon juice (from about 1 small lemon), plus additional to taste

1 clove garlic, minced (about 1 teaspoon)

2 teaspoons honey

½ teaspoon kosher salt

1 teaspoon hot sauce, such as Tabasco, plus additional to taste

---

1. Make the slaw: Place the broccoli slaw, carrots, green onions, and cilantro in a large serving bowl.

2. Make the dressing: In a small bowl or large liquid measuring cup, whisk together the dressing ingredients: oil, lemon juice, garlic, honey, salt, and hot sauce.

3. Pour the dressing over the slaw, then toss to evenly combine. Sprinkle the pepitas and raisins over the top, then toss lightly. Taste and add additional salt, lemon juice, or hot sauce as desired. Enjoy immediately or, if time allows, refrigerate 2 hours prior to serving to let the flavors marry.

STORAGE TIPS:
The slaw tastes best the day it is made but can be refrigerated for 3 days.

PRO TIP:
While I usually purchase premade broccoli slaw mix (because, easy!), you can make your own from fresh broccoli stems. To shred, either use the grater blade of your food processor or, with a knife, cut the stems first into thin planks, then lay the planks flat and cut into very thin strips.

LEFTOVER LOVE:
Use leftovers to top pulled chicken or pork sandwiches, tacos, or grilled fish.

Roasted Beets with Honey Orange Ricotta

ACTIVE TIME: 40 minutes · **TOTAL TIME:** 2 hours · **YIELD:** Serves 6 as a side

I often want to be the person at the potluck who brings the dish everyone raves about most. Actually, I *always* want to be that person, which is why I like to bring these Roasted Beets with Honey Orange Ricotta.

A stunning jewel box on a plate, these ruby-red and golden-yellow gems exemplify the magic of complementary ingredients uniting to create a single, spectacular experience. The tender, earthy beets are brightened by the orange, which is in turn elevated by the honey. Mint adds coolness and pep, and the ricotta? Well, if there's a recipe that *wouldn't* benefit from clouds of lightly sweetened, citrus-kissed ricotta dolloped generously over the top, I haven't met it yet.

---

2 pounds medium red beets, golden beets, or a mix, scrubbed, with tops and root ends trimmed (about 6 beets)

1 cup part-skim ricotta cheese (8 ounces)

Zest (about 2 tablespoons) and 2 tablespoons juice from 1 medium orange, divided

1½ teaspoons honey

1 teaspoon kosher salt, divided, plus an additional pinch for sprinkling on top

1½ tablespoons extra virgin olive oil

1 tablespoon white wine vinegar

¼ teaspoon ground black pepper

3 tablespoons chopped fresh mint, divided

---

1. Place a rack in the center of your oven and preheat the oven to 400 degrees F. Place the beets in a baking dish large enough to hold them comfortably. If you are using a mix of red and golden beets, place them in separate dishes by color to prevent the red beets from tinting the golden. Pour a thin layer of water into the dish(es), cover with aluminum foil, and bake until the beets feel tender in the center when pierced with a small, sharp knife, 50 minutes to 70 minutes, or longer, depending upon the size of your beets. Carefully transfer the beets to a cutting board and let stand until cool enough to handle. If you are concerned about staining your cutting board, lay a sheet of parchment paper over it first.

2. Use a paper towel to rub away the beet skins. If they are stubborn and stick, peel them with a small, sharp knife. Slice the beets crosswise into ¼-inch-thick rounds. If your beets are especially large, cut them in half lengthwise first, then lay them cut-side down on your board and slice each into half moons instead.

3. In a small mixing bowl, stir together the ricotta, orange zest, honey, and ¼ teaspoon of the salt. Set aside.

4. In a separate, larger mixing bowl, whisk together the orange juice, oil, vinegar, pepper, 1 tablespoon of the mint, and remaining ¾ teaspoon salt to make the dressing. If you are using both red and golden beets, pour half of the dressing into a separate bowl. Place the golden beets in one bowl of dressing and the red in the other. (If using only one color of beets, no need to divide the dressing or beets.) Toss to coat.

5. Arrange the dressed beets on a serving plate, mixing the two colors as desired. Drizzle with any dressing that has collected in the bottom of the bowl(s). Sprinkle with a generous pinch of salt, then dollop the ricotta over the top by large spoonfuls. Sprinkle evenly with the remaining 2 tablespoons mint. Enjoy immediately, or refrigerate until ready to serve.

MAKE-AHEAD & STORAGE TIPS:
The beets can be roasted and sliced 2 days in advance and the ricotta mixture prepared up to 1 day in advance. Store ricotta and beets (separated by color if needed) in separate containers in the refrigerator, then make the dressing and assemble the salad up to 4 hours before serving.

PRO TIP:
While this salad is lovely at room temperature, on a hot day it's especially refreshing chilled.

Mediterranean Kale Salad

Killer
Kale
Salad
(3 Ways!)

Mexican Kale Salad

Harvest Kale Salad

Killer Kale Salad (3 Ways!)

ACTIVE TIME: 15 minutes · **TOTAL TIME:** 45 minutes to 1 hour (varies by salad)
YIELD: Serves 6 as a side or 3 or 4 as a main

This cookbook and your life really do need another kale salad.

The utter proliferation of kale salads combined with my general enthusiasm for greens has led me to order dozens of them all over the country. Most have been disappointing. A few have been exceptional. I order one any time I see it on a menu, which means that (a) I am terrible at learning from experience, and (b) I've eaten all the duds so you don't have to.

In this recipe, I've taken everything I've learned about kale salads throughout the years and distilled it into a master formula with three knockout variations. An exciting medley of textures and flavors, these salads are interesting and filling, and they are a meal you will legitimately crave. The leftovers can last for days in your refrigerator even after the dressing is added, so your time spent prepping them will be rewarded all week long.

Every time I make a kale salad, I start with the same base combination of massaged kale, cooked grains—a unique addition that provides an extra dimension of texture, along with protein and fiber—and beans, then change it up with seasonal mix-ins to keep my meals feeling new. Eat your way through these favorites, and don't be afraid to create your own variations too.

◄ A NOT-SO-BASIC KALE SALAD MASTER RECIPE ►

1 (3-ounce) package dry-packed sun-dried tomatoes (about ¾ tightly-packed cup)

1 large bunch curly kale (about 12 ounces or 8 stems) or 2 medium bunches lacinato (dinosaur) kale (about 16 ounces or 18 stems), tough center stems removed

¼ teaspoon kosher salt

1 (15-ounce) can reduced-sodium beans, such as cannellini, black, or chickpeas, rinsed and drained

⅔ cup cooked quinoa, farro, wheat berries, or a similar chewy, nutty grain

½ cup crumbled or shredded cheese, such as feta, cheddar, Parmesan, or gorgonzola

½ cup toasted nuts or seeds, roughly chopped if large

Additional vegetables or mix-ins of choice (as many as you like!)

1 batch Go-to Citrus Dressing (page 89)

VARIATION 1:
Mexican Kale Salad

FOR THE SALAD: Use black beans, queso fresco or feta, and pepitas; add 1 bunch thinly sliced radishes (about 1¾ cups), ½ cup chopped fresh cilantro, and 2 finely chopped medium green onions (about ⅓ cup).

FOR THE DRESSING: Use lime juice.

VARIATION 2:
Mediterranean Kale Salad

FOR THE SALAD: Use chickpeas and feta; omit the nuts; add ½ cup chopped pitted Kalamata olives, 1 (14-ounce) can drained, roughly chopped, and patted-dry artichoke hearts (about 1 heaping cup), ¼ cup finely diced red onion (from about ¼ small red onion), and ½ cup chopped fresh parsley.

FOR THE DRESSING: Use lemon juice; add ¼ teaspoon dried oregano.

VARIATION 3:
Harvest Kale Salad

FOR THE SALAD: Omit the sun-dried tomatoes; use white beans (such as cannellini or great Northern), shredded Parmesan, and walnuts; add 1 small-medium diced and roasted sweet potato (about 1 cup roasted), 1 diced, medium sweet-crisp apple (such as Honeycrisp or Fuji, about 1 cup), and ½ cup dried cranberries.

FOR THE DRESSING: Use orange juice; add 2 teaspoons Dijon mustard.

1. Place the sun-dried tomatoes in a small bowl. Top with very hot water and let sit for a few minutes to rehydrate while you prepare the other ingredients. Drain, pat dry, and roughly chop.

2. Slice the kale into thin ribbons, then chop into bite-sized pieces (you should have about 8 cups of tightly packed kale total). Place the kale in a large bowl, then sprinkle with the salt. Grab the kale by large handfuls and gently squeeze and massage it, working a few handfuls at a time, until the kale is softened and dark green in color. The more you massage, the more tender and tasty the kale will be.

3. Add the sun-dried tomatoes, beans, grains, cheese, nuts, and any other desired mix-ins. Top with half of the dressing (about 2½ generous tablespoons), then toss to coat. Enjoy immediately or refrigerate for up to 3 days. If desired, drizzle the salad with extra dressing prior to serving.

MAKE-AHEAD & STORAGE TIPS:

Cooked grains such as quinoa can be stored in the refrigerator for up to 5 days or frozen for up to 3 months, so you can prepare the grains a few days ahead of when you'd like to assemble the salad. You can also make grains in big batches, then freeze them in individual portions and thaw as needed.

If you're adding roasted vegetables to the salad, such as in the harvest version, start the vegetables roasting first, then chop the kale and prep any other toppings while they bake.

Store leftovers in the refrigerator for 3 to 4 days. If desired, top the leftovers with a little extra dressing or additional squeeze of citrus juice to liven up their flavor.

PRO TIPS:

• Dry-packed sun-dried tomatoes are usually sold in pouch-style packets. Look for them in the produce section beside the fresh tomatoes, by the oil-packed sun-dried tomatoes (which are usually sold in jars), beside the pasta and pasta sauce, or in the dried fruit section. If you can't find dry-packed, swap them for oil-packed. Drain off the oil and pat the tomatoes dry first (no need to rehydrate).

• The biggest trick to transforming a kale salad from something that a bunny wouldn't sniff into a bountiful, healthy lunch you'll truly adore is to massage the kale first. Massaging breaks down the kale's fibers, neutralizing its taste and giving it a smooth, buttery consistency.

MAKE-AHEAD & STORAGE TIPS:
This salad tastes even better after it rests, so feel free to make it a few hours ahead. Store leftovers in the refrigerator for 2 to 3 days and jazz them up with an extra squeeze of lemon juice.

For a hit of protein, this salad tastes wonderful with grilled chicken or grilled shrimp.

Shaved Brussels Sprouts Salad

ACTIVE TIME: 20 minutes · **TOTAL TIME:** 20 minutes · **YIELD:** Serves 4 to 6 as a side or 2 or 3 as a main

Ribbons of Brussels sprouts and vibrant kale tossed in a cheerful lemon dressing, then showered with chewy cranberries, nutty sunflower seeds, and sassy Parmesan, make up this startlingly good salad. It's inspired by one of my favorite Kansas City dinner spots, where I order the shaved Brussels sprouts salad (paired with the house signature cocktail because, balance) every time we go. For reasons of self-preservation, I've resisted completing the necessary number of trial batches to re-create the cocktail at home, but the salad I gleefully pursued and mastered. The ingredient list here is short, so each one is important. Buy real-deal Parmesan and shave it right off the block. Every bite will affirm your decision.

1 medium bunch curly kale (about 8 ounces or 6 stems), stems removed and finely chopped (about 6 cups)

¼ teaspoon kosher salt

⅛ teaspoon ground black pepper

1 pound Brussels sprouts, finely shredded or very thinly sliced (about 4 cups) (see Pro Tip)

1 batch Zippy Lemon Yogurt Dressing (page 89)

⅔ cup shaved or shredded Parmesan cheese (about 2½ ounces)

½ cup dried cranberries

⅓ cup dry-roasted, unsalted sunflower seeds

1. Place the chopped kale in a large serving bowl. Top with the salt and pepper. Massage the kale by grabbing large handfuls and squeezing gently until the kale is darker in color, softened, and more fragrant. Repeat several times, grabbing fresh handfuls of kale as you go. (This step makes the kale more tender and less bitter in taste—don't skip it!) Add the shaved Brussels sprouts, fluffing the strands with your fingers to separate the shreds. Drizzle two-thirds of the dressing over the top. Toss to combine.

2. Sprinkle the Parmesan, cranberries, and sunflower seeds over the top. Toss lightly. Season with additional salt and pepper to taste and add as much extra dressing as you like. Enjoy immediately or refrigerate until ready to serve.

PRO TIP—HOW TO SHRED BRUSSELS SPROUTS:

For the fastest possible shredding, cut the bottom ends off of the Brussels sprouts, then shred the sprouts using a food processor slicing blade.

Alternatively, you can carefully slice the Brussels sprouts with a mandoline, taking care to watch your fingers. I recommend leaving the bottoms untrimmed, holding the bottoms, then slicing starting from the top. When you near the bottom, discard the bit you are still holding (don't risk a cut).

If you do not have a food processor or a mandoline, use a sharp chef's knife: Cut off the bottoms, then slice the sprouts lengthwise into very thin ribbons.

Book Club Salad
(A Great, Green Party Salad)

ACTIVE TIME: 30 minutes · **TOTAL TIME:** 30 minutes · **YIELD:** Serves 8 as a side or 3 or 4 as a main

My friend Erika once brought this salad to our monthly book club, and now, five years later, we still won't let her bring anything else. We refer to it as "The Salad," and its presence at the table is more mandatory than actually reading the book.

This stellar green salad is sized for a crowd, tastes better than any salad I've eaten in a restaurant, and is beautiful and adaptable for the seasons. Peppery arugula tossed with juicy sliced fruit, salty gorgonzola, crunchy almonds, and avocados, "The Salad" manages the elusive feat of tasting wholesome and decadent at the same time. When tossed, the avocados and gorgonzola break down a bit and make the salad creamy. The lemon vinaigrette keeps it bright, and the addition of the fresh fruit and nuts makes every forkful its own enchanting experience. Bring this salad to a party, bask in the applause, then don't be surprised when your friends start insisting that you make it repeatedly too.

For the Salad:

½ small red onion, very thinly sliced (about ½ cup)

10 to 12 ounces baby arugula (12 to 15 lightly packed cups)

2 medium ripe peaches or nectarines, pitted and thinly sliced, peels on or off (about 2 cups)

2 medium ripe avocados, diced (about 2 cups)

⅔ cup toasted sliced almonds

⅔ cup crumbled mild blue cheese, such as gorgonzola (about 3 ½ ounces)

For the Dressing:

¼ cup extra virgin olive oil

¼ cup freshly squeezed lemon juice (from about 1 medium lemon)

½ teaspoon Dijon mustard

1 clove garlic, minced (about 1 teaspoon)

¾ teaspoon kosher salt

¼ teaspoon ground black pepper

1. Make the salad: Place the red onion in a small bowl and cover with water. Let sit while you prepare the rest of the salad. (This will keep the flavor of the onion but remove some of the harsh after-bite.) Place the arugula in a large serving bowl.

2. Make the dressing: In a small bowl or large liquid measuring cup, whisk together the dressing ingredients: the oil, lemon juice, mustard, garlic, salt, and pepper.

3. Drizzle half of the dressing over the greens, then toss to coat. Drain the red onion, then scatter it and the peaches, avocados, almonds, and cheese over the top. Just before serving, drizzle on a bit more dressing and give it a final, gentle toss to combine. Enjoy, with additional dressing as desired.

MARKET SWAPS:
This salad is a delightful base for seasonal swaps. In the fall and winter, replace the peaches and almonds with thinly sliced apples and walnuts; in the spring and early summer, try a mix of sliced strawberries and pecans.

MAKE-AHEAD & STORAGE TIPS:
Prepare right up until the final dressing drizzle and toss in step 3, up to 4 hours in advance. Cover the serving bowl with plastic wrap and store it in the refrigerator.

This salad tastes best the day it is made but (if you don't mind slightly wilted arugula) can be stored in the refrigerator for 1 to 2 additional days. Wake up the leftovers with an extra squeeze of lemon juice.

Main Attractions

Raymonde's Moroccan Lemon Chicken, page 152

Welcome to my happy place. Creating wholesome recipes and sharing them with people I love is deeply entwined with who I am. At no meal do I feel that sense of myself more tangibly than at dinner. Whether I'm hosting friends for an impromptu gathering or preparing a casual dinner for two, even if everything else in my day has gone to pieces, the kitchen has a way of putting them back together.

Healthy, easy-to-make main dishes like the ones you'll find in this chapter play a particularly special, impactful role in my life. They are the recipes I most enjoy creating, as well as the ones for which my blog readers have come to know me best. I know dinnertime is hectic, you don't have extravagant volumes of time to spend cooking, and that you might not even know *what* to cook in the first place. That's why this chapter is here.

I've loaded this section of the book with nourishing recipes that come together quickly, are made with ingredients you can find at an average grocery store, and, above all, taste *incredible*. You don't need fad diets, specialty items, or complicated prep to produce wholesome meals that will leave you feeling satisfied and proud of what you've created, and that your family will adore.

In addition to a lineup of healthy twists on classic comfort foods, sheet pan dinners, and slam-dunk slow cooker recipes, I've loaded this chapter with special quick-fix options for the nights when you walk through the door and no words strike greater terror than *"What's for dinner?"* (Answer: Try 4 Unboring Ways to Use Shredded Chicken, page 154.) To help you make the most of your efforts, I've also included creative ideas for your leftovers (Slow Cooker Bolognese + 3 Ways to Use It, page 192, is one of my favorites). You'll even find clever spins on the same base recipe, like Ultimate Creamy Mac and Cheese (4 Ways!) on page 186.

These recipes will be the dependable, go-to dinners that you feel confident making again and again. The different options and twists will keep them interesting and fresh. It's tried-and-true made a little bit new!

Thai Peanut Chicken Stir-Fry
(The Stir-Fry That Got Me Married)

ACTIVE TIME: 40 minutes · **TOTAL TIME:** 40 minutes · **YIELD:** Serves 4

The first time I cooked this stir-fry for Ben, he demolished the entire pan, collapsed into a food coma, then proposed two weeks later. Coincidence? Or could it be the power of the Thai peanut sauce?

Through the years, this recipe has remained one of our favorite dinners and has become a reader favorite too. This peanut sauce is rich, sassy, and filled with layers of sweet and spicy flavor. Feel free to use any vegetables you have on hand, make the dish vegetarian with tofu (see Market Swaps), or serve it with noodles or quinoa instead of brown rice. Just be careful about *to whom* you serve it. History suggests you may receive a certain question in return!

For the Sauce:

½ cup creamy peanut butter

3 tablespoons water

3 tablespoons honey

2 tablespoons low sodium soy sauce, plus additional to taste

3 tablespoons Thai red curry paste

2 tablespoons rice vinegar

1 tablespoon minced fresh ginger

2 cloves garlic, minced (about 2 teaspoons)

2 teaspoons red pepper flakes, plus additional to taste

For the Stir-Fry:

2 tablespoons extra virgin olive oil, divided

1 medium yellow onion, thinly sliced (about 1½ cups)

1 pound boneless, skinless chicken breasts or thighs, cut into ½-inch dice

6 cups chopped vegetables of choice (about 1½ pounds—see Market Swaps for suggestions)

½ cup chopped dry-roasted, unsalted peanuts, plus additional to taste

½ cup chopped fresh cilantro, plus additional to taste

Prepared brown rice, for serving

1. In a medium bowl, whisk together the sauce ingredients until smooth: the peanut butter, water, honey, soy sauce, red curry paste, vinegar, ginger, garlic, and red pepper flakes. Set aside.

2. Make the stir-fry: In a deep, large nonstick skillet or wok, heat 1 tablespoon of the oil over medium-high heat. Once the oil is hot but not yet smoking, add the onion and cook until fragrant and beginning to soften, about 3 minutes. Add the chicken and sauté, stirring occasionally, until fully cooked through, about 4 minutes. The centers of the pieces will no longer be pink and the juices should run clear when a piece is cut. Remove the chicken and onion from the skillet and set aside.

3. With a paper towel, carefully wipe the skillet clean. Add the remaining 1 tablespoon oil, then the mixed vegetables. Sauté until the vegetables are crisp-tender, 7 to 8 minutes, depending on the vegetables selected.

4. Return the chicken and onion to the skillet. Add the peanut sauce. Toss to coat evenly, and cook until heated through, about 2 minutes. Stir in the peanuts and cilantro. Taste and add additional soy sauce or red pepper flakes as desired. Serve hot over rice, topped with additional chopped peanuts and cilantro as desired.

STORAGE TIPS:
Refrigerate leftovers for up to 4 days or freeze for up to 3 months. Let thaw overnight in the refrigerator and reheat gently in the microwave or on the stove top with a splash of broth or water to keep the stir-fry from drying out.

PRO TIP:
Thai red curry paste is available in the Asian food section or international food section of most grocery stores.

MARKET SWAPS:
- You can use any mix of fresh vegetables you like, or for a true time-saver, use a package of frozen stir-fry vegetables. Thaw and pat the vegetables dry, then add them to the recipe as directed. They won't be as crisp as fresh vegetables, but they'll be yummy, nutritious, and cut the recipe prep time in half.

- When using fresh vegetables, be sure to chop the vegetables to an appropriate size so that the different varieties all cook in the same amount of time. My favorite is a blend of broccoli cut into florets (1 medium, 10-ounce head is about 3 cups), 2 medium red bell peppers thinly sliced into ¼-inch-thick strips (about 2 cups), and 2 medium carrots (about 5 ounces) peeled and cut into thin coins (about 1 generous cup). If you have peas in your freezer, these are easy to toss in at the end. The amount of vegetables is flexible, so if you go a bit over or under, don't worry.

- *Make It Meatless:* Swap the chicken for 1 (12- to 14-ounce) package extra-firm tofu (do not use silken, firm, or any other variety of tofu) and increase the oil to 3½ tablespoons, plus additional as needed. Press the tofu dry, then cut into bite-sized cubes. Begin cooking the stir-fry by heating ½ tablespoon oil over medium-high heat. Once the oil is hot but not yet smoking, sauté the onion until beginning to soften, about 3 minutes. Remove the onion to a plate. Return the pan to the heat and add 2 tablespoons of the oil. Once the oil is hot, add the tofu in a single layer. Sauté until the tofu is golden and crisp on all sides, turning it every few minutes and adding more oil to the pan if the tofu begins to stick. Remove the tofu to the plate with the onion. Add the remaining 1 tablespoon oil, then proceed with sautéing the remaining vegetables as directed, stirring in the onion, tofu, sauce, peanuts, and cilantro at the end.

Kickin' Black Pepper Pork Stir-Fry

ACTIVE TIME: 35 minutes · **TOTAL TIME:** 35 minutes · **YIELD:** Serves 4

No, no, this recipe does not have a typo. That's a full 2 teaspoons of black pepper in the sauce, and yes, you really do want every precious speck. For as ubiquitous as black pepper is, it's a spice I rarely stop to think about for its own individual star power. Here, it steps into the spotlight and elevates this weeknight-friendly meal from something you'll enjoy eating to a dish that will have members of your household calling dibs on the leftovers.

For the Stir-Fry:

4 ounces brown rice noodles

1 small pork tenderloin (about ¾ pound), trimmed and cut into ¾-inch cubes

2 tablespoons cornstarch

¼ teaspoon kosher salt

¼ teaspoon ground black pepper

2 tablespoons canola or grapeseed oil, divided

1 medium head broccoli (about 10 ounces), cut into bite-sized florets (about 3 cups)

4 ounces stemmed shiitake mushrooms, thinly sliced (about 2 cups)

1 small red onion, cut into ¼-inch-thick slices (about 1½ cups)

3 medium green onions, finely chopped (about ½ cup)

1 tablespoon toasted sesame seeds

For the Sauce:

⅓ cup low sodium soy sauce, plus additional to taste

1 tablespoon cornstarch

1½ teaspoons honey

1½ tablespoons rice vinegar

2 teaspoons ground black pepper, plus additional to taste

2 cloves garlic, minced (about 2 teaspoons)

¼ teaspoon ground ginger

1. Make the stir-fry: Cook the noodles according to the package instructions. Reserve 1 cup of the noodle cooking liquid, then drain the noodles into a colander. Rinse briefly under cold water to stop the noodles' cooking. Shake the colander to release excess liquid, then set aside.

2. While the noodles cook, in a medium bowl place the pork, cornstarch, salt, and pepper. Toss to coat.

3. Heat a large nonstick skillet or wok over medium-high heat. Add 1 tablespoon of the oil. Once the oil is hot, add the pork and sauté until lightly browned on all sides, stirring occasionally, until it is cooked through and no longer pink in the center, about 5 minutes. Transfer the pork to a plate or bowl. Set aside.

4. To the skillet, add the remaining 1 tablespoon oil. Once the oil is hot, add the broccoli, mushrooms, and red onion. Sauté for 8 to 10 minutes, stirring occasionally, until the broccoli is crisp-tender and the mushrooms soften.

5. Make the sauce: While the vegetables cook, in a small bowl or large liquid measuring cup whisk together the sauce ingredients until combined: the soy sauce, cornstarch, honey, vinegar, pepper, garlic, and ginger.

6. Once the vegetables have cooked, add the pork, sauce, and noodles to the pan. With a pair of tongs, toss to combine the ingredients and evenly coat the noodles with the sauce, adding a little of the reserved noodle cooking

recipe continues

liquid as needed if the noodles are sticking together. Continue cooking and tossing for 1 to 2 minutes, until the sauce has thickened and the noodles are warmed through. Taste and season with additional soy sauce and pepper as desired. Remove from the heat, sprinkle with the green onions and sesame seeds, and serve immediately.

MAKE-AHEAD & STORAGE TIPS:

For an even faster dinner, cut up the broccoli, mushrooms, and onion up to 2 days in advance and store in an airtight container in the refrigerator. When it's time to add them to the skillet, dump the whole container in at once. Black Pepper Pork, pronto!

Store leftovers in an airtight container in the refrigerator for up to 4 days. Reheat gently in the microwave or on the stove over medium heat with a splash of water or broth to loosen the noodles and keep them from drying out.

MARKET SWAPS:

• Feel free to swap out the broccoli for any other mix of vegetables you enjoy or have on hand. A combo of green and red bell peppers is one of my favorites.

• If you aren't a fan of mushrooms, you can omit them, though the extra depth of flavor shiitakes provide is not to be missed unless it is 100% necessary.

Instant Pot Jambalaya

ACTIVE TIME: 45 minutes · **TOTAL TIME:** 1 hour 30 minutes · **YIELD:** Serves 6

I once made the mistake of packing high-waisted jeans for a trip to New Orleans. As soon as I discovered jambalaya, a spiced mix of rice, meat (usually chicken and sausage), and seafood (usually shrimp), it became abundantly clear that an elastic waistband would have been the prudent choice. A traditional dish you'll find throughout the South, jambalaya is robust, complex, and comforting. Once you start eating it, it's hard to stop!

My lightened-up version is inspired by New Orleans and uses brown rice and extra veggies to make it a true all-in-one meal. Thanks to the Instant Pot, every single component cooks in a single pot, so you have fewer dishes to wash at the end.

This recipe yields a generous amount, so it's ideal for larger groups or anytime you want tasty leftovers. I love making it for casual dinner parties, because it feels fun and a little adventurous but is still familiar enough to be cozy. Be sure to add the fresh lemon, which wakes up the rice and helps the other ingredients shine.

2 tablespoons extra virgin olive oil, divided

12 ounces fully cooked andouille sausage, cut into ¼-inch-thick coins

1 pound large (31/40 count) fresh or frozen raw shrimp, peeled and deveined (if using frozen, thaw, rinse, and pat dry)

1 medium yellow onion, chopped (about 1½ cups)

1 medium green bell pepper, cut into 1-inch pieces (about 1 cup)

1 medium red bell pepper, cut into 1-inch pieces (about 1 cup)

3 cloves garlic, minced (about 1 tablespoon)

1 teaspoon kosher salt

1 teaspoon dried oregano

½ teaspoon dried thyme

¼ teaspoon cayenne pepper

1 large or 2 small bay leaves

1 (14.5-ounce) can low sodium chicken broth, divided

1 (14.5-ounce) can fire roasted diced tomatoes in their juices

1¼ cups uncooked long grain brown rice

1 pound boneless, skinless chicken thighs, trimmed of excess fat

6 dashes hot sauce, such as Tabasco, plus additional to taste

3 medium green onions, finely chopped (about ½ cup)

3 tablespoons freshly squeezed lemon juice (from about 1 small lemon)

1. Add 1 tablespoon of the oil to a 6-quart or larger Instant Pot and select the sauté function. Once the oil is hot but not yet smoking, add the andouille sausage and cook until browned, stirring occasionally so that all sides develop color, about 6 minutes. With a slotted spoon, remove to a plate and set aside.

2. Add ½ tablespoon more oil to the pot, then add the shrimp. Stir and cook just until the shrimp are no longer translucent, about 3 minutes. Remove to the plate with the sausage.

3. Add the remaining ½ tablespoon oil, the onion, and green and red bell peppers. Stir and cook until the onion is translucent, about 5 minutes. Add the garlic, salt, oregano, thyme, cayenne, and bay leaf. Cook just until fragrant, about 30 seconds. Turn the Instant Pot off. Splash in about ½ cup of the broth and stir, using a wooden spoon or sturdy plastic spatula to thoroughly and completely scrape up any bits of food that have stuck to

recipe continues

the bottom of the pot. Scrape up every bit of food so that the Instant Pot does not register a "burn" warning.

4. Stir in the remaining broth. Pour the tomatoes over the top and do not stir. Rinse and drain the rice (this also helps prevent a "burn" warning) and add it on top of the liquid in the Instant Pot. Do not stir. With the back of a spoon or a spatula, gently push the rice down and spread it evenly so that it is submerged in liquid. Arrange the chicken thighs in a single layer on top, tucking the loose side portion of the thigh underneath.

5. Cover and seal the Instant Pot. Cook on high (manual) pressure for 20 minutes. Let the pressure release naturally for 15 minutes, then vent immediately to release any remaining pressure. Carefully open the lid.

6. Remove the chicken thighs to a cutting board and discard the bay leaf. Dice the chicken or shred it with two forks and return it to the pot. Stir in the hot sauce, green onions, lemon juice, and reserved sausage and shrimp, letting the residual heat of the jambalaya warm the shrimp and sausage through. Taste and adjust the seasoning and add additional hot sauce as desired. Serve hot.

STORAGE TIPS:
Refrigerate leftovers for up to 4 days or freeze for up to 3 months. Let thaw in the refrigerator overnight. Reheat gently in the microwave or on the stove over medium heat with a splash of water or broth to keep the rice from drying out.

MARKET SWAPS:
If you can't find andouille sausage, you can substitute kielbasa, which is more widely available. Kielbasa is milder than andouille, so if the jambalaya isn't as spicy as you like, kick it up with a few extra dashes of hot sauce.

Sheet Pan Tandoori Chicken

ACTIVE TIME: 30 minutes · **TOTAL TIME:** 1 hour 15 minutes · **YIELD:** Serves 4

Never have my five senses worked in such a constant state of overdrive than they did during the three weeks I spent in India. Every sight, sound, and smell was saturated with color and energy. While there is much about the country I miss, I crave the food above all else, especially the rich, saucy curries, fluffy naan bread, and tandoori chicken.

Tandoori chicken is a warmly spiced, mouthwateringly juicy chicken dish cooked at a high temperature in a clay oven. Since my cravings for tandoori chicken are frequent (and a return trip to India is not), I created a version using my regular old oven and the spices sold in our Midwest grocery store. While it's certainly not 100% authentic, the robust mix of spices and tenderness of the chicken resemble the dishes I enjoyed abroad. To make this a true all-in-one meal, I added sweet potato, cauliflower, and chickpeas. I like to serve ours with brown rice or a steaming plate of naan with extra Greek yogurt for dipping. Tasty tip: Don't skip the cilantro and lemon juice. They are the final touches that will transport you to a faraway place.

For the Chicken:

1¾ pounds bone-in, skin-on chicken parts (any mix of thighs, drumsticks, or breasts; wings are not recommended, as they will overcook)

½ cup nonfat plain Greek yogurt

4 cloves garlic, minced (about 4 teaspoons)

1 tablespoon minced fresh ginger

1 tablespoon ground cumin

1 teaspoon chili powder

1 teaspoon kosher salt

For the Chickpeas and Vegetables:

1 (15-ounce) can reduced sodium chickpeas

1 small or ½ large head cauliflower (about 1½ pounds), cut into ¾-inch-wide florets (about 4½ cups)

1 small-medium sweet potato (8 to 10 ounces), scrubbed, peel on, and cut into ¾-inch cubes (about 2 cups)

1½ tablespoons extra virgin olive oil

1½ teaspoons chili powder

1 teaspoon ground turmeric

½ teaspoon kosher salt

For Serving:

1 large lemon, halved

Freshly chopped cilantro

Naan or prepared brown rice

Nonfat plain Greek yogurt

1. Prepare the chicken: Remove the skin from the chicken by pulling it with your fingers, then cutting away any stubborn pieces with a knife. If using chicken breasts, with a very sharp, sturdy chef's knife, cut them in half crosswise (that's through the shorter side if you think of the breast from left to right and top to bottom), placing the knife on top of the breast and cutting straight down through the bone. Carefully but firmly wiggle the knife as needed. For each breast, you should be left with 2 pieces of chicken that are roughly the same size (this will help the pieces all cook in the same amount of time). For thighs and drumsticks, remove the skin but leave them whole.

2. To a large ziptop bag, add the Greek yogurt, garlic, ginger, cumin, chili powder, and salt. Seal the bag, removing any air. "Squish" the

recipe continues

ingredients around until they are evenly combined. Open the bag, add the chicken pieces, reseal, then gently squish and turn the bag to coat the pieces evenly with the yogurt mixture. Place the bag in a shallow dish and refrigerate for 30 minutes or up to 24 hours.

3. When you are ready to make the chicken, place a rack in the center of your oven and preheat the oven to 425 degrees F. For easy cleanup, line a large rimmed baking sheet with aluminum foil and coat generously with nonstick spray. If you prefer not to use foil, use parchment paper or coat the baking sheet directly. Remove the chicken from the refrigerator.

4. Prepare the chickpeas and vegetables: Rinse and drain the chickpeas, then spread them onto a double layer of paper towels. Place more paper towels on top and pat them as dry as you can. Remove any chickpea skins that come obviously loose (no need to get them all). Place in a large mixing bowl.

5. To the bowl, add the cauliflower and sweet potato. Drizzle the vegetables and chickpeas with the oil and sprinkle with the chili powder, turmeric, and salt. Toss to evenly coat, then spread into a single layer on the prepared baking sheet.

6. Remove the chicken from the marinade, shaking off any excess, then arrange the pieces on top of the vegetables and chickpeas. Bake for 15 minutes, remove the pan from the oven, then with a small spatula or large spoon, gently turn any vegetables and chickpeas that are visible and not covered by the chicken. No need to perfectly flip them all; simply move them around a little so that you promote even cooking.

7. Return the pan to the oven and continue baking an additional 15 to 20 minutes, until the chicken reaches an internal temperature of 165 degrees F at the thickest part and the juices run clear when sliced. If some of the chicken pieces finish earlier than others, remove the done pieces to a plate and cover to keep warm, then return the pan to the oven and continue baking until the remaining chicken is cooked through.

8. To serve: Return any chicken pieces you removed early back to the baking sheet, then squeeze the lemon over the top of the chicken and vegetables. Sprinkle with cilantro. Serve hot with naan and Greek yogurt.

MAKE-AHEAD & STORAGE TIPS:
For the speediest possible dinner, marinate the chicken up to 24 hours in advance and store it in the refrigerator as suggested in step 2. The vegetables can also be chopped 24 hours in advance and refrigerated in a separate container.

Store leftover chicken and chickpeas/vegetables separately in the refrigerator for up to 3 days. Reheat the chickpeas/vegetables in a 400-degree-F oven for 5 to 10 minutes, until hot. To reheat the chicken, pull it from the bone in large pieces. Rewarm gently in the microwave or on the stove top, covered, with a splash of water or broth to keep it from drying out.

LEFTOVER LOVE:
Chop the leftover chicken and use to top salads throughout the week or to make Chicken Shawarma Wraps (page 156).

Caprese Chicken Skillet

ACTIVE TIME: 45 minutes · **TOTAL TIME:** 45 minutes · **YIELD:** Serves 3 or 4

In a world that's ripe with complication, this recipe is a glorious triumph of the simple. Plump tomatoes, melty mozzarella, sweet balsamic vinegar, and fresh basil unite to create a one-pan wonder that, like the classic Caprese salad that inspired it, is much greater than its individual parts. Don't let the short ingredient list or basic prep fool you—this recipe hits all the right notes on the flavor chord. On your next busy weeknight, take a deep breath and let this easy, healthy, and family-pleasing dish remind you that dinner doesn't need to be difficult to be delicious.

½ cup plus 1 tablespoon balsamic vinegar, divided

1 tablespoon plus 1 teaspoon honey, divided

1½ pounds boneless, skinless chicken breasts

1¼ teaspoons kosher salt, divided

½ teaspoon ground black pepper, divided

2 tablespoons extra virgin olive oil, divided

1 small red onion, diced (about 1 cup)

4 cloves garlic, minced (about 4 teaspoons)

4 cups sliced tomatoes: halved cherry or grape tomatoes (2 pints) or ½-inch-diced peak season plum or other garden tomatoes

¼ teaspoon dried thyme

4 ounces part-skim mozzarella pearls (scant 1 cup) or 4 ounces block-style part-skim mozzarella cheese, cut into bite-sized cubes

¼ cup tightly packed fresh basil leaves, thinly sliced

1. In a small saucepan, combine ½ cup of the vinegar and 1 tablespoon of the honey. Gently simmer over medium-low heat, stirring occasionally, until thickened and reduced by a little more than half, about 15 minutes. Remove from the heat and set aside.

2. While the balsamic reduces, arrange the chicken on a cutting board and stretch a large sheet of plastic wrap over the top. Lightly pound the chicken breasts into an even ½-inch thickness. Discard the plastic, then sprinkle the chicken with ¾ teaspoon of the salt and ¼ teaspoon of the pepper, seasoning both sides.

3. In a large, heavy-bottomed skillet, heat 1 tablespoon of the oil over medium-high heat. Once the oil is hot but not smoking, swirl to coat the pan, then add the chicken breasts

top-sides down, being careful of oil that may splatter. Let cook undisturbed for 4 minutes, or until lightly browned. Flip and cook an additional 3 minutes. Check for doneness. The chicken should reach 165 degrees F at the thickest part when tested with an instant-read thermometer, and when sliced, the juices should run clear. If it needs additional time, flip again and continue cooking for a few minutes on each side, until done. The total cooking time will vary depending upon the size of your chicken. Remove to a plate and cover to keep warm.

4. Without wiping out the pan, reduce the skillet heat to medium. Add the remaining 1 tablespoon oil, swirl to coat the pan, then add the red onion and let cook until slightly softened, about 3 minutes, scraping the

recipe continues

browned bits off the bottom of the pan as it cooks. Add the garlic and let cook 30 seconds, just until fragrant. Add the tomatoes, thyme, remaining 1 tablespoon vinegar, the remaining 1 teaspoon honey, the remaining ½ teaspoon salt, and the remaining ¼ teaspoon pepper. Increase the heat back to medium high and cook until the tomatoes begin to soften, about 2 minutes.

5. Return the chicken to the pan, nestling it into the tomatoes, and scatter the mozzarella throughout. Cover the pan and remove from the heat. Let stand for 1 to 2 minutes to allow the mozzarella to become soft and melty. Uncover, drizzle the balsamic reduction over the top, and sprinkle with the fresh basil. Serve warm.

LEFTOVER LOVE:

Caprese Chicken and Arugula Salad: Chop leftover chicken. Add to a mixing bowl with any remaining leftover tomatoes and mozzarella, and a few handfuls of arugula. Drizzle with a few splashes of olive oil and balsamic vinegar and sprinkle with salt and pepper. Toss to combine.

Instant Pot Spring Green
Farro Risotto

ACTIVE TIME: 35 minutes · **TOTAL TIME:** 1 hour · **YIELD:** Serves 3 or 4 as a main or 6 as a side

The next time you need a little help saying the "L" word, make a pot of risotto instead. Creamy, comforting, and requiring a measure of TLC, risotto expresses caring and love. Traditional stove top risotto can be intimidating, but this pressure cooker method alleviates the pressure. The majority of the cooking happens completely hands free when the pot is sealed. At the end, you'll be left with a cozy dish worthy of the deepest affection.

In place of the usual white rice, which is short on fiber and protein, I use hearty whole grain farro. The end result is just as comforting as classic risotto, but it is far better for you and more filling. This recipe is adaptable for all seasons, so feel free to swap the asparagus for whatever looks best at the market.

2 tablespoons extra virgin olive oil

1 medium shallot, finely chopped (about ½ cup)

1 teaspoon kosher salt, divided

2 cloves garlic, minced (about 2 teaspoons)

1 tablespoon unsalted butter

1½ cups uncooked semi-pearled farro, rinsed and drained

½ cup dry white wine, such as Sauvignon Blanc

4 cups low sodium chicken broth or low sodium vegetable broth, divided

1 pound asparagus, tough ends removed, cut into ¾-inch pieces

1 cup peas, fresh or frozen (no need to thaw)

2 cups lightly packed baby spinach (about 2 ounces)

¼ teaspoon ground black pepper

2 tablespoons freshly squeezed lemon juice (from about ½ medium lemon), plus additional lemon wedges for serving

4 ounces crumbled feta cheese (about ¾ cup), plus additional for serving

1. Set a 6-quart or larger Instant Pot to sauté. Drizzle in the oil. Once the oil is hot but not smoking, add the shallot and ½ teaspoon of the salt. Cook, stirring occasionally, until the shallot is softened but not brown, about 3 minutes. Add the garlic, butter, and farro and cook for 1 minute, stirring to coat the farro in the melted butter. Add the wine and cook, stirring to thoroughly scrape up any browned bits that have stuck to the bottom of the pot. Let the wine reduce for 2 minutes, then stir in 3 cups of the broth.

2. Cover and seal the pot. Cook on high (manual) pressure for 8 minutes. Once the time has elapsed, let the pressure release naturally for 10 minutes, then vent to release any remaining pressure. Carefully open the lid. The farro will be a little liquidy.

3. Turn the Instant Pot to sauté. Stir in the asparagus. Bring the farro to a simmer and cook, stirring often with a wooden spoon and scraping the spoon along the bottom of the pot to prevent sticking. Once the liquid has been absorbed, add the remaining 1 cup broth, a few

recipe continues

generous splashes at a time. Stir between each addition and wait until the broth is mostly absorbed before adding the next few splashes. Continue cooking and stirring until the farro is thickened and creamy and the asparagus is tender, 10 to 12 minutes.

4. Stir in the peas, spinach, pepper, and remaining ½ teaspoon salt until the spinach wilts, about 2 minutes. Stir in the lemon juice and feta. Turn the Instant Pot off. Let cool a few minutes, then taste and adjust the seasoning as desired. Enjoy hot, topped with a sprinkle of additional feta and extra squeeze of lemon juice as desired.

STORAGE TIPS:
Refrigerate leftovers in an airtight container for up to 4 days. Reheat gently in the microwave or on the stove top with a splash of water or broth to loosen the farro as needed.

NEXT LEVEL:
For an extra hit of protein, top with diced grilled chicken breast, sliced and sautéed chicken sausage, or grilled or sautéed shrimp.

MARKET SWAPS:
This is a farro risotto for all seasons! Try it with any mix of your favorite in-season veggies. Butternut squash and mushrooms are two of our favorites in the fall, and cherry tomatoes and zucchini are ideal for summer. If using firm vegetables (such as butternut squash or eggplant) or juicy vegetables (such as cherry tomatoes or zucchini), cook them in olive oil in the Instant Pot using the sauté setting before beginning the recipe. Remove the cooked vegetables to a plate, make the recipe as directed, then stir the sautéed vegetables back in at the end.

Italian Turkey Sausage Skillet with Farro, Greens, and Beans

ACTIVE TIME: 20 minutes · **TOTAL TIME:** 45 minutes · **YIELD:** Serves 4

Meet the MVP of "Well Plated Tapas," the nickname our friends gave to the nights that followed my twelve-hour marathon recipe-testing days writing this book. While I worked on the recipes, we regularly had a small group of friends over for dinner (good friends who didn't mind the state of the kitchen or the fact that I still had food in my hair), as much to help assuage the mega-influx of leftovers as to offer valuable feedback on the recipes themselves. Each time, we had so many different dishes to try, I served them in tapas-sized portions and coursed them out as logically as I could. Inevitably, we were stuffed by the end, but everyone at the table managed second helpings of this Italian Turkey Sausage Skillet.

This is exactly the kind of meal we all need more of in our repertoire. It's uncomplicated to prepare, the flavors are lusty and robust, and it includes every food group you need in a healthy dinner. It comes together in a reasonable amount of time, reheats like a dream, and the entire recipe cooks in the same skillet, so you have only one pan to wash in the end. MVP indeed!

1 tablespoon extra virgin olive oil

1 pound uncooked Italian turkey or chicken sausage, either ground sausage or sausage links in casings

1 small red onion, cut into ¼-inch dice (about 1 cup)

3 cloves garlic, minced (about 1 tablespoon)

1 small bunch curly kale (about 6 ounces or 4 to 5 stems) or 1 medium bunch lacinato (dinosaur) kale (about 8 ounces or 9 stems), stemmed and roughly chopped

1 (15-ounce) can reduced sodium white beans, such as cannellini, great Northern, or white kidney, rinsed and drained

1 (14.5-ounce) can fire roasted diced tomatoes in their juices

1 cup uncooked semi-pearled farro, rinsed and drained

2½ cups water

1½ teaspoons Italian seasoning

½ teaspoon kosher salt

½ cup finely grated Parmesan cheese (about 1½ ounces)

1. In a large, deep skillet, heat the oil over medium-high heat. Once the oil is hot but not yet smoking, add the sausage (if it is in casings, squeeze the sausage from the casings directly into the pan, then discard the casings). Cook, crumbling and breaking apart the meat into small pieces, until the sausage is lightly browned and cooked through, 5 to 7 minutes.

2. Reduce the heat to medium. Add the onion and cook until the onion is beginning to soften, about 3 minutes. Add the garlic

and cook an additional 30 seconds, just until fragrant. Add the kale a few handfuls at a time, stirring until it begins to wilt and cook down, then continuing to add handfuls as you are able to fit more into the pan, about 2 minutes total. Add the beans, tomatoes, farro, water, Italian seasoning, and salt. Stir to combine.

3. Increase the heat to high. Bring the mixture to a boil, then reduce the heat to a gentle simmer. Let simmer uncovered until most of

recipe continues

the liquid is absorbed and the farro is tender but still retains some chew, 25 to 30 minutes. Stir the mixture periodically as it cooks, to prevent sticking, and add a little water if the farro starts to become dry. Remove the pan from the heat and sprinkle with the Parmesan. Serve hot.

STORAGE TIPS:
Refrigerate leftovers for up to 4 days or freeze for up to 2 months. Let thaw overnight in the refrigerator. Rewarm gently in the microwave or on the stove top with a spash of water or broth to keep it from drying out.

NEXT LEVEL:
For a gourmet crunch, sprinkle the finished dish with chopped toasted walnuts or toasted pine nuts.

MARKET SWAPS:
- In place of Parmesan, this recipe is also delicious with feta. The white beans can also be swapped for chickpeas, which have a nuttier flavor and more chew but are still very yummy.
- *Make It Meatless:* Swap the sausage for an additional can of white beans. Season with a pinch of red pepper flakes, additional Italian seasoning, and salt to taste.

Sheet Pan Spicy Garlic Shrimp and Vegetables

ACTIVE TIME: 30 minutes · **TOTAL TIME:** 35 minutes · **YIELD:** Serves 2 to 4

So, this thing about dinner: It happens every night. Does my stomach care if I've had a no-good-long-exhausting day and the idea of any action more tasking than opening a box of crackers sounds preposterous? My stomach does not. Hungry family members seem to share its zero-sympathy sentiments.

Since dinnertime reliably arrives without a shred of respect for whether I'm in the mood to cook, it's tremendously helpful to have a collection of fast, easy meals that fulfill the basics—thirty minutes ago, I was contemplating selling my grandmother's necklace in exchange for pizza; now I'm not—and that I legitimately crave. This Sheet Pan Spicy Garlic Shrimp and Vegetables is one of those recipes. Using frozen, peeled and deveined shrimp cuts the recipe down to mere minutes and the seafood seasoning blend gives it a complex flavor that tastes anything but rushed.

---

1 large head broccoli, cut into florets (about 5 cups)

1 pint cherry or grape tomatoes, left whole

4 cloves garlic, minced, divided (about 4 teaspoons)

1½ tablespoons extra virgin olive oil, divided

1½ teaspoons seafood seasoning, such as Old Bay, divided

1 pound jumbo (26/30 count) shrimp, peeled and deveined with tails on (fresh or frozen and thawed)

1 small bunch green onions, chopped, white and light green parts divided from dark green parts (about 5 medium or ¾ cup chopped)

1 tablespoon hot sauce, such as Frank's RedHot Original, plus additional to taste

1 small lemon, cut into wedges

---

1. Place a rack in the center of your oven and preheat the oven to 425 degrees F. For easy cleanup, line a large, rimmed baking sheet with aluminum foil and lightly coat with nonstick spray. If you prefer not to use foil, omit it and coat the pan directly.

2. Place the broccoli, tomatoes, and 2 cloves of the minced garlic in the center of the prepared baking sheet. Drizzle with 1 tablespoon of the oil, then sprinkle with ½ teaspoon of the seafood seasoning. Toss to coat, then spread into an even layer. Bake for 20 to 23 minutes, until the broccoli is tender and

becoming crispy at the tips of the florets and the cherry tomatoes begin to burst, turning the vegetables once with a spatula halfway through.

3. While the vegetables bake, pat the shrimp dry, then place in a medium mixing bowl. Add the white and light green parts of the green onions, the hot sauce, remaining 2 cloves garlic, remaining ½ tablespoon olive oil, and the remaining 1 teaspoon seafood seasoning. Toss to coat.

recipe continues

4. Once the vegetables have baked, remove the pan from the oven and carefully pour the shrimp and any extra oil and spices that have collected in the bottom of bowl over the top. With a spatula, carefully toss the shrimp and vegetables together, then spread them back into an even layer.

5. Return the pan to the oven and bake just until the shrimp go from blue/gray to white/pink and are no longer translucent, 4 to 6 minutes. Watch carefully so that the shrimp does not overcook. Remove the pan from the oven and squeeze the lemon wedges over the top. Sprinkle with the reserved dark green onion tops. Enjoy immediately.

STORAGE TIP:
This recipe is best enjoyed the day it is made, as shrimp tends to dry out when reheated. If I do have leftover shrimp, I love to let it sit at room temperature for a few minutes, then add it to salads.

PRO TIPS:
• For the fastest possible prep, purchase deveined, easy-peel shrimp. Since fresh shrimp can be pricey, I typically purchase frozen shrimp, let it thaw, then rinse it under cool water before using it in the recipe.

• To stretch the recipe for a larger (or hungrier) group, serve it with a side of cooked brown rice or quinoa.

• As written, the recipe has a nice kick. If you are sensitive to spice, reduce the hot sauce to 2 teaspoons or omit it entirely and allow each diner to add it to his or her serving.

MARKET SWAPS:
This recipe works well with almost any mix of vegetables. Try replacing the broccoli with trimmed, halved asparagus in the spring, green beans in the summer, and diced sweet potatoes in the fall. Note that if you use different vegetables, you may need to alter the roasting time in Step 2. Keep an eye on the vegetables towards the end of the baking time and add or subtract a few minutes as needed.

One Pot Creamy Sun-Dried Tomato Orzo with Spinach

ACTIVE TIME: 35 minutes · **TOTAL TIME:** 35 minutes · **YIELD:** Serves 4 as a main or 8 to 10 as a side

Early in my marriage, I entered what I now call the Risotto Period. I cooked a giant, decadent pot of it once or twice a week, thinking nothing of standing at the stove and babysitting it on a Tuesday night. Now that I'm older, wiser, and (I don't want to call myself lazy, so can we agree on "efficient"?), I make this one pot creamy orzo instead.

Orzo is a short, rice-shaped pasta. Like the traditional Arborio rice used to make risotto, it has a creamy, velvety texture once cooked. When made with a reduced amount of liquid, it becomes starchy and rich just like a rice-based risotto, but it doesn't require the prolonged micromanagement. For maximum nutritional benefit, I use whole wheat orzo, which cooks in about 8 minutes, a fraction of the time you'd need for a comparable brown rice risotto.

You can use this orzo cooking method for a wide variety of vegetables, cheeses, and mix-ins, but the combination of sun-dried tomatoes, spinach, Parmesan, and lemon I've suggested here is my truest love. It's creamy, bright, tangy, and the right amount of indulgent. On its own, it's hearty enough for a vegetarian main, or you can serve it as a side with roasted or grilled chicken, salmon, or shrimp.

1 (3-ounce) package dry-packed sun-dried tomatoes (about ¾ tightly-packed cup)

2 tablespoons extra virgin olive oil

1 small yellow onion, cut into ¼-inch dice (about 1 cup)

1 pound dry whole wheat orzo pasta (about 2½ cups)

3 cloves garlic, minced (about 1 tablespoon)

1 teaspoon kosher salt

¼ teaspoon ground black pepper

2 cups nonfat milk

2 to 3 cups low sodium chicken broth or low sodium vegetable broth, divided

5 ounces baby spinach, coarsely chopped (about 5 cups)

¼ teaspoon red pepper flakes, plus additional to taste

Zest and juice of 1 medium lemon (about 1 teaspoon zest and ¼ cup juice)

⅔ cup shredded Parmesan cheese (about 2½ ounces), plus additional for serving

¼ cup loosely packed fresh basil leaves, thinly sliced, divided

1. Place the sun-dried tomatoes in a small bowl and cover with very hot water. Let sit to rehydrate while you prepare the orzo.

2. In a large Dutch oven or similar large, heavy-bottomed pot with a tight-fitting lid, heat the oil over medium-high heat. Once the oil is hot but not yet smoking, add the onion and sauté until fragrant and beginning to soften, about 3 minutes. Add the orzo, garlic, salt, and black pepper. Sauté, stirring to combine the ingredients and coat the orzo with the onion and oil. Cook just until the garlic is fragrant, about 30 seconds. Be careful not to let the garlic burn.

3. Slowly stir in the milk and 2 cups of the broth. Bring to a gentle boil, stirring very frequently with a wooden spoon and scraping

recipe continues

the spoon along the bottom of the pot to prevent the orzo from sticking. Cover the pot and reduce the heat to a light simmer. Cook until the orzo is al dente, most of the liquid is absorbed, and the orzo is very creamy, 8 to 10 minutes. Lift the lid every few minutes to stir and run the spoon along the bottom to prevent sticking. If the pasta looks dry at any point, add several splashes of broth as needed to loosen it.

4. Drain and roughly chop the sun-dried tomatoes. Add them to the pot. Stir in the spinach, red pepper flakes, lemon zest and juice, Parmesan, and half of the basil. Continue to cook and stir until the spinach is just wilted and the cheese melts, about 1 minute. Taste and season with additional salt, black pepper, and red pepper flakes as desired. Serve hot, sprinkled with the remaining basil and additional Parmesan.

STORAGE TIPS:
Refrigerate leftovers for up to 3 days. Reheat gently on the stove top or in the microwave with a splash of water, broth, or milk to keep the leftovers from drying out.

PRO TIP:
For suggestions on where to find dry-packed sun-dried tomatoes, see Killer Kale Salad Pro Tips (page 113).

5-Ingredient Maple Dijon Salmon

ACTIVE TIME: 10 minutes · **TOTAL TIME:** 30 minutes · **SERVES:** 2 or 3

Cooking fish terrified me for years. I considered it something that belonged only in fancy restaurants or on the tables of home cooks more accomplished than myself. Then one fateful day, a moment of impulsive bravery collided with a sale on salmon too good to refuse. When I got home with my purchase, I set it on the counter and stared at it for a full ten minutes, thinking, "NOW WHAT?"

Fortunately, I had recently checked out a stack of cookbooks from the library and I found a recipe for baked salmon that looked so simple I reasoned that even I, a true fish nincompoop, could not completely mess it up.

We've now eaten our way through many iterations of baked salmon. Each time I make it, I am freshly amazed that something this straightforward to prepare can taste so special. This maple Dijon combination is the variation I come back to again and again. It's buttery, tangy, and sweet, and the zip of the Dijon perfectly balances the richness of the salmon. This back-pocket recipe is only five ingredients, cooks in fifteen minutes, and by the second time you make it you'll have it memorized.

---

1 pound skin-on salmon fillet, wild caught if possible

½ teaspoon kosher salt

1 tablespoon extra virgin olive oil

1 tablespoon pure maple syrup

2 teaspoons Dijon mustard

---

1. Using aluminum foil or parchment paper, line a baking dish large enough to hold the salmon and lightly coat the foil with nonstick spray. Place the salmon in the center. With a paper towel, pat it dry, then sprinkle the salt over the top.

2. Place a rack in the center of your oven and preheat the oven to 425 degrees F. In a small bowl or liquid measuring cup, whisk together the oil, maple syrup, and mustard. Pour over the salmon. With a pastry brush or your fingers, lightly rub the mixture over the top of the salmon so that the surface is nicely coated. Let the salmon stand at room temperature for 10 minutes while the oven continues to preheat.

3. Bake until the salmon is cooked through and flakes easily at the thickest part. The cooking time will vary based on the thickness of your salmon. Estimate 8 to 12 minutes for a thinner fillet (½ to ¾ inch at the thickest part), 13 to 19 minutes for a thicker fillet (1 inch to 1½ inches at the thickest part), or 20 to 22 minutes for a very thick fillet (1¾ to 2 inches at the thickest part). You can also use an instant-read thermometer to test for doneness, removing the salmon when it reaches 145 degrees F at the thickest part. Slice crosswise into individual servings. Enjoy immediately.

PRO TIP:

Cooking times can vary widely based on the thickness of your salmon, as well as your personal preference. If you're new to cooking salmon, write down how thick your fillet was and how long you needed to cook it to your liking so you'll have it next time for reference.

LEFTOVER LOVE:

Because fish easily dries out when reheated, I like to use my leftovers in ways that the salmon can be enjoyed cold or at room temperature. Try serving it over a salad or adding it to an omelet with goat cheese and dill. Or for something fancy, flake the leftovers over avocado toast and sprinkle with a pinch of salt and red pepper flakes.

LEFTOVER LOVE:
Make an extra-large batch of the sauce, then use it for a classic stir-fry later in the week.

Sheet Pan Sweet Chili Asian Baked Fish and Vegetables

ACTIVE TIME: 15 minutes · **TOTAL TIME:** 45 minutes · **YIELD:** Serves 4

In my hierarchy of Asian dipping sauces (you have one of those, don't you?), sweet chili sauce is second only to peanut sauce (which you can find smothering my Thai Peanut Chicken Stir-Fry, page 122). Sweet, sticky, and just a little spicy, it's the flavor inspiration behind this all-in-one sheet pan dinner. Unlike the sweet chili sauces you'll find at the grocery store or a restaurant table, this one is naturally sweetened with a moderate amount of honey. The fish bakes up tender and flaky, the vegetables are colorful and fresh, and the sauce is oh-so addictive. You can enjoy this as a simple fish-and-veggie dish on its own or serve it over brown rice to stretch the portions and give it a stir-fry vibe. If you go the rice route (or share my passion for sauce), consider multiplying the sauce portion of this recipe by one-and-a-half or even doubling it.

For the Fish and Vegetables:

4 medium carrots, peeled and cut into ¼-inch-thick diagonal slices (about 10 ounces or heaping 1½ cups)

2 cups sugar snap peas (about 8 ounces)

1 medium red bell pepper, cut into ¾-inch dice (about 1 cup)

4 (6-ounce) cod fillets (or similar firm, flaky white fish, such as halibut, wild caught if possible)

For the Sauce:

¼ cup low sodium soy sauce

3 tablespoons honey

1 tablespoon extra virgin olive oil

2 teaspoons sambal oelek (fresh chili paste; reduce to 1 teaspoon if sensitive to spice)

3 cloves garlic, minced (about 1 tablespoon)

1 tablespoon minced fresh ginger

For Serving:

1 small lime, cut into wedges

Chopped green onion

Prepared brown rice or quinoa (optional)

1. Prepare the fish and vegetables: Generously coat a large rimmed baking sheet with nonstick spray. Place a rack in the center of your oven and preheat the oven to 400 degrees F. Place the carrots, peas, and bell pepper in the center of the sheet.

2. Prepare the sauce: In a mixing bowl or large liquid measuring cup, whisk together the soy sauce, honey, oil, sambal oelek, garlic, and ginger. Pour half of it over the vegetables and toss to coat. Spread the vegetables into a single layer and bake for 15 minutes.

3. Remove the pan from the oven and carefully push the vegetables to the sides. Arrange the fish fillets in the center. Drizzle the fish with half of the remaining sauce, then brush the sauce evenly over the tops of the fillets. Reserve the remaining sauce for serving. Bake for 11 to 13 additional minutes, until the fillets are opaque and flake easily with a fork.

4. To serve: Drizzle a little extra sauce over the fish, then squeeze lime wedges over the whole pan. Sprinkle with green onion. Serve hot with prepared rice and extra sauce as desired.

Raymonde's Moroccan Lemon Chicken

ACTIVE TIME: 35 minutes · **TOTAL TIME:** 1 hour · **YIELD:** Serves 4

When I studied abroad in France, I lived with two of the most vibrant, energetic individuals I've ever known: Raymonde and her husband, Marcel. Eight years later, they were brave enough to welcome me back into their home, along with my very new, very non-French-speaking husband. We spent the evenings dining in their lovely outdoor garden, Marcel pouring me more wine as I struggled to play translator. I don't remember if the wine helped or hindered my attempts, but I'll never forget the Moroccan-inspired lemon chicken that Raymonde served. Fall-apart tender, richly aromatic, and filled with the warm spices of faraway places, this one-pan chicken recipe is adapted from my memories of Raymonde's dish. Its flavors are inspired by North African cuisine, but every bite takes me back to that early-summer evening in a cozy garden in France.

2 tablespoons extra virgin olive oil

2½ pounds boneless, skinless chicken thighs, trimmed of excess fat

1 teaspoon kosher salt

½ teaspoon ground black pepper

1 pound carrots, peeled and cut into ½-inch-thick diagonal slices, slices halved if large (about 3 cups or 6 medium carrots)

1 medium yellow onion, cut into ¼-inch dice (about 1½ cups)

5 cloves garlic, minced (about 5 teaspoons)

2½ teaspoons ground ginger

2 teaspoons ground cumin

1 teaspoon ground cinnamon

½ teaspoon ground coriander

2 large lemons, divided

1 cup whole green, pitted or unpitted olives (see Pro Tips)

½ cup raisins (golden or regular)

½ cup low sodium chicken broth

Prepared whole wheat couscous or brown rice, for serving

1. In a Dutch oven or large, deep skillet with a tight-fitting lid, heat the oil over medium-high heat. Sprinkle the chicken on both sides with the salt and pepper. Once the oil is hot but not yet smoking, place the chicken in the pan in a single layer and cook on both sides until lightly golden, about 5 minutes total, moving it as little as possible to ensure it browns nicely. If all of the chicken will not fit in a single layer, brown it in two batches. Remove the chicken to a plate and set aside.

2. To the pan, add the carrots and onion. Cook, stirring occasionally, until the vegetables just begin to soften, about 4 minutes. Reduce the heat to medium and stir in the garlic, ginger, cumin, cinnamon, and coriander.

Let cook until very fragrant, 30 seconds to 1 minute.

3. Slice one of the lemons into wedges, then add the wedges to the pan. Add the olives and raisins. Juice the second lemon over the top, then pour in the broth. Stir, scraping up any browned bits that have collected on the bottom of the pan.

4. Return the chicken to the pan, nestling it among the carrots and onion. Increase the heat to high and bring to a boil. Cover the pan, reduce the heat to low, and let simmer until the chicken is cooked through and tender, 25 to 30 minutes. Serve hot with the prepared couscous.

PRO TIPS:

Raymonde included green olives in her version, but if you prefer to omit them, the recipe will still be delicious. Since olives are salty, if you leave them out, be sure to taste the final dish and add extra salt as needed.

The French tend to leave the pits in their olives, but if you are concerned about the choking hazard (or having guests spitting olive pits at the table), you can purchase pitted olives or pit them yourself prior to adding them to the recipe.

4 Unboring Ways
to Use Shredded Chicken

Don't let the bland, dry chicken breast dishes you've suffered through scare you into skipping these recipes. Despite its abuse and overuse, chicken has celebrity potential. It's a lean source of protein, affordable, and as these four recipes demonstrate, full of versatile and delicious opportunity.

All four of these recipes start with cooked, shredded or diced chicken. You can cook the chicken yourself using one of the methods I've suggested on page 161 (you'll love how ready for the week you feel when you prepare a week's worth in advance) or source it in a hurry by picking up a cooked rotisserie chicken from the store. These recipes are designed to be ready in about 30 minutes once your chicken is cooked, making them ideal options when you're short on time. Lightning fast and tasty, these meals will make bad chicken dishes of the past a distant memory!

Asian Noodle Salad with Spicy Peanut Dressing

ACTIVE TIME: 15 minutes · **TOTAL TIME:** 30 minutes · **YIELD:** Serves 4 to 6

For the Salad:

6 ounces dry soba noodles or whole grain spaghetti or linguine noodles

2 cups cooked, shredded chicken (about 2 medium breasts) (see page 161)

1 (12-ounce) package broccoli slaw (about 4 cups; see Pro Tip, page 107)

3 cups shredded carrots (about 1 pound or 6 medium)

1 small red bell pepper, thinly sliced (about 1 cup)

2 green onions, thinly sliced (about ⅓ cup)

½ cup dry-roasted, unsalted peanuts, roughly chopped

½ cup chopped fresh cilantro

For the Dressing:

¼ cup rice vinegar

3 tablespoons low sodium soy sauce

3 tablespoons creamy peanut butter

2 tablespoons plus 1 teaspoon toasted sesame oil

2 tablespoons plus 1 teaspoon extra virgin olive oil

1 tablespoon plus 1 teaspoon honey

1 tablespoon plus 1 teaspoon minced fresh ginger

3 cloves garlic, minced (about 1 tablespoon)

2 teaspoons Sriracha or sambal oelek (fresh chili paste), plus additional to taste

1. Make the salad: Bring a large pot of salted water to a boil. Cook the noodles until al dente, according to the package instructions. Reserve ½ cup of the pasta cooking liquid. Drain the remaining pasta and rinse the noodles briefly with cool water. Shake out as much water as possible, then transfer to a large serving bowl. Top with the chicken, broccoli slaw, carrots, and bell pepper.

2. While the pasta cooks, whisk together the dressing: the vinegar, soy sauce, peanut butter, sesame oil, olive oil, honey, ginger, garlic, and Sriracha. Pour over the noodle mixture and, with a long pair of tongs, toss to combine. Add the green onions, peanuts, and cilantro and toss once more. If the pasta is stickier than you would like, splash in a little of the reserved pasta water to loosen it. Taste and adjust the seasoning as desired. Serve chilled or at room temperature.

MAKE-AHEAD & STORAGE TIPS:
Prepare the dressing up to 3 days in advance and store in the refrigerator. Whisk back together just before topping the salad.

Refrigerate leftovers for up to 3 days. The noodles tend to absorb some of the dressing, so if you know you'd like leftovers and want to keep them nicely coated, make one-and-a-half times the dressing, then reserve a portion for topping the leftovers.

PRO TIP:
Don't skip the sesame oil—it's what gives this salad its complex and bewitchingly addictive flavor. You can find sesame oil (along with the Sriracha and sambal oelek) in the Asian food section of most grocery stores.

Chicken Shawarma Wraps

ACTIVE TIME: 15 minutes · **TOTAL TIME:** 15 minutes · **YIELD:** Serves 4

For the Shawarma Filling:

3 cups cooked, shredded chicken (about 3 medium breasts) (see page 161), warm or at room temperature

1 cup nonfat plain Greek yogurt

1½ teaspoons ground cumin

1 teaspoon garlic powder

¾ teaspoon kosher salt

¾ teaspoon ground allspice

¼ teaspoon ground turmeric

¼ teaspoon ground cinnamon

¼ teaspoon cayenne pepper (reduce to ⅛ teaspoon if sensitive to spice)

2 tablespoons freshly squeezed lemon juice (from about ½ medium lemon)

For Serving:

4 whole wheat pita halves or wraps

Prepared hummus of choice

Sliced cucumber, thinly sliced red onion, sliced tomatoes, or a mix

Crumbled feta cheese

Chopped fresh parsley

1. Make the shawarma filling: In a medium saucepan, combine the chicken, Greek yogurt, cumin, garlic powder, salt, allspice, turmeric, cinnamon, and cayenne. Heat over medium low so that you gently warm the chicken but do not curdle the yogurt. Stir in the lemon juice. Taste and adjust the seasoning as desired.

2. To serve: Place the pitas on a microwave-safe plate and heat gently in the microwave for a few seconds to warm. Alternatively, you can warm the pitas on a baking sheet in a 300-degree-F oven for a few minutes. To assemble, spread or fill the pitas with hummus. Add the cucumber, red onion, and tomatoes, then fill with the warm chicken. Sprinkle with feta and parsley. Enjoy immediately.

STORAGE TIPS:
Refrigerate leftover chicken for up to 3 days. Fill pitas just before serving.

LEFTOVER LOVE:
- *Chicken Shawarma Salad:* Serve the chicken over a salad of chopped romaine, sliced cucumbers, and halved cherry tomatoes. Top with Zippy Lemon Yogurt Dressing (page 89).
- *Shawarma Pita Pizzas:* Gently warm leftover chicken in the microwave or on the stove. Arrange whole pita rounds in a single layer on a baking sheet. Place in a 425-degree-F oven and bake until lightly crisp, 6 to 8 minutes. Spread with hummus, then top with the chicken filling and any other desired toppings.

Lemon Chicken Pasta Salad with Tarragon and Grapes

ACTIVE TIME: 15 minutes · **TOTAL TIME:** 30 minutes · **YIELD:** Serves 4

8 ounces dry whole wheat bowtie, fusilli, penne, or similar pasta (about 3 cups)

1¼ cups nonfat plain Greek yogurt

Zest and juice of 1 small lemon (about ¾ teaspoon zest and 3 tablespoons juice)

1 tablespoon plus 1 teaspoon honey

1 teaspoon Dijon mustard

1¼ teaspoons kosher salt

½ teaspoon ground black pepper

3 cups cooked, shredded chicken (about 3 medium breasts) (see page 161), cooled to room temperature or chilled

3 cups chopped baby spinach (about 3 ounces)

2 cups seedless red grapes, halved (about 12 ounces)

½ cup toasted sliced almonds

1 tablespoon chopped fresh tarragon leaves

3 green onions, finely chopped (about ½ cup)

1. Cook the pasta to al dente, according to the package instructions. Drain, and run cold water over the pasta to stop the cooking. Shake off any excess water. Let the pasta rest 5 minutes, then shake again. You want to remove as much water as possible so that it doesn't water down the dressing. Transfer to a large serving bowl.

2. While the pasta is cooking, stir together the Greek yogurt, lemon zest, lemon juice, honey, mustard, salt, and pepper. Pour over the cooked pasta and stir to coat.

3. Add the chicken, spinach, grapes, and almonds. Stir again until all ingredients are evenly combined. Stir in the tarragon and green onions. Taste and adjust the seasoning as desired.

STORAGE TIPS:
Refrigerate leftovers in an airtight container for up to 2 days. Stir to recombine just before serving. I also like to squeeze a bit of extra lemon juice over the top of the leftovers to restore their zip.

Baked Avocado Chicken Taquitos

ACTIVE TIME: 30 minutes · **TOTAL TIME:** 45 minutes · **YIELD:** 12 taquitos (serves 3 or 4)

2 medium ripe avocados

1 (15-ounce) can reduced sodium pinto beans, rinsed and drained

½ cup prepared salsa, plus additional for serving

2 tablespoons freshly squeezed lime juice (from about 1 medium lime)

½ teaspoon kosher salt

½ teaspoon garlic powder

2 cups cooked, shredded chicken (about 2 medium breasts) (see page 161)

1 cup shredded pepper Jack cheese (use Monterey Jack if sensitive to spice), about 4 ounces

12 fajita-size (6-inch) whole wheat flour tortillas

1. Place racks in the upper and lower thirds of your oven and preheat the oven to 425 degrees F. Generously coat two large rimmed baking sheets with nonstick spray.

2. Into a large mixing bowl, scoop the avocado flesh. Add the pinto beans, salsa, lime juice, salt, and garlic powder. With a potato masher or fork, lightly mash and stir the ingredients. Make sure the ingredients are well combined, but leave the mixture a little bit chunky. Fold in the chicken and cheese. Taste and add a bit of extra salt as desired.

3. To assemble the taquitos: Scoop a scant ⅓ cup of the filling onto each tortilla, then spread it so that it forms a line across the center of the tortilla, leaving a little space uncovered on each end. Roll up each tortilla tightly so that the filling is wrapped in the center, then arrange on a prepared baking sheet, seam-side down. Repeat with the remaining tortillas, dividing them between the baking sheets and leaving space between each. Lightly mist the tops of the tortillas with additional nonstick spray.

4. Bake in the upper and lower thirds of the oven until the tops are golden and crisp and the filling is hot and bubbly, 15 to 20 minutes, switching the pans' positions on the upper and lower racks halfway through. Serve hot, topped with additional salsa as desired.

STORAGE TIPS:
Because the tortillas will soften once the filling is rolled inside, these are best enjoyed the day they are made. If you don't plan to eat all of the taquitos right away, store extra filling separately in an airtight container with plastic wrap pressed directly against its surface to deter the avocado from browning. Refrigerate for up to 1 day. Assemble and bake just before serving.

LEFTOVER LOVE:
Mexican-ish Super Toast: Warm leftover filling and spread generously over toasted bread. Sprinkle with shredded cheese and broil in the oven for 1 to 3 minutes, until the cheese is hot and bubbly. Enjoy immediately, topped with additional avocado and salsa as desired.

How to Cook Boneless, Skinless Chicken Breasts

2 to 3 medium chicken breasts (about 10 ounces each)	Yield: 2 to 3 shredded cups, about 1 cup per breast

Stove Top

Place the chicken breasts in a medium saucepan, then season them lightly with salt and pepper. If you are cooking several chicken breasts, you can overlap them slightly. (If you have a large amount of overlap, use a larger pot or divide between two smaller pots.) Cover the chicken with 1 inch of water. Place the pot on the stove and bring the water to a boil. Once the liquid is boiling, reduce the heat and let simmer, uncovered, until the chicken reaches an internal temperature of 165 degrees F on an instant-read thermometer, 8 to 16 minutes, depending upon the size and number of chicken breasts that you are cooking and how vigorously they simmer. A 10-ounce chicken breast will need to simmer for 12 to 14 minutes. Remove the chicken from the water and let rest until cool enough to handle, then dice, slice, or shred as desired.

Slow Cooker

Arrange the chicken breasts in a single layer on the bottom of your slow cooker (do not overlap multiple layers or the chicken will not cook evenly). Season lightly with salt and pepper. Cover (no need to add liquid) and cook on low for approximately 2½ to 3 hours, until the chicken reaches 165 degrees F on an instant-read thermometer. The cooking time depends upon how crowded the slow cooker is and your exact model, so check early to avoid overcooking. Remove the chicken from the slow cooker and let rest until cool enough to handle, then dice, slice, or shred as desired.

Instant Pot

Pour 1 cup of water in the bottom of an Instant Pot. Add the trivet, then the chicken breasts. Season lightly with salt and pepper. Cover and seal the Instant Pot. Cook on high (manual) pressure for 8 minutes (for 10-ounce breasts; add or subtract a minute if your breasts are larger or smaller). Once the pressure has built and the cooking time is complete, vent to release any remaining pressure. Carefully open, then remove the chicken. With an instant-read thermometer, check to make sure the chicken has reached 165 degrees F. If your chicken hasn't fully cooked through, add it back to the Instant Pot, reseal, and cook on high (manual) pressure for a few additional minutes, then vent, uncover, and check again. Let rest until cool enough to handle, then dice, slice, or shred as desired.

4 Things to Do
with a Can of Chickpeas

I'll spare you the unabridged version of the poem "Ode to a Chickpea" that I published in my blog's early days, but since it does feel too fitting to not share here, I've chosen a few select lines to express my sentiment: *Chickpea, Sweet Chickpea, I profess my love to thee, More precious than a pearl is your lumpy round self to me. Mighty protein do you pack, my modest little bean, Some call you a garbanzo; I call you hero to cuisine!*

Fortunately for our healthy-eating needs, a can of chickpeas has far greater potential than I do as a poet. Here are four of my favorite ways to use 1 (15-ounce) can of reduced sodium chickpeas, rinsed and drained, to create fast protein and fiber-rich meals.

Better Avocado Toast

YIELD: Serves 2 to 4

1. In a large bowl, use a fork or potato masher to lightly mash the **chickpeas,** leaving the mixture fairly chunky. Scoop the flesh of 1 medium ripe **avocado** into the bowl with the chickpeas, then add 3 tablespoons **nonfat plain Greek yogurt**, ½ teaspoon **kosher salt**, and ¼ teaspoon **red pepper flakes**. With a fork, stir to combine, breaking up the avocado and leaving the mixture with a bit of texture. Taste and adjust the seasoning as desired.

2. Divide the mixture between 4 slices of toasted **whole wheat bread**, using the back of a spoon to smooth it into an even, thick layer. Sprinkle with a pinch of additional salt.

Chickpea Veggie Stir-Fry

YIELD: Serves 2

1. In a small bowl or large liquid measuring cup, whisk together ¼ cup **low sodium soy sauce**, ¼ cup **water**, 2 tablespoons **honey**, 2 tablespoons **rice vinegar**, 1 clove **minced garlic**, and ¼ teaspoon **red pepper flakes**.

2. In a large skillet, heat 2 tablespoons **canola oil** over medium high. Add 1 thinly sliced **red bell pepper** (about 1¼ cups), 1 small head **broccoli** cut into florets (about 2½ cups), and 1 thinly sliced small **red onion**. Sauté until the vegetables are crisp-tender, about 5 minutes.

3. Stir in the **chickpeas** and half of the sauce. Serve hot with **brown rice or soba noodles**, drizzled with additional sauce.

Quick Chickpea Pasta

YIELD: Serves 2

1. Bring a large pot of salted water to a boil and cook 8 ounces **dry, short whole wheat pasta,** such as orechiette, shells, or farfalle (about 3 cups) until al dente, according to package instructions. While it cooks, in a medium saucepan, heat 1 tablespoon **extra virgin olive oil** over medium heat. Add **chickpeas** and cook until they begin to pop, 3 to 4 minutes, stirring every minute or so. Add 3 cloves minced **garlic** (about 1 tablespoon) and cook, stirring constantly just until fragrant, 30 seconds. Add 1½ cups **good-quality prepared tomato-based pasta sauce,** stir to combine, then reduce the heat to low and cover to keep warm while you finish cooking the pasta.

2. Reserve 1 cup of the **pasta cooking liquid,** then drain the pasta and immediately add the noodles to the sauce. Stir to combine, splashing in the reserved pasta water as needed to thin the sauce.

3. Stir in ¼ cup shredded **Parmesan** (about 1 ounce). Taste and season with **kosher salt** and **ground black pepper.** Serve hot, topped with **fresh basil, thyme, or parsley** (or any other herbs you have hanging out in your refrigerator) and an additional sprinkle of Parmesan. For bonus veggies, add **Every-Night Roasted Vegetables** (Classic Salt and Pepper, page 262, or Parmesan and Herb, page 265).

Tu-No Melts

YIELD: 8 melts (serves 4)

1. Place a rack in the upper third of your oven and preheat the oven to 375 degrees F. Line a large baking sheet with aluminum foil or parchment paper. Place ¼ cup finely chopped **red onion** (about ¼ small) in a small bowl and cover with cold water. Let sit for 5 minutes, then drain. In a medium bowl with a fork or potato masher, lightly mash the **chickpeas,** leaving them fairly chunky. Add ¼ cup **nonfat plain Greek yogurt,** 1 tablespoon freshly squeezed **lemon juice,** 1 teaspoon **honey,** 1 teaspoon **Dijon mustard,** ¼ teaspoon **kosher salt,** ⅛ teaspoon **ground black pepper,** and 2 to 4 dashes of **hot sauce,** to taste. Continue to mash the chickpeas, combining them with the other ingredients. Everything should be mixed, but the chickpeas should still have a good amount of texture. Stir in 3 tablespoons

dry-roasted, unsalted sunflower seeds, 1½ tablespoons chopped **fresh parsley,** and the drained red onion. Taste and adjust the seasoning as desired.

2. Arrange 8 split **whole wheat English muffin halves** (from 4 whole muffins) in a single layer on the prepared baking sheet, split-sides up. Divide the chickpea mixture between the halves (each will have a scant ¼ cup). With the back of a spoon, gently spread it into an even layer. Bake for 5 minutes. Remove the pan from the oven and top each melt with a slice of **Havarti, baby Swiss, or provolone cheese.** Return the pan to the oven and turn the oven to broil. Let cook until the cheese is melted and bubbly, about 3 minutes. Watch carefully so that the cheese does not burn. Let cool on the sheet pan for a few minutes. Enjoy hot.

Butternut Squash, Chicken, and Wild Rice Casserole

ACTIVE TIME: 1 hour · **TOTAL TIME:** 1 hour 30 minutes · **YIELD:** Serves 6

If a harvest-scented candle and an oversized fuzzy blanket got together to cook dinner, they'd make this Butternut Squash, Chicken, and Wild Rice Casserole. It is the essence of cozy, manifested as a healthy dinner, with a bounty of fabulous ingredients for fall and winter cooking: nutty wild rice, golden butternut squash, tangy dried cranberries, earthy thyme, and savory Parmesan. Here, the quintessential casserole "Throw it all in a baking dish and see what happens!" *laissez-faire* doesn't merely work, it triumphs. As you stir the different components together, it might seem like the casserole won't be creamy enough, but fear not. The Parmesan holds it all together.

---

1 cup uncooked wild-and-brown-rice blend

1½ pounds boneless, skinless chicken thighs, trimmed of excess fat

4 tablespoons extra virgin olive oil, divided

½ teaspoon kosher salt, divided

½ teaspoon ground black pepper, divided

1 small butternut squash (about 1½ pounds)

1 medium yellow onion, cut into ¼-inch dice (about 1½ cups)

1 tablespoon chopped fresh thyme, plus additional for garnish

¾ cup dried cranberries

½ cup shredded Parmesan cheese (about 2 ounces), divided

½ cup roughly chopped raw pecans or walnuts

---

1. Cook the rice according to the package instructions and set aside (you should have about 3 cooked cups).

2. Place a rack in the center of your oven and preheat the oven to 425 degrees F. For easy cleanup, lay a large piece of aluminum foil or parchment paper in the bottom of a 9×13-inch baking dish. Arrange the chicken thighs in a single layer on top, tucking the loose side portion of each thigh underneath. Drizzle with 2 tablespoons of the oil. Sprinkle with ¼ teaspoon salt and ¼ teaspoon pepper. Bake until the chicken thighs reach 165 degrees F on an instant-read thermometer at the thickest part, about 20 minutes. Immediately transfer from the dish to a plate and cover. Let rest 10 minutes. Reduce the

oven temperature to 350 degrees F. Discard the foil or parchment and keep the pan handy.

3. While the chicken cooks, peel the butternut squash and trim off the top and bottom ends. Cut the neck away from the round base, then stand the base up on its flat end and cut it in half from top to bottom. Scoop out the seeds and discard. Cut the squash (both base and neck) into ½-inch cubes (you should have about 4 cups of cubes).

4. In a large, deep skillet with a tight-fitting lid, heat the remaining 2 tablespoons oil over medium heat. Add the squash, onion, remaining ¼ teaspoon salt, and remaining

recipe continues

¼ teaspoon pepper. Sauté until the onion begins to soften, about 2 minutes. Cover and cook, stirring occasionally, until the squash is tender but still retains some chew, 6 to 8 minutes.

5. Once the chicken has rested, cut it into bite-sized pieces. Add it to the pan with the squash, then add the thyme, cranberries, ¼ cup of the Parmesan, and the rice. Stir to combine.

6. Lightly coat with nonstick spray the same 9×13-inch dish you used to bake the chicken (no need to wash it in between). With a large spoon, scoop the squash and rice mixture into the dish, spreading it into an even layer.

7. Bake for 15 minutes, then remove the casserole from the oven and sprinkle the nuts and remaining ¼ cup Parmesan on top. Bake 8 to 10 additional minutes, until the cheese is melted and the nuts are toasted and crisp. Sprinkle with additional chopped fresh thyme and serve warm.

MAKE-AHEAD & STORAGE TIPS:

For even faster dinner prep: Prepare the rice up to 2 days in advance (or make it in big batches and freeze individual portions for up to 3 months). The chicken and butternut squash can be cooked up to 1 day in advance. You can also swap the cooked chicken thighs for 3 cups of shredded rotisserie chicken.

The entire casserole can be assembled through step 6 and stored in the refrigerator, unbaked, for up to 1 day. Let come to room temperature, then bake as directed.

To freeze: Bake the casserole completely, then let cool to room temperature. Cover it tightly, then freeze for up to 3 months. Let thaw overnight in the refrigerator, bring to room temperature, then cover with foil and reheat in a 350-degree-F oven until warmed through.

NEXT LEVEL:

For extra decadence, in step 5, stir ½ to 1 cup of shredded Gruyère or fontina cheese into the filling with the Parmesan.

MARKET SWAPS:

Make It Meatless: Swap the chicken for 2 (15-ounce) cans of rinsed-and-drained reduced sodium white beans, such as great Northern or cannellini beans. Add the beans to the squash in step 5.

Almond-Crusted Trout
with Lemon-Butter Caper Sauce

ACTIVE TIME: 45 minutes · **TOTAL TIME:** 45 minutes · **YIELD:** Serves 4

One of my definite I-could-move-here-tomorrow towns is Park City, Utah. In addition to being captivated by the conspicuous—hello, gorgeous mountains, adorable main street, and year-round access to the outdoors—I have developed a serious affinity for trout, which is especially fresh in Utah. The first time I visited, I ordered the most sublime almond-crusted fillet in a light lemon-butter caper sauce. It was simple yet had an elevated, memorable touch that didn't feel too contrived or stuffy.

Trout is now one of the fish I buy most regularly. It's affordable, you can often find it sustainably caught, and it cooks ultra quickly, making it ideal for weeknight meals. This recipe is inspired by that first trout I had in Utah and it is still my favorite way to prepare it. Capers, lemon, and a touch of butter create a luscious sauce, and the almonds give the trout a lightly crispy, nutty crust. This recipe comes together quickly, so be sure to have the ingredients prepped and at the ready. In the end, you'll have a dish that will make you feel accomplished in the kitchen and that you'd be proud to serve to even the fanciest of company.

½ cup raw whole almonds

¼ cup whole wheat panko bread crumbs

1 teaspoon kosher salt

½ teaspoon ground black pepper

1 large egg

4 (6-ounce) skin-on trout fillets

⅔ cup dry white wine, such as Sauvignon Blanc

Zest and juice of 1 medium lemon (about 1 teaspoon zest and ¼ cup juice)

3 tablespoons capers, drained

3 tablespoons extra virgin olive oil, divided

4 tablespoons unsalted butter

2 tablespoons chopped fresh parsley, plus additional for serving

1. Place the almonds, panko, salt, and pepper in the bowl of a food processor fitted with a steel blade. Pulse in 10-second bursts, until the almonds are ground into a coarse crumb mixture. Transfer the crumbs to a shallow baking dish. Beat the egg in a small bowl.

2. Place the trout fillets on a large plate. Pat each trout fillet dry, then brush the tops with egg so that they are moistened (no need to brush the skin). Place each fillet flesh-side down in the almond mixture, lifting up the fillet and using your hands to adhere the crumbs as needed. No need to coat the skin side with crumbs or to pack the crumbs on

thickly; simply ensure each piece has a nice coating. Depending upon the size of your fish, you will likely have some coating left over. Transfer the fillets back to the plate as you go.

3. In a large liquid measuring cup, combine the wine, lemon zest, lemon juice, and capers. Set near the stove. Have the butter close at hand.

4. Heat a large stainless-steel or similar sturdy-bottomed skillet over medium-high heat. Add 1½ tablespoons of the oil and swirl to

recipe continues

coat. Once the oil is hot but not yet smoking, add the first 2 fillets, crust (flesh)-side down, and let cook undisturbed until golden brown, about 3 minutes. Flip and continue cooking on the other side, until the fish is cooked through and flakes easily with a fork at the thickest part, 2 to 3 additional minutes, depending upon the thickness of your fillets. Remove to a clean plate and cover to keep warm. With a paper towel, carefully wipe out the skillet to remove any burned bits of the coating that may have fallen into the pan. Add the remaining 1½ tablespoons oil. Once the oil is hot, cook the remaining 2 fillets, following the same method. Remove the fillets to the same clean plate and cover.

5. Wipe the skillet once more, then return to the stove. Reduce the heat to medium. Add the wine mixture (stand back, as the wine will splatter when it hits the hot pan) and butter. Increase the heat back to medium high and let cook, stirring occasionally for 4 to 5 minutes, until reduced by half. Stir in the parsley. Arrange the fillets on individual plates, then spoon the sauce generously over the top. Enjoy immediately, sprinkled with extra parsley as desired.

STORAGE TIPS:
This fish tastes best the day it is made but can be reheated gently in a skillet on the stove. Store and rewarm the sauce separately, then spoon the sauce over the reheated fillets just before serving.

PRO TIPS:
- While you prepare and cook the fish, you can have a pan of Classic Salt and Pepper Every-Night Roasted Vegetables (page 262) in the oven. By the time the vegetables finish, the fish will be ready to serve, and you'll have a complete meal.

- The trout is also delicious with a simple green salad. Toss arugula (or a mix of arugula and spinach) with Go-to Citrus Dressing (page 89) and a handful of Parmesan. Perfect!

- I usually make this recipe with lake trout, which is large, so you use only a portion (fillet) of the fish, but you can also make the recipe with whole, boned and butterflied rainbow trout, which are much smaller. If using whole, ask for the heads to be removed, if you prefer, or if you will be serving to guests who might not appreciate the bonus anatomy lesson.

MARKET SWAPS:
This recipe is delicious with any fairly firm-bodied, thin fish fillets, such as arctic char or a thin (about ½-inch-thick) fillet of salmon.

Better-Than-a-Restaurant Baked Cauliflower Parmesan

ACTIVE TIME: 15 minutes · **TOTAL TIME:** 50 minutes · **YIELD:** Serves 2 as a main or 4 as a side

Before I met my husband, I had a particular attraction to punk rockers, lead guitarists, and men who wear jeans that are too tight. Every single one of them broke my heart. Fortunately, I eventually developed a crush on a nice, all-American boy whose pants weren't trendy, and now I feel lucky to have missed the boys that I *thought* were good for me and even luckier to have found the one who actually is.

Which brings me to this baked cauliflower Parmesan. It's the better, take-home-to-Mom version of chicken Parmesan, a dish I am forever drawn to at Italian restaurants but that, with its soggy breading and excessively heavy topping, consistently and mercilessly disappoints. This Parmesan, on the contrary, makes my heart sing. The coating is light and crisp, the cauliflower is tender, and the shower of mozzarella on top is exactly the right amount to feel indulgent but not to leave you with feelings of regret.

This dish is scrumptious served over whole wheat pasta noodles, though I find it shines brightest on its own, perhaps with a crisp green salad and hunk of crusty baguette.

1 large head cauliflower (about 3 pounds)

3 tablespoons extra virgin olive oil

1 teaspoon Italian seasoning

1 teaspoon garlic powder

½ teaspoon kosher salt

¼ teaspoon ground black pepper

½ cup finely grated Parmesan cheese (about 2½ ounces)

1 cup good-quality prepared tomato-based pasta sauce, plus additional for serving, if desired

¾ cup shredded part-skim mozzarella cheese (about 3 ounces)

¼ cup thinly sliced fresh basil

For serving (optional): prepared whole wheat spaghetti, linguini, or similar long pasta noodles, or zucchini noodles

1. Place racks in the center and upper third of your oven. Preheat the oven to 425 degrees F. Line a large baking sheet with parchment paper.

2. Place the cauliflower on a cutting board and slice off the base so that it forms a flat surface. Cut away the thick green stems. Stand it up on its cut end, with the florets-side up. Working from top to bottom, slice the head into 1-inch-thick "steaks" (I recommend starting at the center, then working your way out). Some of the slices may break apart and florets on the sides will fall away. Arrange all of the cauliflower, both steaks and florets, in a single layer on the prepared baking sheet.

3. In a small bowl, stir together the oil, Italian seasoning, garlic powder, salt, and pepper. Brush over both sides of the cauliflower steaks and florets. Turn any loose florets so that their flat, cut sides are facing down and touching the surface of the pan.

4. Bake the cauliflower on the center rack for 20 minutes. Remove from the oven and

recipe continues

with a thin, flexible spatula, gently turn the steaks and florets over. Sprinkle the Parmesan over the top. Return the pan to the oven and continue baking until the Parmesan turns golden and the cauliflower is tender and caramelized at the edges, 18 to 20 additional minutes. Remove the pan from the oven and turn the oven to broil.

5. While the cauliflower bakes, prepare any noodles you'd like to serve with the cauliflower. If you'd like additional sauce to serve on the side or with the noodles, warm it in a small saucepan over medium heat (reserve 1 cup sauce for baking the cauliflower).

6. Once the cauliflower has baked, spoon the 1 cup sauce over the top. Sprinkle with the mozzarella. Return the cauliflower to the oven, placing the pan on the upper rack. Broil until the cheese is melted and turning golden, 1 to 3 minutes. Do not walk away from the oven, to ensure the cauliflower does not burn. Sprinkle with the basil. Enjoy immediately, with noodles and warmed sauce if desired.

MAKE-AHEAD & STORAGE TIPS:
The cauliflower steaks and florets can be cut and stored in the refrigerator up to 1 day in advance.

Refrigerate leftovers in an airtight container for up to 3 days. If serving with pasta or vegetable noodles, store the noodles in a separate container. Rewarm the cauliflower in a 400-degree-F oven for 8 to 10 minutes, until heated through.

Grammy's Green Chile Chicken Enchiladas

ACTIVE TIME: 40 minutes · **TOTAL TIME:** 1 hour 15 minutes · **YIELD:** 8 enchiladas (serves 4)

Meet the very first recipe I ever posted on my blog. I didn't think anyone even noticed I'd hit "publish" until a high school girlfriend texted to say she'd made the recipe and loved it, and asked, "Did I have any other healthy recipe ideas?" As a matter of fact, I did. So I published another. Then another. Then a thousand more. Fast-forward eight years, and those same enchiladas have made it into the cookbook you hold in your hands!

These enchiladas are a lightened-up version of the legendary green-chile sour cream chicken enchiladas that my grammy makes every year for Christmas dinner (because why *wouldn't* you want enchiladas on Christmas?). For their cookbook debut, I made a few improvements to the recipe; the biggest is that I have replaced the canned green-enchilada sauce with homemade. I pinky promise that the sauce is easier than you ever imagined possible—we're talking shove a sheet pan of veggies into the oven, blend them up, DONE—and it tastes so deeply rewarding, it will ruin the canned stuff for you in the best possible way.

As sweet and surreal as it feels to see this cherished recipe in print, this book isn't the recipe's consummation or peak. These enchiladas reach their ultimate at *your* table!

1 tablespoon extra virgin olive oil

2 medium red, yellow, or orange bell peppers, cut into ¼-inch dice (about 2 cups)

1 medium yellow onion, cut into ¼-inch dice (about 1½ cups)

1 pound boneless, skinless chicken breasts, cooked and shredded (about 1½ heaping cups); see page 161 for easy cooking methods

1½ teaspoons kosher salt, divided

1 teaspoon chili powder

¾ teaspoon garlic powder

½ teaspoon ground cumin

½ teaspoon ground black pepper

2 cups shredded Monterey Jack cheese (about 8 ounces), divided

1½ cups nonfat plain Greek yogurt

2 (4-ounce) cans diced green chiles, drained

8 taco-size (8-inch) whole wheat flour tortillas

2 cups Green Enchilada Sauce (page 176)

Diced fresh tomatoes, fresh cilantro, diced avocado, diced red onion, for serving, as desired

1. Place a rack in the center of your oven and preheat the oven to 350 degrees F. Lightly coat a 9×13-inch casserole dish with nonstick spray and set aside.

2. Heat the oil in a large skillet over medium heat. Once the oil is hot, add the bell peppers and onion. Cook, stirring occasionally, until the vegetables soften and the onion becomes translucent, 8 to 10 minutes.

3. To the skillet, add the chicken, ½ teaspoon of the salt, the chili powder, garlic powder, cumin, and black pepper. Stir to coat evenly, then remove the skillet from the heat and let cool.

4. In a large bowl, combine 1 cup of the cheese, the Greek yogurt, green chiles, and remaining

recipe continues

1 teaspoon salt. Once the chicken and veggie mixture has cooled to near room temperature, add it to the bowl with the yogurt mixture and, with a large spoon or spatula, stir until the chicken and vegetables are coated evenly with the yogurt.

5. Lay a tortilla on a work surface and spread one-eighth of the chicken-yogurt mixture down the middle, leaving a bit of space on each end of the filling (you will use about a heaping ½ cup per enchilada). Roll the tortilla as tightly as you can without the filling squishing out, and place in the prepared dish, seam-side down. Repeat with the remaining tortillas. Pour 1½ to 2 cups of the green enchilada sauce evenly over the top (use more if you like a saucier enchilada). Cover the pan with aluminum foil, then bake for 30 minutes.

6. Remove the pan from the oven, uncover, and sprinkle with the remaining 1 cup cheese. Bake, uncovered, for 5 additional minutes, or until the cheese is melted. Sprinkle with the desired toppings and enjoy!

STORAGE TIPS:
Refrigerate leftovers for up to 4 days or freeze for up to 3 months. Reheat in a 350-degree-F oven, either from the refrigerator or directly from frozen (no need to thaw first). Except if freezing in a glass dish (such as a Pyrex), the cold dish may shatter if it's placed directly into a hot oven. To avoid this, you can either thaw the enchiladas in the refrigerator overnight or let the dish warm up at room temperature first (the dish can be cool but not cold). Cover the pan with foil, then bake until heated through, 20 to 30 minutes (if refrigerated) or 45 minutes (if frozen).

For speedier reheating, warm individual servings in the microwave.

Green Enchilada Sauce

ACTIVE TIME: 25 minutes · **TOTAL TIME:** 1 hour 15 minutes · **YIELD:** 2½ cups

1 pound small tomatillos, husked, scrubbed, and left whole (9 to 10; see Pro Tips)

2 poblano peppers, stemmed, seeded, and coarsely chopped into ¾- to 1-inch pieces (about 2 cups)

2 medium jalapenos, seeds and membranes removed and chopped into ¼- to ½-inch pieces (about ½ cup)

1 small yellow onion, chopped into ¼- to ½-inch pieces (about 1 cup)

4 cloves garlic, peels on and left whole

3 tablespoons extra virgin olive oil

1 teaspoon kosher salt

¼ teaspoon ground black pepper

½ cup chopped fresh cilantro

¼ teaspoon ground cumin

1 cup water

1. Place a rack in the center of your oven and preheat the oven to 400 degrees F. For easy cleanup, line a large rimmed baking sheet with parchment paper. Place the tomatillos, poblanos, jalapenos, onion, and garlic in the center of the baking sheet. Drizzle with the oil and sprinkle with the salt and pepper. Toss to coat, then spread the veggies into an even layer. Bake for 25 to 30 minutes, until the peppers and onion are golden brown and soft and the tomatillos begin to break down, flipping the tomatillos over and tossing the onion and peppers once halfway through. Set aside and let cool for 15 minutes.

2. Peel the garlic and discard the skins. Working in batches if needed, transfer the roasted vegetables to a blender and add the cilantro. Puree until smooth, then add the cumin and water. Blend again until smooth. Taste and adjust the seasoning as desired. If you'd like a thinner sauce, add more water, 1 tablespoon at a time, until you reach your desired consistency.

STORAGE TIPS:
Refrigerate leftover sauce for up to 1 week or freeze for up to 3 months. Let thaw overnight in the refrigerator.

PRO TIPS:
Look for tomatillos with tight-fitting husks and firm flesh. If the husks are dark brown and shriveled, the tomatillos are past their prime. To remove the husks, simply peel the husks back from the smooth, green skin. Rinse the flesh under warm water and rub away the light, sticky film.

LEFTOVER LOVE:
In addition to being delicious with enchiladas, this sauce is dynamite drizzled over scrambled eggs, Instant Pot Confetti Rice and Beans (page 258), or Cheesy Southwest Breakfast Casserole (page 32).

Salmon Quinoa Cakes
with Creamy Sriracha Dipping Sauce

ACTIVE TIME: 45 minutes · **TOTAL TIME:** 1 hour · **YIELD:** 8 cakes (serves 4)

Ben and I are two seafood lovers living in the landlocked Midwest. As a result, we have planned entire vacations around eating as much fresh seafood as possible, scouting seafood shacks up and down the East and West Coasts. Because traveling every time I'm craving seafood isn't an option, I created a do-anywhere recipe for one of my favorite seafood dishes: salmon cakes. Instead of fresh fish, this recipe uses good-quality canned salmon, so you can find all the ingredients at your average grocery store. The salmon cakes are packed with colorful veggies and a tasty array of spices, and are budget-friendly too. The outsides are dark golden and crisp, while the insides are moist and fall-apart tender. Don't skip the dipping sauce. Its note of spice and creaminess completes these cakes.

For the Salmon Quinoa Cakes:

1 tablespoon plus 2 teaspoons extra virgin olive oil, divided

1 small red onion, finely chopped (about 1 cup)

1 large red bell pepper, cut into ¼-inch dice (about 1½ cups)

1 teaspoon seafood seasoning, such as Old Bay

¼ teaspoon kosher salt

¼ teaspoon ground black pepper

2 cups lightly packed baby spinach, torn or roughly chopped (about 2 ounces)

1 large egg

6 tablespoons nonfat plain Greek yogurt

¼ cup white whole wheat flour

1 tablespoon Dijon mustard

½ teaspoon hot sauce, such as Sriracha or Tabasco (more if you like a feisty kick)

½ teaspoon Worcestershire sauce

15 ounces canned boneless, skinless wild-caught salmon in water, drained

1 cup cooked, cooled quinoa

For the Creamy Sriracha Dipping Sauce:

1 cup nonfat plain Greek yogurt, plus additional to taste

2 tablespoons nonfat milk or milk of choice, plus additional to taste

1½ teaspoons hot sauce, such as Sriracha or Tabasco, plus additional to taste

1½ teaspoons white vinegar

½ teaspoon kosher salt

¼ teaspoon garlic powder

1. If you'd like to keep the cakes warm between batches, place a rack in the center of your oven and preheat the oven to 200 degrees F. Heat 2 teaspoons of the oil in a large nonstick skillet over medium-low heat. Once the oil is hot but not yet smoking, add the onion, bell pepper, seafood seasoning, salt, and black pepper. Sauté gently until the vegetables are soft, 10 to 15 minutes. Add the spinach, stirring until it wilts, 1 to 2 minutes. Remove the pan from the heat and let the vegetables cool to room temperature.

2. While the vegetables cool, prepare the sauce: In a small bowl, stir together the Greek yogurt, milk, hot sauce, vinegar, salt, and garlic powder. If you would like the sauce a little thinner, add milk, 1 teaspoon at a time, until you reach your desired consistency. Taste and adjust the seasoning as desired; if the sauce is

recipe continues

too spicy, add a bit more Greek yogurt to cool it down; if you'd like it hotter, dash in extra Sriracha. Set aside for serving.

3. In a large mixing bowl, lightly beat the egg. Stir in the Greek yogurt, flour, mustard, hot sauce, and Worcestershire sauce until combined. Flake the drained salmon into the bowl. Add the quinoa and the cooled vegetable mixture (keep the skillet nearby for cooking the patties). With a fork, lightly mix the ingredients together until they are evenly combined.

4. Portion the batter by slightly heaped ⅓ cupfuls and shape into eight ¾-inch-thick patties. If time allows, refrigerate the patties for 15 minutes. Refrigerating will help them hold together more easily as you cook them. If you are in a hurry, you can cook them right away; just be a bit more delicate when flipping.

5. With a paper towel, carefully wipe the skillet clean. Add ½ tablespoon of the oil and heat over medium-low heat. Once the oil is hot, swirl to coat the bottom of the pan, then add the salmon patties, four at a time. Cook 7 to 8 minutes on the first side, until deeply golden, then very gently flip and cook on the other side for 5 to 6 minutes, until cooked through. Transfer to a paper towel–lined plate or place on a baking sheet and keep warm in the oven. Repeat with the remaining patties, adding the remaining ½ tablespoon oil to the skillet if needed to prevent sticking. Serve hot with the dipping sauce.

MAKE-AHEAD & STORAGE TIPS:
Uncooked shaped patties can be tightly wrapped in plastic and refrigerated for up to 1 day. Cook as directed.

To freeze in advance: Form the salmon patties (do not cook). Arrange in a single layer on a parchment-lined baking sheet, then place in the freezer until firm. Wrap each patty tightly in plastic and transfer to a ziptop bag. Freeze for up to 1 month. Defrost overnight in the refrigerator, then cook as directed.

Cooked salmon cakes taste best the day they are made but can be refrigerated for up to 1 additional day. Reheat gently in a nonstick skillet over medium-low heat. I find that the reheated cakes lose a bit of their seasoning, so be sure you have some dipping sauce on hand to liven them back up.

PRO TIPS:
Pan-frying will give you a lightly crispy exterior and moist, flaky interior, similar to a classic crab cake. If you prefer a more even texture throughout (or want a more hands-free cooking method), you can bake the patties instead: Place a rack in the center of your oven and preheat the oven to 400 degrees F. Line a baking sheet with parchment paper and lightly coat the paper with nonstick spray. Place the shaped patties on the prepared baking sheet. Bake for 10 minutes on the first side, gently flip the patties, then return to the oven and continue baking until lightly golden, dry to the touch, and cooked through, about 5 additional minutes.

NEXT LEVEL:
• Try these cakes as sliders on soft whole wheat buns with the sauce, a few pieces of crisp lettuce, some sliced tomato, and very thinly sliced red onion. A piece of crispy bacon would not be remiss.

• Top with sautéed spinach and a poached egg for a lighter twist on a crab cake Benedict.

• Serve on top of a bed of arugula, drizzled with either Zippy Lemon Yogurt Dressing (page 89) or Go-to Citrus Dressing made with lemon juice (page 89).

Slow Cooker Apricot-Glazed Pork and Vegetables

ACTIVE TIME: 45 minutes · **TOTAL TIME:** 3 hours 30 minutes · **YIELD:** Serves 4 to 6

This recipe caused me to seriously consider if I could apricot-glaze everything. The sweet, sticky sauce bathes the pork in a wonderful, fruity flavor that reminds me of classic pork chops and applesauce but all grown up and decidedly more interesting. Every forkful leaves you with a new taste to discover and appreciate. Sometimes it's the orange that stands out to me. Sometimes it's the rosemary. Sometimes I can't quite put my finger on why I can't stop eating it, so I have no choice but to drizzle on a little extra glaze and contemplate it further.

To ensure your pork comes out perfectly moist and fork tender, check its temperature for doneness early the first time you make it. All slow cookers are a little different, and because pork loin is lean, it can go from *juuuust* right to overdone more quickly than you expect. If the worst should happen and you do overcook it, fear not. A few extra spoonfuls of the magical apricot glaze will moisten the pork right back up.

2½ pounds boneless pork loin roast, trimmed of excess fat (do not use pork tenderloin, which is a bit too lean for slow cooking)

2 teaspoons kosher salt, divided

½ teaspoon ground black pepper, divided

2 tablespoons extra virgin olive oil, divided

1 large yellow onion, thinly sliced (about 3 cups)

1 (10-ounce) jar apricot jam or preserves (look for a pure-fruit variety sweetened with only fruit and fruit concentrate or honey)

½ cup freshly squeezed orange juice (from about 1 medium orange)

2 tablespoons Dijon mustard

1 tablespoon chopped fresh rosemary leaves, from about 2 (6-inch) rosemary stems

1 pound green beans, ends trimmed, halved crosswise (about 2¾ cups)

1 pound carrots, peeled and cut into ¼-inch-thick diagonal slices, slices halved if large (about 3 cups or 6 medium)

10 dried apricot halves, thinly sliced

2 tablespoons cornstarch mixed with 2 tablespoons water to create a slurry

1. Lightly coat a 6-quart or larger slow cooker with nonstick spray. Season the pork loin with 1 teaspoon of the salt and ¼ teaspoon of the pepper. In a large skillet, heat 1½ tablespoons of the oil over medium-high heat, swirling to coat the pan. Once the oil is hot but not yet smoking, sear the pork on all sides until browned, about 2 minutes per side. Remove to a plate and leave the drippings in the pan.

2. Reduce the skillet heat to medium. Add the remaining ½ tablespoon oil. Add the onion and ½ teaspoon of the salt. Cook, stirring occasionally, until the onion is golden brown and very soft, about 15 minutes.

3. In a medium mixing bowl, whisk together the jam, orange juice, mustard, rosemary, and the remaining ½ teaspoon salt and the remaining ¼ teaspoon pepper.

recipe continues

4. Place the green beans and carrots in the bottom of the slow cooker and scatter half of the sautéed onion and half of the apricot slices over the top. Place the pork on top of the vegetables, then scatter the remaining onion and apricot slices over the pork. Pour the apricot glaze over the top. Cover and cook on low for 2 to 3 hours, until the pork is cooked through and reaches an internal temperature of 145 degrees F on an instant-read thermometer at the thickest part. Be sure to check a little before the 2-hour mark to monitor the pork's progress and ensure it does not overcook. Remove the pork to a cutting board, cover with aluminum foil, and let rest for 10 minutes. With a slotted spoon, transfer the vegetables to a serving plate and cover to keep warm.

5. Strain the cooking liquid from the slow cooker into a medium saucepan. Stir in the cornstarch slurry. Place the pan on the stove and bring to a boil over medium-high heat, stirring very frequently. Continue cooking and stirring until the sauce has thickened, 3 to 5 minutes. Stir constantly in the last minutes to ensure the glaze stays smooth.

6. Uncover the pork and vegetables. Slice the pork and arrange the pieces in the center of the vegetables. Spoon ⅓ cup glaze over the top of the pork. Serve hot, drizzled with additional glaze as desired.

STORAGE TIPS:
Refrigerate leftover pork, vegetables, and glaze in separate containers for up to 3 days. To rewarm: Heat the vegetables gently in the microwave or on the stove top. Cut the pork into thin slices and warm in a single layer in a lightly oiled pan over medium heat. Cover the pan with a lid as the pork warms to help it cook evenly, and turn it every minute or so. As soon as the pork is warmed through, 2 to 3 minutes depending upon the thickness of your slice, remove it from the pan and serve. Warm the glaze separately on the stove or in the microwave and brush over the pork slices.

PRO TIP:
To round out the meal, serve the pork and vegetables over brown rice with the apricot glaze spooned generously over the top.

LEFTOVER LOVE:
Sweet and Tangy Pork Sandwich: Spread one side of 2 slices of whole wheat bread with honey mustard. Rewarm the sliced pork as described in Storage Tips. Top 1 slice of bread with the warmed pork, a slice of cheddar cheese, thinly sliced red onion, and pickles. Add the other bread slice on top, mustard-side down, then butter the outsides of the bread. Grill the sandwich in a skillet heated over medium-low heat for 3 to 4 minutes on each side, until the bread is golden and the cheese is melted. Serve immediately.

STORAGE TIPS:

Refrigerate leftovers in an airtight container for up to 4 days. Rewarm gently in the microwave or a lightly oiled skillet.

MARKET SWAPS:

This recipe is delicious with a wide combination of fall vegetables. Try diced sweet potatoes, carrots, parsnips, butternut squash, and even beets. Harder vegetables will need longer to cook, so either cut them into smaller pieces than the other vegetables or pop them in the oven ahead of time to give them a head start.

Autumn Sheet Pan Sausages
with Apples and Harvest Vegetables

ACTIVE TIME: 25 minutes · **TOTAL:** 1 hour · **YIELD:** Serves 4

Estabrook Park, a large, lively outdoor beer garden in Milwaukee, is a little piece of paradise on earth. It's sunny and surrounded by trees; the picnic tables are long and communal; and every time you visit, you catch a slice of life that ranges from rosy-cheeked babies in strollers, to white-whiskered men playing cards, to blushing couples on awkward first dates. Count on a live polka band. Dancing is encouraged.

In addition to German beer, the little food stall in the center of the garden serves up hearty sausages with sauerkraut and mustard. While I've never been a fanatic for German food, I can appreciate the way it hits the spot on chilly fall days. This sheet-pan adaptation satisfies in much the same way. In place of bratwurst, which I find to be pretty bland, I use precooked apple chicken sausages, which have a savory-sweetness that works magnificently here. The sauerkraut, made with cabbage, is represented by Brussels sprouts, which is a relative. Red onion and apples complete the harvest picture, and mustard and apple cider vinegar provide balance and punch. I'd like to think any beer garden would be pleased to add this dish to its menu—or at least offer me a full stein in exchange for a serving!

1 pound Brussels sprouts, trimmed and halved (about 4 cups)

1 medium red onion, cut into ¼-inch-thick slices (about 2 cups)

4 cloves garlic, minced (about 4 teaspoons)

3 tablespoons Dijon mustard, plus additional for dipping the sausages

2 tablespoons extra virgin olive oil

1 tablespoon honey

1 teaspoon apple cider vinegar

1½ teaspoons kosher salt

½ teaspoon ground black pepper

1 medium sweet-crisp apple, such as Fuji, Gala, or Honeycrisp, peel-on, cored and cut into 1-inch cubes (about 1¼ cups)

12 ounces precooked apple chicken or apple turkey sausages, sliced into ½-inch-thick coins

1 tablespoon chopped fresh thyme

1. Place a rack in the center of your oven and preheat the oven to 400 degrees F. For easy clean up, line a large, rimmed baking sheet with aluminum foil or parchment paper.

2. Place the Brussels sprouts and onion in the center of the baking sheet. In a small bowl or large liquid measuring cup, whisk together the garlic, mustard, oil, honey, vinegar, salt, and pepper. Pour over the vegetables. Toss to coat, then spread the vegetables into an even layer. They will overlap somewhat.

3. Bake for 10 minutes. Remove the pan from the oven. Add the apple and sausage to the pan, then with a large spoon, stir to combine with the vegetables and mustard mixture, intermixing the pieces with the vegetables. Spread into an even layer.

4. Bake for 15 to 20 additional minutes, until the vegetables are tender and caramelized and the sausage is lightly browned, stirring once halfway through. Sprinkle fresh thyme over the top. Serve hot, with extra mustard for dipping.

Ultimate Creamy Mac and Cheese (4 Ways!)

ACTIVE TIME: 35 minutes · **TOTAL TIME:** 1 hour · **YIELD:** Serves 6 as a main or 10 to 12 as a side

When my grammy allowed my sisters and me to select our own birthday dinner menus growing up, I'm not entirely sure she was prepared for all three of us to pick homemade macaroni and cheese every year for eighteen years straight—or for us to grow up, move out, get married, and then come home for holidays and request she make it once more.

Given my family's attachment to mac and cheese, creating a lighter version that honored the memories and distinct feelings of being loved that I still associate with it was no small task. This Ultimate Creamy Mac and Cheese succeeds. It's a pan of warmth, abundance, and unapologetic cheesy celebration. Every time I eat it, I feel like a little girl whose birthday wish came true.

Thanks to Greek yogurt and whole wheat pasta, this decadent-tasting dish is loads lighter than other mac and cheese recipes you'll try, but it doesn't skimp an ounce of satisfaction. In addition to my tried-and-true classic mac and cheese, I also have three yummy spin-offs. Make one for your birthday, one for your half birthday, one for your quarter birthday, and one just because there isn't a day on the calendar that won't benefit from a gooey, steaming pan of homemade macaroni and cheese.

◄ CLASSIC, PERFECT MAC AND CHEESE MASTER RECIPE: ►

1 pound dry short whole wheat pasta, such as shells, penne, rigatoni, or elbow macaroni

3 tablespoons unsalted butter

½ small yellow onion, diced (about ½ cup)

4 cloves garlic, minced (about 4 teaspoons)

½ cup white whole wheat flour

4 cups nonfat milk

1½ teaspoons kosher salt

½ teaspoon ground black pepper

¼ teaspoon cayenne pepper, plus additional to taste

¾ cup nonfat plain Greek yogurt

1½ cups shredded melty, flavorful cheese, such as sharp cheddar, fontina, Gouda, or Gruyère (about 6 ounces)

½ cup shredded Parmesan cheese (about 2 ounces)

VARIATION 1: Broccoli Cheddar

Add: 1 small head broccoli (about 8 ounces), very finely chopped (about 2 cups)

Add: 1 teaspoon dry mustard

For the melty cheese: use sharp cheddar

VARIATION 2: Tomato Basil

Add: ½ cup thinly sliced fresh basil, divided

Add: 4 small plum tomatoes, cut into thin, round slices

For the melty cheese: use any combination of sharp cheddar, mozzarella, or fontina (if using mozzarella, I recommend also incorporating cheddar, since mozzarella is quite mild and will benefit from the extra flavor boost)

VARIATION 3: Spicy Cajun

Add: 1 tablespoon extra virgin olive oil

Add: 8 ounces precooked andouille sausage, cut into ¼-inch-thick coins

Add: 1 medium red or green bell pepper, diced (about 1 cup)

Add: 1 tablespoon Cajun seasoning blend

For the melty cheese: use a combination of sharp cheddar and Monterey Jack

recipe continues

Classic, Perfect

Tomato
Basil

Spicy
Cajun

Broccoli
Cheddar

For Classic, Perfect:

1. Bring a large pot of salted water to a boil. Add the pasta and cook according to the package instructions until barely al dente. Drain and set aside.

2. Place racks in the center and upper third of your oven and preheat the oven to 350 degrees F. Coat a 9×13-inch casserole dish or similar 3- to 3½-quart casserole dish with nonstick spray.

3. While the pasta cooks: In a Dutch oven or similar large, heavy-bottomed pot, heat the butter over medium heat. Once melted, add the onion and cook until the onion is fragrant and beginning to soften but is not yet brown, about 2 minutes. Add the garlic, then sprinkle the flour over the top. With a whisk, stir continually until the flour turns golden brown and the white bits disappear, about 1 minute. The flour will be lumpy at first but will smooth out as you continue with the recipe.

4. Pour in the milk a few splashes at a time, whisking constantly to break up any lumps. Bring to a simmer and cook, stirring often, until the sauce thickens, 5 to 7 minutes.

5. Remove the pot from the heat and stir in the salt, black pepper, and cayenne pepper. Let the mixture cool for 1 minute, then stir in the Greek yogurt and melty cheese. Add the drained pasta. With a large spoon or spatula, stir and fold gently to combine the ingredients and lovingly coat each piece of pasta with the sauce. Taste and add additional salt, black pepper, or cayenne pepper to taste.

6. Transfer the mixture to the prepared dish. Sprinkle the Parmesan over the top. Bake on the center rack until hot and bubbly, 15 to 20 minutes. If you'd like a crispy top, turn the oven to broil and transfer the dish to the upper rack. Broil for 2 to 3 minutes, until the top is as dark golden and as crispy as you like, watching it carefully so that it does not burn. Let rest 5 minutes. Enjoy hot.

For Broccoli Cheddar:

At the beginning of step 5, add the broccoli and dry mustard to the pot with the other spices. Proceed with the recipe as directed.

For Tomato Basil:

Stir half of the basil into the cheese sauce with the pasta in step 5. Before putting the dish in the oven, arrange the tomato slices on top, overlapping slightly if needed. Proceed with the recipe. When the mac and cheese has finished baking, sprinkle the remaining basil on top.

For Spicy Cajun:

1. Reduce the salt to ½ teaspoon and omit the black pepper and cayenne pepper.

2. Begin the recipe by heating the olive oil in a Dutch oven or similar, heavy-bottomed pot over medium-high heat. Add the sliced sausage and sauté until lightly golden on all sides, 6 to 7 minutes. Remove to a plate and set aside. Proceed with the recipe as directed, adding the diced bell pepper to the pot with the onion in step 3. In step 5, add the Cajun seasoning with the other spices and fold the cooked sausage in with the pasta. Proceed with the recipe as directed.

STORAGE TIPS:

Refrigerate leftovers in an airtight container for up to 4 days. Reheat individual servings gently in the microwave with a splash of milk to keep them from drying out, stirring periodically. Rewarm a larger portion in a casserole dish loosely tented with foil in a 350-degree-F oven until heated through. The amount of time needed to reheat in the oven will vary based upon the portion size. Start with 15 minutes, then check periodically.

    To freeze: Use a freezer-safe casserole dish. Instead of baking in step 6, let the mixture cool in the dish completely, then cover tightly and freeze for up to 3 months. Let thaw overnight in the refrigerator. Unwrap, loosely cover with foil, then reheat in a 350-degree-F oven until heated through, 30 to 45 minutes.

NEXT LEVEL:

• One of my favorite ways to add extra pizzazz to the classic version is changing up the variety of melty cheeses. While sharp cheddar is my go-to, grocery stores now offer many fun flavors, such as cheeses infused with dill, pesto, and even caramelized onion. For even more variation, try a blend of different cheeses.

• *Crispy Breadcrumb Topping* (especially tasty on the Classic, Perfect and Broccoli Cheddar versions): In a medium microwave-safe bowl in the microwave or in a saucepan over medium heat, melt 3 tablespoons unsalted butter. Stir together with ¾ cup panko bread crumbs and the ½ cup Parmesan listed in the recipe. Sprinkle over the top of the unbaked pasta, then bake as directed.

Slow Cooker Bolognese
+ 3 Ways to Use It

Stuffed
Zucchini
Boats

Slow Cooker
Hearty Turkey
Bolognese

Spaghetti Pie

Slow Cooker Bolognese
+ 3 Ways to Use It

When I decided to publish a recipe for something as brazenly traditional as Bolognese sauce, I could not rest until it was endorsed by the highest level of Italian sauce authority I know: my mother-in-law.

My in-laws are Italian, and every year my mother-in-law cooks an epic pot of homemade red sauce to serve with the family's (also homemade) pasta at Christmas dinner. When she first tasted a spoonful of my version, I watched anxiously and awaited her verdict. V–I–C–T–O–R–Y! By the end of the meal, she'd asked me for the recipe three times, and now you have it too.

Like any Bolognese sauce worthy of the name, this healthier version does require some up-front prep. Once it makes its way into the slow cooker, however, all you need to do is sit back, relax, and try to remain patient while the alluring scent of slow-simmering garlic, tomatoes, and wine perfumes your kitchen. I've loaded this sauce with vegetables and slimmed it down with ground turkey in place of the usual pork and beef, but it turns out so impressively thick and rich, no one will suspect. By your second or third bite, you might forget too!

This recipe yields a large batch of sauce. I'm so confident you'll love having it on hand regularly, I've also included three spin-off recipes that use it.

Slow Cooker Hearty Turkey Bolognese

ACTIVE TIME: 45 minutes · **TOTAL TIME:** 7 hours · **YIELD:** About 7 cups (serves 6)

For the Sauce:

2 tablespoons extra virgin olive oil

1 pound carrots, peeled and finely chopped into ¼-inch or smaller dice (about 3 cups or 6 medium)

2 medium zucchini (about 8 ounces each), peeled and finely chopped into ¼-inch or smaller dice (about 2 cups)

1 large yellow onion, finely chopped (about 2 cups)

2½ teaspoons kosher salt

1¼ teaspoons ground black pepper

2 pounds 93% lean ground turkey

6 cloves garlic, minced (about 2 tablespoons)

2 tablespoons dried oregano

½ teaspoon dried thyme

½ teaspoon red pepper flakes, plus additional to taste

1½ cups dry white wine, such as Sauvignon Blanc

1 (28-ounce) can crushed tomatoes

1 teaspoon granulated sugar

⅓ cup half-and-half

For Serving:

Cooked whole wheat pasta, zucchini noodles, or baked and "fluffed" spaghetti squash strands

Or try any of the following recipe variations!

1. Make the sauce: Lightly coat a 6-quart or larger slow cooker with nonstick spray. In a Dutch oven or similar large, heavy-bottomed pot, heat the oil over medium-high heat. Once the oil is hot but not yet smoking, add the carrots, zucchini, onion, salt, and black pepper and cook until the vegetables are beginning to soften, 5 to 7 minutes. Add the ground turkey and cook, breaking up the meat into small bits with a spoon or spatula, until it is starting to brown, 5 to 7 minutes more.

2. Drain off any excess liquid that has gathered in the pot, then return the pot to the stove. Stir in the garlic, oregano, thyme, and red pepper flakes and cook just until fragrant, about 1 minute.

3. Add the wine and stir. Return to a simmer and let the wine cook until it is reduced by half, 7 to 10 minutes, stirring occasionally.

4. Transfer the mixture to the slow cooker. Add the crushed tomatoes and sugar and stir to combine. Cover and cook on low for 6 hours. Uncover and stir in the half-and-half.

5. To serve: Taste and add additional salt, black pepper, or red pepper flakes as desired. Serve hot over cooked pasta, zucchini noodles, spaghetti squash strands, or try any of the variations on the following pages.

STORAGE TIPS:

Refrigerate leftovers for up to 5 days or freeze for up to 3 months. I find it easiest to freeze in individual portions. Let thaw overnight in the refrigerator, then rewarm gently on the stove or in the microwave with a splash of water or broth to thin the sauce if needed. Season with a bit of additional salt, black pepper, and red pepper flakes to taste. A little splash of red wine vinegar and a glug of half-and-half also work wonders.

Forget to thaw your sauce? Remove the frozen Bolognese from the container and place it in a pot on the stove. Cover and warm over very low heat, checking periodically to stir and break apart the sauce.

PRO TIPS:

• Low and slow is the name of the game with Bolognese. Avoid the temptation to crank the slow cooker to high. This recipe needs time to allow the flavors to develop.

• If you don't have half-and-half on hand, I recommend omitting it versus substituting milk, as milk will make the sauce too thin. The sauce has excellent flavor without the half-and-half, but the cream's special touch is what elevates the Bolognese from satisfying to supreme.

MARKET SWAPS:

In place of the turkey, try 93% lean ground beef, ground bison, or a mix.

Spaghetti Pie

ACTIVE TIME: 20 minutes · **TOTAL TIME:** 55 minutes · **YIELD:** One 9-inch pie (serves 4 to 6)

8 ounces dry whole wheat spaghetti noodles

2½ cups Slow Cooker Hearty Turkey Bolognese (page 192)

8 ounces low-fat (1% or 2%) cottage cheese (about 1 cup)

2 large eggs

2 tablespoons finely chopped fresh parsley

1 teaspoon kosher salt

1 (10-ounce) package frozen spinach, thawed

½ cup shredded part-skim mozzarella cheese (about 2 ounces), divided

4 tablespoons finely grated Parmesan cheese (about ¾ ounce), divided

1. Place a rack in the center of your oven and preheat the oven to 350 degrees F. Generously coat a deep 9-inch pie dish with nonstick spray.

2. Bring a large pot of salted water to a boil. Add the spaghetti and cook for 3 to 4 minutes less time than the package recommends. It should be very al dente and too chewy to eat. Drain, shaking off as much excess water as possible.

3. While the water boils and the pasta cooks, in a large bowl, whisk together the Bolognese sauce, cottage cheese, eggs, parsley, and salt.

4. Squeeze as much excess water from the spinach as possible, wrapping it in paper towels and changing the towels if needed, then stir it into the Bolognese mixture, using a fork to break apart the leaves. Stir in ¼ cup of the mozzarella and 2 tablespoons of the Parmesan. Last, add the cooked spaghetti. Toss to evenly combine the ingredients, then transfer the mixture to the prepared pie dish. Sprinkle the remaining ¼ cup mozzarella and 2 tablespoons Parmesan over the top.

5. Bake until the cheese is bubbling and golden brown and the pie is hot and set in the center, 28 to 30 minutes. Let rest for 5 minutes, then cut into wedges and serve.

STORAGE TIPS:
Refrigerate leftovers for up to 4 days. Reheat gently in the microwave or a 350-degree-F oven, tented with foil. You can also tightly wrap the entire pie or individual slices with plastic and freeze in a ziptop bag for up to 3 months. Let thaw overnight in the refrigerator.

Stuffed Zucchini Boats

ACTIVE TIME: 20 minutes · **TOTAL TIME:** 40 minutes · **YIELD:** 8 boats (serves 4)

4 medium zucchini of similar size (7 to 8 inches, or 8 ounces each)

1½ teaspoons extra virgin olive oi

2¼ cups Slow Cooker Hearty Turkey Bolognese (page 192)

1½ cups shredded part-skim mozzarella or provolone cheese (about 6 ounces)

1. Place a rack in the center of your oven and preheat the oven to 400 degrees F. Coat a 9×13-inch casserole dish with nonstick spray.

2. Halve the zucchini lengthwise. With the tip of a spoon, scrape out and discard the seeds. Then, scoop out the remaining center flesh, reserving the flesh, to create shallow zucchini boats, leaving a wall about ¼ inch thick all around. Transfer the reserved zucchini flesh to a cutting board and roughly chop. Arrange the zucchini boats in the prepared dish.

3. Heat the oil in a large nonstick skillet over medium-high heat. Once the oil is hot but not yet smoking, add the reserved chopped zucchini. Cook until it begins to give up its liquid, about 2 minutes. Add the Bolognese sauce and simmer for 2 to 3 minutes, until warmed through. Remove from the heat.

4. With a spoon, mound the Bolognese filling generously into the zucchini boats. Sprinkle the mozzarella over the top.

5. Bake until the zucchini is heated through and the cheese is melted, about 20 minutes. Enjoy hot.

STORAGE TIPS:
Refrigerate leftovers for up to 3 days. Reheat gently in the microwave (I like to cut the boats into a few big pieces to help them warm evenly) or in a 375-degree-F oven until warmed through.

Polenta Lasagna

ACTIVE TIME: 30 minutes · **TOTAL TIME:** 1 hour 15 minutes · **YIELD:** Serves 6 to 8

---

2 cups low-fat (1% or 2%) cottage cheese or part-skim ricotta cheese

1 tablespoon extra virgin olive oil

1 pound sliced cremini (baby bella) mushrooms (about 5 cups)

½ teaspoon kosher salt, divided

2 cloves garlic, minced (about 2 teaspoons)

5 ounces baby spinach (about 5 cups)

1 large egg

¼ teaspoon ground nutmeg

1 cup shredded part-skim mozzarella cheese (about 4 ounces), divided

4 tablespoons finely grated Parmesan cheese (about ¾ ounce), divided

1 (8-ounce) can no-salt-added tomato sauce

1 (18-ounce) tube cooked polenta, cut into 24 slices (the slices will be about ¼ inch thick)

2 cups Slow Cooker Hearty Turkey Bolognese (page 192)

---

1. Place the cottage cheese in a mesh strainer set over a bowl and let drain while you prepare the other ingredients. Place racks in the center and upper third of your oven and preheat the oven to 375 degrees F. Lightly coat a 9×13-inch casserole dish with nonstick spray.

2. Heat the oil in a large nonstick skillet over medium-high heat. Once the oil is hot but not yet smoking, add the mushrooms and ¼ teaspoon of the salt. Cook until the mushrooms soften and brown and give up most of their liquid, 8 to 10 minutes, stirring occasionally. Add the garlic and sauté for 30 seconds. Add the spinach a few handfuls at a time, stirring until it wilts, 1 to 2 minutes. Continue cooking until any remaining liquid has cooked off, about 30 additional seconds.

3. In a medium mixing bowl, lightly beat the egg. Add the strained cottage cheese (discard any liquid that has collected at the bottom of the bowl—it might not be much, which is fine), nutmeg, ½ cup of the mozzarella, 2 tablespoons of the Parmesan, and the remaining ¼ teaspoon salt. Stir to combine.

4. Drizzle about ⅓ cup of the tomato sauce (you can eyeball this—it will be about one-third of the can) in the bottom of the prepared dish. With the back of a spoon, spread it into a thin, even layer. Arrange half of the polenta slices on top so that they form an even layer. Next, scatter on half the mushroom-spinach mixture, then dollop on half of the cottage cheese mixture. With the back of a spoon, spread it into an even layer. Next, add half of the Bolognese (1 cup) and drizzle on the next ⅓ cup tomato sauce. Spread evenly.

5. Repeat layering with the remaining polenta slices, mushrooms and spinach, cottage cheese, Bolognese, and tomato sauce. Sprinkle the remaining ½ cup mozzarella and remaining 2 tablespoons Parmesan over the top.

6. Bake the lasagna on the center rack for 30 to 40 minutes, until very hot and bubbly. If desired, transfer the dish to the upper rack and turn the oven to broil to brown the cheese, 2 to 3 minutes (do not walk away or the cheese will burn when you are least expecting it). Remove from the oven and let rest at least 10 minutes prior to serving. With a spatula or spoon, scoop big, messy slices onto your plate. Enjoy hot.

Stuffed Sweet Potatoes (5 Ways!)

ACTIVE TIME: 5 to 15 minutes · **TOTAL TIME:** 1 hour (including baking the sweet potato)
YIELD: 1 sweet potato (multiply by as many times as you like)

Meet my single-lady-dinner-turned-married-lady-who-doesn't-always-have-time-to-cook dinner: stuffed sweet potatoes! Sweet potatoes are rich in fiber; vitamins A, B, and more; and can serve as tasty, nourishing vehicles for as many toppings as your imagination allows. When I was cooking for only myself, I turned to stuffed sweet potatoes often because I could scale them to meet my needs—be it one for dinner that night or two or more for easy-to-reheat, packable lunches. Today, I still make stuffed sweet potatoes, because they're effortless, healthy, budget-friendly, and we happily devour them with gusto. The next time you need a fast, filling meal, try one of these super-loaded spuds.

◀ **HOW TO BAKE A SWEET POTATO: START HERE!** ◀

1 small-medium sweet potato (8 to 10 ounces)

1. Place a rack in the center of your oven and preheat the oven to 400 degrees F. For easy cleanup, line a rimmed baking sheet with aluminum foil or parchment paper. Scrub the sweet potato and pat it dry. Prick it all over with the tines of a fork, then place on the prepared baking sheet. Bake until the potato is fork tender, 45 minutes to 1 hour, depending on the size. Remove from the oven and let rest until cool enough to handle.

2. To stuff: Make a slit from end to end down the top of the potato. With a fork, open the slit and lightly fluff the insides to make space for the toppings. Stuff with any of the delicious combos on the following pages.

MAKE-AHEAD & STORAGE TIPS:
For quick meals throughout the week, you can bake a big batch of sweet potatoes one night, leave them unstuffed, then reheat them individually and fill as desired. To reheat: Remove the baked sweet potato from the refrigerator and let it come to as close to room temperature as time will allow. Rewarm in a 425-degree-F oven for 10 to 15 minutes, turning it over once, halfway through. The oven is the ideal option, but you can also reheat baked sweet potatoes in the microwave. Place them on a microwave-safe plate, slice into a few large pieces to promote even heating, then microwave on medium until heated through.

Baked sweet potatoes will keep in the refrigerator for up to 5 days.

California-Style

¼ cup cherry or grape tomatoes

½ medium ripe avocado

1 teaspoon extra virgin olive oil

1 large egg

Generous pinch each kosher salt and ground black pepper

1. Slice the tomatoes in half. Cut the avocado into chunks. Stuff the avocado and tomatoes inside the baked, split sweet potato.

2. In a small nonstick skillet over medium-high heat, heat the olive oil. Once the oil is hot but not yet smoking, swirl to coat the pan, then gently crack the egg into the center. Immediately reduce the heat to low. Let the egg cook gently until the white is completely set and the yolk reaches your desired doneness, 4 to 5 minutes.

3. Immediately top the sweet potato with the egg. Sprinkle with salt and pepper. Enjoy right away.

Barbecue Chicken

½ cup cooked, shredded chicken breast (see page 161)

3 tablespoons prepared barbecue sauce of choice

¼ teaspoon garlic powder

⅛ to ¼ teaspoon cayenne pepper

Generous pinch each kosher salt and ground black pepper

¼ cup shredded sharp cheddar cheese (1 ounce)

1 tablespoon chopped green onion

Place the chicken, barbecue sauce, garlic powder, ⅛ teaspoon cayenne pepper, salt, and black pepper in a small saucepan and heat over medium-low heat. Stir to combine and coat the chicken with the sauce. Cook until the sauce is warm and the chicken is heated through, about 2 minutes. Alternatively, you can stir the ingredients together in a microwave-safe bowl, then heat them gently in the microwave, stirring periodically. Taste and adjust the salt, black pepper, and cayenne pepper as desired. Stuff inside the baked, split sweet potato and top with the cheddar and green onion. Enjoy warm.

Barbecue Chicken

Power Breakfast

California-Style

Mediterranean

Hawaiian

Mediterranean

3 tablespoons prepared hummus of choice

1 tablespoon unsweetened almond milk or nonfat milk, plus additional as needed

½ small red bell pepper, diced (about ½ cup)

2 tablespoons diced red onion

2 tablespoons crumbled feta cheese

1 tablespoon chopped fresh parsley (optional)

Generous pinch each kosher salt and ground black pepper

1. In a small bowl, stir together the hummus with the almond milk to thin. Add a little more almond milk as needed, until it reaches a pourable consistency.

2. Stuff the baked, split sweet potato with the bell pepper and red onion, then drizzle with the hummus. Sprinkle with the feta and parsley and season with the salt and pepper. Enjoy warm.

Power Breakfast

⅓ cup nonfat plain Greek yogurt

1 tablespoon peanut butter or nut butter of choice

½ medium banana, sliced (about generous ¼ cup)

2 tablespoons Ridiculously Addictive Maple Quinoa Granola (page 26) or prepared granola of choice

In a small bowl, stir together the Greek yogurt and peanut butter. Spoon half of the mixture inside the baked, split sweet potato. Top with the banana slices, then the remaining yogurt mixture. Sprinkle the granola over the top. Enjoy immediately.

Hawaiian

2 ounces Canadian bacon slices (about four 3-inch round slices)

¼ cup diced pineapple (fresh, frozen and thawed, or canned in 100% juice and drained)

¼ cup shredded sharp cheddar or Monterey Jack cheese (about 1 ounce)

1 tablespoon finely chopped green onion or red onion

1. Place a rack in the center of your oven and preheat the oven to 400 degrees F. Heat a small nonstick skillet over medium heat. Add the Canadian bacon slices in a single layer and crisp on one side until warm and slightly browned, 1 to 2 minutes. Flip and cook until browned on the other side, about 30 additional seconds. Transfer to a cutting board and let cool slightly. Chop into small, bite-sized pieces.

2. Stuff the baked, split sweet potato with the pineapple and Canadian bacon. Sprinkle with the cheese. For easy cleanup, line a baking sheet or small baking pan with aluminum foil or parchment paper. Transfer the sweet potato to the sheet and bake until the pineapple is warm and the cheese is melted, about 3 minutes. Let cool slightly, then sprinkle with the onion. Enjoy warm.

Beyond the Bread:
Sandwiches and Other Hand-Helds

Slow Cooker
Crispy Pineapple
Pork Carnitas, page 217

Portobello Philly Melts · **Steak Fajita 'Dillas**

Greek Pita Pizzas with Skinny Tzatziki Sauce

Buffalo Chicken Burgers with Blue Cheese Sauce

On-Purpose Veggie Burgers with Roasted Red Pepper Sauce

Slow Cooker Crispy Pineapple Pork Carnitas · **Asian Lettuce Wraps**

Grown-Up Grilled Cheese (3 Ways!)

Garlicky Sweet Potato Spinach · *Roasted Broccoli-Cauli Cheddar*

The Beautiful Bs: Blackberry, Basil, Balsamic, Brie

———•———

A dutiful brown-bagger who packed PB&Js well into my twenties, I sought sandwiches not for pleasure so much as efficiency. I considered them standard-issue fare to be eaten for the sake of convenience and my grocery budget. Then I married Ben, who happily ate a sandwich almost every single day for lunch, then would come home and devour another for dinner. I began to suspect that there might be more to this whole sandwich idea, and I started to play around. Fast-forward a few years and a few hundred slices of bread, and we're arrived at this chapter!

Sandwiches—and their hand-held cousins: wraps, melts, tacos, and burgers—are quick, convenient, and (literally) filled with delicious possibility. I've stacked this chapter with an array of tasty options. You'll find inventive new combinations you might not have thought of, lightened-up twists on classics you've loved for years, and even fresh ways to expand the very meaning of the word "sandwich." As you'll see, bread isn't the only vessel you'll enjoy picking up and polishing off with your fingers. From tortillas to pitas to even crisp lettuce cups, the "sandwiches" in this chapter will suit every craving.

Portobello Philly Melts

ACTIVE TIME: 35 minutes · **TOTAL TIME:** 40 minutes · **YIELD:** 4 melts

I realize I am baiting the wrath of the entire city of Philadelphia with this recipe, but it is so scrumptious, I'm willing to risk it. A slimmed-down version of the notorious Philly cheesesteak, this marvelous melt swaps the beef for thick slices of portobello mushrooms. A splash of Worcestershire and soy sauce are my secret ingredients. They give the mushrooms a deeply satisfying and (forgive me, but there really is no other way to explain this) *meaty* flavor that even the staunchest of cheesesteak purists would struggle to resist. My other departure from cheesesteak tradition is ditching the ho-hum hoagie bun in favor of thick slices of good-quality bread and serving them as a melt. The melt approach allows the filling to play the starring role, and ensures that the gooey, golden cheese works its way into every bite.

---

4 slices thick-cut good-quality whole wheat or sourdough bread

1 tablespoon extra virgin olive oil

1 medium yellow onion, cut into ¼-inch-thick slices (about 2 cups)

4 large portobello mushrooms, stems and gills removed (see Pro Tips), cut into ¼-inch-thick slices

1 medium red bell pepper, cut into ¼-inch-thick strips (about 1¼ cups)

1 medium green bell pepper, cut into ¼-inch-thick strips (about 1¼ cups)

½ teaspoon dried thyme

½ teaspoon ground black pepper

1 tablespoon all-purpose flour

¼ cup water

1 tablespoon low sodium soy sauce

1 tablespoon Worcestershire sauce (see Pro Tips)

1 cup shredded part-skim provolone or mozzarella cheese (about 4 ounces)

---

1. Place a rack in the upper third of your oven and preheat the oven to 400 degrees F. Line a baking sheet with aluminum foil or parchment paper, then arrange the bread slices in a single layer on top. Bake for 5 minutes, then flip the slices, return the pan to the oven, and continue baking until the slices are lightly toasted, 4 to 5 additional minutes. Remove from the oven and set aside. Turn the oven to broil.

2. Meanwhile, in a large nonstick skillet, heat the oil over medium-high heat. Once the oil is hot but not yet smoking, add the onion and sauté, stirring often, until beginning to brown, about 4 minutes. Add the mushrooms, red and green bell peppers, thyme, and black pepper. Cook, stirring often, until the vegetables are soft and beginning to lightly brown, 10 to 15 minutes.

3. Reduce the skillet heat to low. Sprinkle the flour over the top of the vegetables and stir to coat. Stir in the water, soy sauce, and Worcestershire. Turn the heat back to medium high and continue to cook and stir until the liquid evaporates, about 1 additional minute. Remove the pan from the heat.

4. Scoop the filling on top of the toasted bread, dividing it evenly among the slices (you will have about ¾ cup filling per slice). Spread the filling into an even layer, then sprinkle each slice with ¼ cup of the provolone. Place in the oven and broil until the cheese is melted and golden brown on top, 3 to 4 minutes. Watch closely during the last few minutes to ensure the bread and cheese do not burn. Let cool a few minutes on the pan. Enjoy hot.

MAKE-AHEAD & STORAGE TIPS:

This filling can be stored in the refrigerator for up to 4 days, so it's a great make-ahead option for quick dinners. It's also perfect for a casual get-together with friends. Simply multiply the filling by as many people as you will be serving (days in advance if you like!), then just before serving, warm the filling and bake as directed.

PRO TIPS:

- The dark gills on the underside of portobellos are edible, but the texture can be off-putting. To remove them, use a spoon to gently scrape them away.

- Not all Worcestershire sauce is vegetarian, so if you will be serving this meal to those who follow a strict vegetarian diet, be sure to find a brand labeled as such. In a pinch, you can omit the Worcestershire and add a bit more soy sauce to taste.

LEFTOVER LOVE:

This filling is also delicious with brown rice. For an extra hit of protein, top with a fried or poached egg.

Steak Fajita 'Dillas

ACTIVE TIME: 45 minutes · **TOTAL TIME:** 55 minutes · **YIELD:** 8 quesadillas (serves 4 to 6)

You know that feeling of envy when you are sitting at a Mexican restaurant and a server strides by with a different table's order of sizzling hot fajitas? The smell! The sound! The tantalizing aroma!

Making these Steak Fajita 'Dillas feels like sitting at the fajita table. In this killer sheet pan recipe, the steak and veggies bake on a single baking sheet in a matter of minutes, so you won't have to stand at the stove and brave oil splatters to cook them. Then, you do the restaurant one better. Stuff the tender fajita steak and vegetables along with some melty Monterey Jack cheese into tortillas and toast them up, quesadilla-style, until they're browned and crispy on the outside and hot and melty on the inside. Now *that* is what I call sizzle!

1 large red bell pepper, cut into ¼-inch-thick strips (about 1¾ cups)

1 large yellow or orange bell pepper, cut into ¼-inch-thick strips (about 1¾ cups)

1 large green bell pepper, cut into ¼-inch-thick strips (about 1¾ cups)

1 medium yellow onion, cut into ¼-inch-thick slices (about 2 cups)

3 tablespoons freshly squeezed lime juice (from about 2 small limes)

2 tablespoons extra virgin olive oil

1 tablespoon Worcestershire sauce

1½ teaspoons honey

2 teaspoons ground cumin

2 teaspoons chili powder

1 teaspoon kosher salt

½ teaspoon red pepper flakes

½ teaspoon ground black pepper

1 pound flank steak, very thinly sliced across the grain

8 taco-size (8-inch) whole wheat flour tortillas

2 cups shredded Monterey Jack cheese (about 8 ounces), divided

For serving: sliced fresh avocado, salsa, nonfat plain Greek yogurt, lime wedges

1. Place racks in the upper and lower thirds of your oven. Set a large, rimmed baking sheet on the upper rack. Preheat the oven (with the baking sheet in it) to broil. In a medium mixing bowl, place the red, yellow, and green bell peppers and onion.

2. In a small mixing bowl or large liquid measuring cup, whisk together the lime juice, oil, Worcestershire, honey, cumin, chili powder, salt, red pepper flakes, and black pepper. Pour half of the mixture over the vegetables. With a large spoon or spatula, stir to coat.

3. Carefully remove the baking sheet from the oven and coat with nonstick spray. Add the vegetables to the pan and, with a spatula, spread into a single layer. Broil on the upper rack for 8 to 10 minutes, until the vegetables are tender. Keep the bowl handy.

4. While the vegetables bake, add the steak to the bowl. Pour the remaining lime/Worcestershire mixture over the top. Stir to coat, and let sit while the vegetables bake.

recipe continues

5. Remove the vegetables from the oven, carefully push them to one side of the pan (they will overlap), then scoop the steak onto the open side of the pan, discarding any excess liquid that has collected in the bowl. Spread the steak slices into as even a layer as you can. Broil on the upper rack for 3 minutes, or until the steak reaches your desired doneness. Watch very carefully towards the end to ensure the steak does not overcook. Remove the pan from the oven and turn the oven off.

6. For the first quesadilla: Warm a large nonstick skillet over medium heat. Lightly coat the skillet with nonstick spray or lightly brush with olive oil. Lay a tortilla in the skillet and sprinkle 2 tablespoons of the cheese over half of it, leaving the other half uncovered. Top the cheese with one-eighth of the steak slices (about ¼ cup) and one-eighth of the onion and peppers (about ⅓ cup). Sprinkle an additional 2 tablespoons cheese on top, then fold the open side of the tortilla in half over the top to create a half moon. Slide the quesadilla to one side of the skillet so that the folded, straight edge runs down the center, as though it is dividing the skillet in half.

7. For the next quesadilla: Nestle a second tortilla into the open skillet space, folding it the opposite direction of the first tortilla (the open sides of the quesadillas will point away from each other). Top the side of the tortilla touching the skillet with 2 tablespoons of the cheese, one-eighth of the meat, one-eighth of the veggies, and 2 tablespoons additional cheese. Fold the tortilla over itself to create a second half moon.

8. Cook the quesadillas on both sides until the tortillas are golden and the cheese is melted, 5 to 6 minutes total. If desired, transfer the cooked quesadillas to a clean baking sheet and place on the lower rack of the oven to keep warm while you finish cooking the remaining quesadillas (the oven should still be warm from cooking the steak and vegetables, but if not, heat it to 200 degrees F). Repeat with the remaining tortillas.

9. Transfer the quesadillas to a cutting board and let rest 1 to 2 minutes. Slice into wedges and serve hot with your desired toppings.

STORAGE TIPS:
Refrigerate leftover steak-and-vegetables filling in an airtight container for up to 3 days. Rewarm gently in the microwave or on the stove top, then assemble and cook the quesadillas prior to serving.

Greek Pita Pizzas
with Skinny Tzatziki Sauce

ACTIVE TIME: 50 minutes · **TOTAL TIME:** 1 hour · **YIELD:** 4 pizzas and 1½ cups sauce

When a girlfriend rings to see if you'd be interested in joining her for a ten-day trip to Greece, the proper response is "should I bring one swimsuit or two?" (I brought three.) It was on our whirlwind, blue-sky and turquoise-water-tinted Grecian adventure that I fell in love with lamb. With a flavor that is a bit like beef (but lighter) and a bit like chicken (but more exciting), lamb is a fresh, invigorating option to add to your cooking repertoire.

These pita "pizzas" are inspired by my trip to Greece. The familiar, friendly pizza format makes it extra appealing, especially for someone who might be new to lamb. Whole wheat pita acts as the crust, the toppings are bright and fresh, and the combination of the lamb and seasonings will transport you straight to the Mediterranean. Be sure to top the pizzas generously with the tzatziki sauce. Its creamy texture and garlicky bite make the recipe complete.

For the Tzatziki Sauce:

½ large English cucumber, peel on (about 8 ounces)

1 cup nonfat plain Greek yogurt

2 cloves garlic, minced (about 2 teaspoons)

1 tablespoon freshly squeezed lemon juice

1 tablespoon finely chopped fresh dill

2 teaspoons extra virgin olive oil

¼ teaspoon kosher salt

For the Pita Pizzas:

1 pound ground lamb (my favorite!) or 93% lean ground beef

2 cloves garlic, minced (about 2 teaspoons)

1½ teaspoons dried oregano

¾ teaspoon ground cumin

¾ teaspoon ground cinnamon

½ teaspoon kosher salt

½ teaspoon ground black pepper

Zest of 1 medium lemon (about 1 teaspoon)

4 whole wheat pita breads

2 teaspoons extra virgin olive oil

⅓ cup thinly sliced red onion (about ½ small)

½ cup crumbled feta cheese (about 3 ounces)

1. Prepare the tzatziki sauce: Grate the cucumber onto a double stack of paper towels. Fold the towels around the cucumber. Over the sink, squeeze out as much excess water as possible, adding another layer of paper towels as needed. Transfer the cucumber to a medium bowl and discard the paper towels. Add the Greek yogurt, garlic, lemon juice, dill, oil, and salt. Stir to combine. Cover and refrigerate for at least 30 minutes or up to 3 days.

2. Make the pizzas: Place a rack in the upper third of your oven and preheat the oven to 400 degrees F. Line a large baking sheet with parchment paper.

3. Heat a large nonstick skillet over medium-high heat. Add the lamb and cook, breaking apart the meat into crumbles and stirring occasionally until it is brown and no longer pink, about 5 minutes. Drain or use a paper

recipe continues

towel to blot away all but about 1 tablespoon of the extra fat. You don't want the meat to be greasy but ensure it is not completely dry either. Add the garlic, oregano, cumin, cinnamon, salt, and pepper. Stir and cook until the garlic is fragrant, about 30 seconds. Stir in the lemon zest. Remove from the heat.

4. Arrange the pitas on the prepared baking sheet. Brush the top of each pita with ½ teaspoon of the oil. Divide the lamb mixture among the 4 pitas, scooping about ⅓ cup onto each. Top with the red onion slices and sprinkle with the feta. Bake until the cheese is warmed and the pitas are lightly toasted, 11 to 14 minutes. Remove from the oven and transfer to a cutting board. Cut each pita into quarters. Serve hot, topped generously with the sauce.

MAKE-AHEAD & STORAGE TIPS:
The ground lamb topping can be cooked and refrigerated for up to 4 days or frozen for up to 3 months. Assemble the pizzas just before baking.

Store the tzatziki in the refrigerator for up to 3 days. Stir before serving.

LEFTOVER LOVE:
• Warm leftover lamb topping and mix it with cooked brown rice. Top with a sprinkle of chopped fresh parsley and tzatziki sauce.

• Dip extra tzatziki sauce with pita chips, spoon generously over roasted or grilled vegetables, or serve on top of On-Purpose Veggie Burgers (page 214).

Buffalo Chicken Burgers
with Blue Cheese Sauce

ACTIVE TIME: 30 minutes · **TOTAL TIME:** 30 minutes
YIELD: 4 burgers and about ¾ cup sauce

If you've glimpsed the inside of my refrigerator, we must be *very* good friends. It's a three-dimensional game of Tetris, especially the shelf of condiments. Before you gently suggest I dispose of a few, please know that I have no intention of parting with either identical jar of hot sauce. Once you taste these burgers, you'll know why!

These juicy burgers take the classic, ever-appealing spicy Buffalo flavor that prompted you to stop on this page in the first place, and they turn it into a lean, healthy, and crowd-pleasing dinner. My secret ingredient is shredded carrots. They keep the burgers moist, and their natural sweetness is an ideal foil to the spiciness of the hot sauce. Another carrot plus: Their orange hue blends seamlessly with the color of the hot sauce–spiked patties, so they are nearly invisible. Picky eaters will never suspect your wily ways.

For the Buffalo Chicken Burgers:

1 pound ground chicken

1 cup peeled and finely shredded carrots (about 5 ounces or 2 medium; do not use the preshedded kind sold in grocery stores, as they will be too dry)

¼ cup classic hot sauce, such as Frank's RedHot Original

¾ teaspoon garlic powder

½ teaspoon kosher salt

¼ teaspoon cayenne pepper

3 medium green onions, finely chopped (about ½ cup), divided

Canola oil, for grilling

4 pretzel (our favorite) or whole wheat hamburger buns

For the Blue Cheese Sauce:

½ cup nonfat plain Greek yogurt

2 tablespoons nonfat milk

½ teaspoon white vinegar

¼ teaspoon ground black pepper

½ cup crumbled blue cheese (about 2 ounces)

1. Make the burger patties: In a large mixing bowl, place the ground chicken, carrots, hot sauce, garlic powder, salt, cayenne, and ¼ cup of the green onions. With a fork or your fingers, lightly combine to evenly distribute the ingredients, being careful not to compact the meat. Divide and shape into 4 patties that are ¾ inch thick. Cover and place in the refrigerator while you prepare the blue cheese sauce.

2. Preheat an outdoor grill or indoor grill pan to medium heat. If you would like to toast the buns in the oven, place a rack in the upper third of your oven and preheat the oven to 350 degrees F.

3. In a small mixing bowl, stir together the blue cheese sauce ingredients: Greek yogurt, milk, vinegar, pepper, and blue cheese. Set aside for serving, or refrigerate for up to 3 days.

4. When ready to cook the burgers, lightly brush the grill with canola oil. Grill the burgers for 4 minutes on the first side, then flip and grill for an additional 3 to 5 minutes, until cooked through and the internal temperature reaches 165 degrees F on an instant-read thermometer.

5. If desired, toast the buns on the grill or place cut-side up on an ungreased baking sheet and toast in the oven for 8 minutes, or until lightly toasted. Serve the burgers on the buns, topped with a generous portion of the blue cheese sauce, and sprinkled with the remaining ¼ cup green onions. Enjoy immediately.

STORAGE TIPS:
Shaped, uncooked patties can be tightly wrapped in plastic and refrigerated for 1 day or frozen for up to 1 month. Let thaw overnight in the refrigerator, then cook as directed.

Cooked burgers are best enjoyed the day they are made but can be tightly wrapped in plastic and refrigerated for up to 3 days. Reheat in a small saucepan over medium heat. Add a little water to the pan, cover, and let cook a few minutes, then remove the cover and continue cooking until the burgers are warmed through and most of the water has cooked off, flipping them a few times to heat both sides.

MARKET SWAPS:
• Swap the blue cheese for the same amount of crumbled feta.

• If you'd like to skip the sauce entirely, try the burgers topped with sliced provolone or cheddar cheese.

On-Purpose Veggie Burgers
with Roasted Red Pepper Sauce

ACTIVE TIME: 40 minutes · **TOTAL TIME:** 50 minutes · **YIELD:** 6 burgers and ¾ cup sauce

The first time I witnessed my carnivorous husband order a veggie burger in a restaurant, I interrupted to inform him that, *um, there's no meat in that.* Apparently he was aware and had ordered it on purpose. I asked our server to change my order to match, reasoning that if a veggie burger was enticing enough for my meat-loving man to select it at will, I needed to try it too.

Those veggie burgers turned out to be one of the best ordering decisions we've ever made. The texture was moist but not mushy or crumbly, the flavor was rich and complex, and the roasted red pepper sauce made every bite sing and zing. Years later, they are still our favorite burger—meat or nonmeat—in Milwaukee. This recipe is inspired by them and will be a fast favorite at your table too.

For the Burgers:

½ cup raw walnut halves

3 tablespoons extra virgin olive oil, divided

8 ounces sliced cremini (baby bella) mushrooms (about 2½ cups)

2 cloves garlic, minced (about 2 teaspoons)

1 medium shallot, minced (about ½ cup)

1 (12-ounce) jar roasted red peppers, drained and cut into ¼-inch dice (about 1 cup), divided

1 teaspoon kosher salt, divided

1 (15-ounce) can reduced sodium black beans, rinsed and drained

¾ cup old-fashioned oats, plus additional as needed

1 tablespoon smoked paprika

1½ teaspoons ground cumin

1 tablespoon Worcestershire sauce (see Pro Tips)

¼ teaspoon ground black pepper

¼ cup chopped fresh parsley

6 whole wheat hamburger buns, for serving

For topping (optional): sliced avocado, arugula

For the Roasted Red Pepper Sauce:

¾ cup nonfat plain Greek yogurt

¼ teaspoon kosher salt

⅛ teaspoon cayenne pepper

---

1. Make the burger patties: Place racks in the center and upper third of your oven and preheat the oven to 350 degrees F. Spread the walnuts in a single layer on an ungreased baking sheet. Place in the oven and bake on the center rack until toasted and fragrant, 8 to 10 minutes. Watch carefully towards the end to ensure the nuts do not burn. Transfer to a small bowl. Keep the baking sheet handy and leave the oven heated for toasting the buns.

2. Heat 1 tablespoon of the oil in a large skillet over medium-high heat. Add the mushrooms, garlic, shallot, half of the roasted peppers (reserve the other half for the sauce), and ½ teaspoon of the salt. Let cook until the mushrooms brown, the shallot softens, and the liquid has cooked off, 6 to 8 minutes. Transfer to the bowl of a food processor fitted with a steel blade. Keep the skillet handy to cook the burgers.

recipe continues

3. To the food processor, add the black beans, oats, smoked paprika, cumin, Worcestershire, black pepper, remaining ½ teaspoon salt, and the toasted walnuts. Pulse the mixture in 5-second bursts until it is combined but still a little chunky (3 or 4 pulses or 15 to 20 seconds total). If the mixture is very wet and not holding together, pulse in additional oats, 1 tablespoon at a time, until the mixture easily holds together when shaped into a patty. If it seems too dry, add a little water. The mixture will be moist but should be easy to shape. Transfer the filling to a mixing bowl. With a spatula or spoon, stir in the parsley.

4. Scoop the mixture by rough ⅓ cupfuls and shape into six ¾-inch-thick patties. Let the patties rest for 5 minutes while you prepare the red pepper sauce.

5. Make the red pepper sauce: In a small bowl, stir together the Greek yogurt, salt, and cayenne. With a paper towel, pat the remaining chopped peppers dry, then stir them into the sauce. Taste and adjust the seasoning as desired.

6. Cook the burgers: Gently wipe the skillet clean. Add 1½ tablespoons of oil and heat over medium-high heat. Once the oil is hot but not yet smoking, swirl to coat the bottom of the pan. Cook the burgers, three at a time, until crisp on the first side, 2 to 3 minutes. Flip and cook until crisp on the other side and hot throughout, 2 to 3 additional minutes. Remove the burgers to a paper towel–lined plate. Repeat with the remaining burgers, adding the final ½ tablespoon olive oil to the pan as needed to prevent sticking.

7. Toast the buns: Grab the baking sheet you used to toast the walnuts (dust off any crumbs). Place the buns on it, cut-sides up. Bake in the upper third of the oven for 6 to 8 minutes, until lightly toasted.

8. Serve the burgers on the buns with the Roasted Red Pepper Sauce and desired toppings. Enjoy immediately.

MAKE-AHEAD & STORAGE TIPS:

Shaped, uncooked burger patties can be individually wrapped in plastic and stored in the refrigerator for up to 4 days. Cook as directed. Leftover cooked burgers can be stored in the refrigerator for up to 3 days. Reheat gently in a lightly oiled skillet.

To freeze: Fully cook the patties, let them cool, then wrap tightly in plastic. Place in a ziptop bag and freeze for up to 3 months. Let thaw overnight in the refrigerator. To reheat, microwave on high for 1 to 2 minutes, or bake in a 350-degree-F oven for 12 to 15 minutes, until warmed through.

PRO TIPS:

- If you are making these burgers for strict vegetarians, be sure to use a vegetarian Worcestershire sauce made without anchovies.

- To bake the burgers instead: Preheat the oven to 400 degrees F. Line a baking sheet with parchment paper. Generously brush both sides of the shaped patties with extra virgin olive oil. Bake for 15 minutes on the first side, flip, then continue baking 5 additional minutes, or until cooked through.

Slow Cooker Crispy Pineapple Pork Carnitas

ACTIVE TIME: 40 minutes · **TOTAL TIME:** 6 hours 30 minutes · **YIELD:** Serves 4 to 6

I recommend eating these tacos with someone whom you either (a) know very well or (b) won't mind being intimately acquainted with by the end of the meal because when these tacos are on, table manners are *off*. Finger licking, plate scraping, and inappropriately loud *MMMM*s are inevitable. The melt-in-your-mouth pork filling begins with a warm, complex blend of spices, along with pineapple to balance the heat. The low-and-slow cooking method makes the pork drippy, juicy, and fall-apart tender. From there, a quick trip under the broiler crisps the pork's edges and reduces its cooking juices into a lightly sweet, scrape-the-pan yummy sauce that bathes every morsel. Though it's difficult, refrain from eating all of the crispy bits the moment they come out of the oven. The pork makes a fantastic taco filling that will have you (and any lucky guests with whom you share it) ditching your manners and fighting for the last bite.

2½ pounds boneless pork shoulder, trimmed of excess fat

2 teaspoons kosher salt

1 teaspoon ground black pepper

2 tablespoons extra virgin olive oil

1 tablespoon chili powder

2 teaspoons ground cumin

2 teaspoons dried oregano

½ teaspoon red pepper flakes

¼ teaspoon ground cloves

2 (8-ounce) cans crushed pineapple in 100% juice, left undrained

4 cloves garlic, minced (about 4 teaspoons)

2 tablespoons white vinegar

1 tablespoon low sodium soy sauce

For serving: corn or flour tortillas, fresh cilantro, lime wedges

Even more toppings: shredded pepper Jack cheese or queso fresco, sliced avocado, finely chopped red onion

---

1. Lightly coat a 6-quart or larger slow cooker with nonstick spray. Season the pork with the salt and black pepper. Heat the oil in a medium skillet over medium-high heat. Once the oil is hot but not yet smoking, add the pork. Brown the meat on all sides for 10 minutes, or until the pork has a nice crust. Turn it every few minutes and do not disturb it more often than needed to ensure it browns properly. Transfer the pork to the slow cooker.

2. While the pork browns, in a small bowl, stir together the chili powder, cumin, oregano, red pepper flakes, and cloves. In a separate bowl, stir together the pineapple with its juice, garlic, vinegar, and soy sauce. Sprinkle the

spice mixture over the pork, then rub to coat. Next, pour the pineapple mixture over the top. Cover and cook on low for 5 to 7 hours, until the meat is ultratender and shreds easily with two forks.

3. Place a rack in the upper third of your oven and preheat the oven to broil. For easy cleanup, line a large, rimmed baking sheet with aluminum foil and coat the foil with nonstick spray (if you prefer not to use foil, leave the pan unlined and coat it with nonstick spray).

4. With two forks, shred the pork directly in the slow cooker. Once it is shredded, give it

recipe continues

a big stir to coat it with cooking liquid and pineapple, then transfer the pork and any juices to the prepared baking sheet, spreading it into an even layer. Broil for 4 minutes, or until the edges of the pork are beginning to crisp. Remove from the oven, then with a spoon or spatula, toss the pork in its juices. Spread back into an even layer, then return to the oven and broil for 3 to 4 additional minutes, until nicely crisp at the edges. Watch carefully to ensure the pork does not overcook.

5. While the pork broils, heat a dry skillet over medium heat. Warm the tortillas on both sides for about 30 seconds each, until they are toasty and pliable. Or if you prefer, wrap the tortillas in a damp paper towel and warm them in the microwave.

6. Assemble the tacos: Fill the tortillas with the pork and top with cilantro, a squeeze of lime juice, and any extra toppings you desire. Enjoy immediately.

STORAGE TIPS:
Refrigerate leftover pork filling for up to 3 days or freeze for up to 3 months. Let thaw overnight in the refrigerator. Rewarm in a covered saucepan over medium-low heat with a splash of water or broth to keep the meat from drying out.

PRO TIP:
You can cook the pork in the slow cooker on high in 3 to 4 hours with decent results, but it will not be as fork tender or shred as easily as pork that is cooked on low. Marbled, tougher cuts like pork shoulder truly benefit from the low-and-slow cooking.

Asian Lettuce Wraps

ACTIVE TIME: 25 minutes · **TOTAL TIME:** 25 minutes · **YIELD:** Serves 2 to 4

When a P.F. Chang's opened in my hometown of Wichita, Kansas, it was A Big Deal. Two-hour wait times persisted for the better part of a year. When my family finally scored a table, our server insisted that we order the lettuce wraps. They lived up to the restaurant's hometown hype!

This recipe is a lightened-up version of the wraps we ate that night. A dead-ringer for the addictive original, they're made with tofu and mushrooms and they are one of my blog's most all-time popular recipes. Dozens of readers have reported that they *thought* they hated tofu, until they tried these wraps. They've also reported that you can keep the ingredient list a secret, serve them to someone who refuses to touch tofu, and receive rave reviews in return. I'll leave the level of trickery up to you.

---

3 tablespoons hoisin sauce

3 tablespoons low sodium soy sauce

2 tablespoons rice vinegar

1 teaspoon toasted sesame oil

1 (12- to 14-ounce) package extra firm tofu (do not use silken, firm, or any other variety of tofu)

2 teaspoons canola oil

8 ounces cremini (baby bella) mushrooms, finely chopped (about 2¾ cups)

1 (8-ounce) can sliced water chestnuts, drained and finely chopped

2 cloves garlic, minced (about 2 teaspoons)

2 teaspoons grated fresh ginger

¼ teaspoon red pepper flakes, plus additional to taste

4 green onions, thinly sliced (about ⅔ cup), divided

8 large Bibb lettuce leaves or large inner romaine lettuce leaves

For serving: shredded carrots

---

1. In a small bowl, stir together the hoisin, soy sauce, vinegar, and sesame oil. Set aside.

2. Press the tofu between paper towels to squeeze out as much liquid as possible. Refresh the paper towels and press again.

3. Heat the canola oil in a large nonstick skillet over medium-high heat. Once the oil is hot, crumble in the tofu. With a wooden spoon or spatula, break it into very small bits and sauté. Continue cooking for 5 minutes, stirring periodically so that the tofu cooks evenly. Add the mushrooms. Continue cooking until the liquid cooks off and the tofu starts to turn golden, about 3 minutes more. Stir in the water chestnuts, garlic, ginger, red pepper flakes, and half of the green onions. Cook until fragrant, about 30 seconds.

4. Pour the reserved hoisin mixture over the top and stir to coat. Cook just until you hear bubbling and the sauce is warmed through, 30 seconds to 1 minute.

5. To serve, spoon the tofu mixture into individual lettuce leaves. Top with the remaining green onions, some shredded carrots, and additional red pepper flakes as desired. Enjoy immediately.

LEFTOVER LOVE:
Try leftovers scrambled with eggs and a small drizzle of sesame oil. A little oil goes a long way, so start small.

STORAGE TIPS:
The tofu filling can be refrigerated for up to 5 days. Reheat gently in the microwave or in a small skillet over medium heat with a small splash of water or broth to prevent it from drying out.

Garlicky
Sweet Potato
Spinach

Grown-Up Grilled Cheese (3 Ways!)

The secret is out! Cookbook author and food blogger Erin Clarke eats grilled cheese for dinner. With a list like these Grown-Up Grilled Cheeses, however, can you blame me?

Grilled cheese has become our defacto "I Don't Feel Like Making Dinner" dinner. The flavor possibilities are endless, you can usually come up with a filling based on what you have in your refrigerator, and rarely is so little effort rewarded as richly as it is with a buttery, gooey grilled cheese sandwich. These recipes include creative twists you are sure to love. The next time you're tempted to order takeout, flip to this page, pull out your skillet, and give one of these Grown-Up Grilled Cheeses a whirl instead.

1. Heat a nonstick skillet over medium-low or preheat your panini press to medium-high heat.

2. Butter the outsides of the assembled sandwiches, then once the skillet is warm or the panini press is preheated, grill on the stove top for 4 to 5 minutes on the first side and 1 to 2 minutes on the second side, or until the bread is toasty and golden and the cheese is melted. Be patient. Low and slow will guarantee the most melty, perfectly cooked grilled cheese—or cook in the panini press for about 3 minutes. Remove the sandwich from the pan or press and transfer to a plate or cutting board. Let rest 1 to 2 minutes, then slice and enjoy hot.

Garlicky Sweet Potato Spinach

ACTIVE TIME: 30 minutes · **TOTAL TIME:** 30 minutes · **YIELD:** 2 sandwiches

1 tablespoon plus 1 teaspoon olive oil, divided

1 small sweet potato (about 6 ounces), peeled and cut into ¼-inch-thick rounds

½ teaspoon kosher salt

⅛ teaspoon ground black pepper

3 tablespoons water

3 cups baby spinach (about 3 ounces)

¼ teaspoon garlic powder

⅛ teaspoon ground nutmeg

4 slices good-quality whole wheat bread

3 ounces shredded Havarti cheese (about ¾ cup), or 4 thin deli slices

1 tablespoon light butter spread or unsalted butter, softened

1. Heat a large nonstick skillet with a tight-fitting lid over medium heat. Add 1 tablespoon of the oil and swirl to coat. Once the oil is hot but not yet smoking, add the sweet potato slices in a single layer. Cover the skillet and cook for 3 minutes, or until the slices turn golden underneath. Flip the sweet potatoes, sprinkle with the salt and pepper, and add the water (be careful, it will splatter). Re-cover the skillet and let the sweet potatoes steam for 5 additional minutes, or until fork tender. Remove to a plate and set aside.

2. Add the remaining 1 teaspoon oil to the skillet. Add the spinach, then sprinkle the garlic powder and nutmeg over the top. Working quickly with a rubber spatula, push the spinach around the pan to evenly coat the leaves in the spices. Let cook just until the spinach wilts, about 1 minute. Remove the skillet from the heat.

3. To assemble the sandwiches: For the first sandwich, top 1 slice of the bread with one-quarter of the cheese, half of the sweet potato slices, half of the spinach, and the next one-quarter of cheese. Place a second bread slice on top. Repeat with the second sandwich. Cook according to "How to Cook a Perfect Grilled Cheese," carefully wiping the skillet clean prior to cooking the sandwich if necessary.

Roasted Broccoli-Cauli Cheddar

ACTIVE TIME: 20 minutes (if vegetables are roasted in advance), 30 minutes (if vegetables are not roasted in advance)
TOTAL TIME: 20 minutes (if vegetables are roasted in advance), 55 minutes (if vegetables are not roasted in advance)
YIELD: 2 sandwiches

¼ cup nonfat plain Greek yogurt

1 tablespoon Dijon mustard

½ teaspoon garlic powder

⅛ teaspoon cayenne pepper

4 slices good-quality whole wheat bread

2 ounces shredded sharp cheddar cheese (about ½ cup), or 2 thin deli slices

1 cup roughly chopped mixed roasted broccoli and roasted cauliflower (see Classic Salt and Pepper Every-Night Roasted Vegetables, page 262)

1 tablespoon light butter spread or unsalted butter, softened

1. In a small bowl, stir together the Greek yogurt, mustard, garlic powder, and cayenne. Spread over one side of each of the 4 slices of bread, dividing evenly among the slices.

2. For the first sandwich, top 1 slice of bread with half of the cheese, then ½ cup chopped roasted vegetables. Place a second bread slice on top, yogurt-side down. Repeat for the second sandwich. Cook according to "How to Cook a Perfect Grilled Cheese" (page 223).

The Beautiful Bs: Blackberry, Basil, Balsamic, Brie

ACTIVE TIME: 20 minutes
TOTAL TIME: 20 minutes
YIELD: 2 sandwiches

½ cup fresh blackberries

2 teaspoons balsamic vinegar

1 teaspoon honey

⅛ teaspoon kosher salt

4 slices good-quality whole wheat bread

4 ounces thinly sliced Brie cheese, enough to put 2 layers on each sandwich (4 to 6 slices, depending upon the size of your piece of Brie)

2 tablespoons thinly sliced fresh basil

1 tablespoon light butter spread or unsalted butter, softened

1. In a small bowl with the back of a fork, smash the blackberries together with the vinegar, honey, and salt, leaving the mixture a little chunky.

2. To assemble the sandwiches: For the first sandwich, top 1 slice of bread with a layer of Brie slices, arranging the slices so that when the cheese melts, it will cover the entire sandwich. Spoon on half of the berry mixture, using only the chunky, pulpy part and not too much of the juice so that the bread does not become soggy. Sprinkle with half of the basil, then add a second layer of Brie. Place a second bread slice on top. Repeat for the second sandwich. Cook according to "How to Cook a Perfect Grilled Cheese" (page 223).

NEXT LEVEL:
Sneak in an extra "B" by adding a few slices of crispy bacon.

The Beautiful Bs:
Blackberry, Basil,
Balsamic, Brie

Soup's On!

Chicken Pot Pie Stew with Buttery Garlic "Crust" Croutons, page 233

Blue Ribbon Chili · Cozy Roasted Parsnip Apple Soup
Chicken Pot Pie Stew with Buttery Garlic "Crust" Croutons
Slow Cooker Sweet Potato Peanut Soup
Slow Cooker Golden Coconut Lentil Soup · Instant Pot Pasta e Fajioli

⎯⎯⎯⎯●⎯⎯⎯⎯⎯●⎯⎯⎯⎯

When the wicked winter wind blows, we turn up our coat collars, wrap our scarves more snugly, and pull on our thickest socks, and I crave soup. When it's the halfway point of a long week and I'm tired and can't imagine surviving the days that stand between myself and the weekend, I crave soup. When I'm energized and prepping to feed a group of friends, soup has it in the bag (er, bowl) then too.

No matter my need, be it quick, healthy lunches I can reheat all week, a big pot of chili for a game-day crowd, or an arctic-grade warm-up to survive our long Wisconsin winters, I can find a soup recipe to match.

This collection of soups is here to comfort and sustain you. You'll find my wholesome spins on classics like Blue Ribbon Chili (page 228), slow cooker and Instant Pot options, and soups that feature fresh combinations and star ingredients you might not have tried before. Pick a page, pull out your ladle (and a loaf of crusty bread), and rest assured that every one of these recipes will nourish you inside and out.

Blue Ribbon Chili

ACTIVE TIME: 1 hour · **TOTAL TIME:** 2 hours · **YIELD:** Serves 6 to 8 (about 11 cups)

Growing up, our hometown's chili cook-off was one of my most anticipated events of the year. My sisters and I would strut around like food critics, sampling batches with our pinkies extended. We feverishly debated which booth would receive our coveted voting tokens. Now whenever I make a pot of chili, I fondly wonder if my childhood self would have deemed it a champion.

If ever there were a pot of chili to enter into a competition, here it is. Rich, thick, and aromatic, it seamlessly blends the sensations of warmth and caring that emanate from a slow-simmered dish with the unexpected, elevated touches that make it worthy of a bold, blue ribbon. A pinch of cinnamon gives this chili a winning flavor in the arena where it matters most: your dining table.

1 pound 93% lean ground beef

2 teaspoons kosher salt

½ teaspoon ground black pepper

1 tablespoon extra virgin olive oil

1 large yellow onion, chopped (about 2 cups)

2 medium green bell peppers, chopped (about 2 cups)

1 medium red bell pepper, chopped (about 1 cup)

2 small-medium sweet potatoes (about 1¼ pounds), peeled and cut into ½-inch dice (about 3½ cups)

4 cloves garlic, minced (about 4 teaspoons)

2 bay leaves

1½ tablespoons chili powder

2 teaspoons ground cumin

2 teaspoons chipotle chili powder

2 teaspoons dried oregano

¼ teaspoon cayenne pepper

⅛ teaspoon ground cinnamon

12 ounces dark or light beer (my favorite is an amber beer)

2 (15-ounce) cans fire roasted diced tomatoes in their juices

1 (14.5-ounce) can low sodium chicken broth

1 (15-ounce) can reduced sodium dark or light red kidney beans, rinsed and drained

1 (15-ounce) can reduced sodium cannellini or great Northern beans, rinsed and drained

1 (15-ounce) can reduced sodium black beans, rinsed and drained

½ teaspoon granulated sugar

The works, for serving: sliced avocado, nonfat plain Greek yogurt, crushed tortilla chips or tortilla strips, lime wedges, shredded cheese such as Monteray Jack or cheddar

1. Heat a large Dutch oven or similar large, heavy-bottomed pot over medium-high heat. Add the beef, salt, and black pepper. Brown the meat, breaking it apart into small pieces and stirring occasionally until it is fully cooked through, about 5 minutes. With a slotted spoon, transfer it to a paper towel–lined plate. Lightly pat dry and set aside.

2. Reduce the heat to medium and add the oil. Once the oil is hot but not yet smoking, add the onion, green and red bell peppers,

and sweet potatoes. Cook, stirring frequently, until the onion is softened and turning golden brown, 10 to 15 minutes. Add the garlic, bay leaves, chili powder, cumin, chipotle chili powder, oregano, cayenne, and cinnamon. Cook until very fragrant, about 1 minute.

3. Add the beer, scraping up any browned bits from the bottom of the pot. Let simmer 3 minutes. Add the diced tomatoes, broth, kidney beans, cannellini beans, black beans, and reserved beef. Reduce the heat to medium

low and partially cover the pot. Simmer
gently, stirring occasionally, until the chili is
thickened and tantalizingly fragrant, 1 hour to
1 hour 15 minutes.

4. Remove and discard the bay leaves. Stir in
the sugar. Taste and adjust the seasoning as
desired. Serve hot, garnished with any and all
desired toppings. Eat up and enjoy your blue-
ribbon victory!

STORAGE TIPS:
Refrigerate leftover chili for up to 5 days
or freeze for up to 3 months. Reheat on
the stove top or in the microwave, with a
splash of water or broth to thin as needed.

Cozy Roasted Parsnip Apple Soup

ACTIVE TIME: 30 minutes · **TOTAL TIME:** 1 hour · **YIELD:** Serves 4 to 6 (about 10 cups)

Knobby, a little awkward, and haphazardly placed at the outskirts of the grocery shelf, parsnips are a little like that guy or girl you overlooked in high school who eventually went on to become a devastatingly attractive business executive. Recognize their potential now or forever wistfully wonder what might have been.

Roasted parsnips are tender, lightly sweet, and earthy, and they taste both soothingly familiar and seductively unique. For this soup, I blended them with roasted apples, which provide a clean, tart counterpoint. By the time you've added a touch of nutmeg and maple syrup for warmth, you'll be ready to call those parsnips up and make your love official!

2½ pounds parsnips, peeled and cut into ½-inch dice (about 8 cups or 10 medium parsnips)

2 large tart apples, such as Granny Smith, peeled, cored, and cut into ¼-inch-thick slices (about 3 cups)

2 large cloves garlic, peeled and left whole

1 medium yellow onion, thinly sliced (about 1½ cups)

3 tablespoons extra virgin olive oil

1¼ teaspoons kosher salt, divided

1 teaspoon dried thyme

¼ teaspoon ground black pepper

4 cups low sodium chicken broth or low sodium vegetable broth

1 cup unsweetened almond milk, plus additional as needed

1 tablespoon pure maple syrup

¼ teaspoon ground nutmeg

1. Place racks in the upper and lower thirds of your oven and preheat the oven to 400 degrees F. Generously coat two rimmed baking sheets with nonstick spray. Set aside.

2. Place the parsnips, apples, garlic, and onion in a large bowl. Drizzle with the oil, then sprinkle with 1 teaspoon of the salt, the thyme, and pepper. Toss to evenly coat, then divide the mixture between the two prepared baking sheets and spread each into an even layer. Roast until the vegetables and apples are tender and lightly browned in a few places, 22 to 28 minutes, turning twice throughout. Let cool on the pans for 10 minutes.

3. To puree with an immersion blender: Transfer the vegetable mixture to a large, deep pot such as a Dutch oven. Add the broth and almond milk. Puree until smooth.

To puree with a blender: Place one-third to one-half of the vegetable mixture and 1 cup of the broth in a high-powered blender. Carefully puree until smooth, adding more broth as needed so that the mixture blends. Transfer to a large, deep pot such as a Dutch oven, then repeat with the remaining vegetable mixture and additional broth, adding the puree to the pot as you go. Once all of the mixture is blended, add any remaining broth and the almond milk to the pot and stir to combine.

recipe continues

4. Bring the soup to a simmer over low heat, stirring often. Stir in the maple syrup, nutmeg, and remaining ¼ teaspoon of salt. If the soup is thicker than you would like, add additional almond milk to reach your desired consistency. Taste and season with additional salt and pepper. Enjoy hot.

MAKE-AHEAD & STORAGE TIPS:

The vegetables can be roasted up to 1 day in advance and stored in the refrigerator. When you are ready to make the soup, start the recipe at step 3.

Refrigerate leftover soup for up to 5 days or freeze for up to 3 months. Let thaw overnight in the refrigerator. Reheat gently on the stove or in the microwave, with a splash of water, broth, or almond milk to thin the soup as needed.

NEXT LEVEL:

- Top with Buttery Garlic "Crust" Croutons (see page 233).

- For an extra boost of protein, try topping your soup with a big dollop of Greek yogurt. It makes the soup extra creamy and filling.

MARKET SWAPS:

- Any variety of sweet or tart apple is delicious in this recipe, depending upon your preferred level of sweetness. Since parsnips are fairly sweet on their own, I prefer tarter apples like Granny Smiths to help balance the overall flavor.

- For a unique, fresh-from-the-market flavor, try swapping a portion of the parsnips for sweet potatoes, butternut squash, carrots, or a mix.

Chicken Pot Pie Stew
with Buttery Garlic "Crust" Croutons

ACTIVE TIME: 1 hour · **TOTAL TIME:** 1 hour · **YIELD:** Serves 4 (about 7 cups soup and 4 cups croutons)

In grade school I mastered the art of holding the thermometer up to a lightbulb until it registered a fever. The goal: Stay home "sick." I'd laze in my PJs all day, enjoy full reign over the remote, and my mom (who is likely only learning about this little charade now, as she reads this—sorry, Mom!) would make me a special lunch, usually a warm and creamy soup.

Now that I'm an adult, sick days have lost their allure, but creamy soups have not. No matter my mood or need, be it a warm-up on a damp day, a fast and healthy dinner, or a comforting meal for an all-PJs afternoon, this chicken pot pie stew never lets me down. Like classic chicken pot pie, it's homey, packed with tender vegetables and juicy chicken, and eating it feels like being scooped into a warm hug. *Unlike* chicken pot pie, this stew is light on calories, and doesn't ask you to fuss with pie crust. I've swapped the pie dough for quick, crispy baked croutons that are made with whole wheat bread. They're salty, garlicky, and the ideal counterpoint to the stew's more mellow flavor.

For the Stew:

2 tablespoons extra virgin olive oil

8 ounces sliced cremini (baby bella) mushrooms (about 2½ cups)

3 medium stalks celery, cut into ¼-inch dice (about 1 cup)

2 teaspoons garlic powder

1 teaspoon kosher salt

½ teaspoon dried thyme

½ teaspoon rubbed sage

¼ teaspoon ground black pepper

¼ cup all-purpose flour

2 cups unsweetened almond milk or nonfat milk

1 (14.5-ounce) can low sodium chicken broth

2 medium Yukon gold potatoes, peeled and cut into ½-inch dice (about 2 cups)

1 (12-ounce) bag frozen mixed vegetables, such as a blend of carrots, green beans, corn, and peas

2 cups cooked, shredded chicken (about 2 medium breasts; see page 161)

For the Croutons:

4 slices whole wheat bread, cut into 1-inch cubes (about 4 cups)

½ teaspoon kosher salt

½ teaspoon garlic powder

2 tablespoons unsalted butter, melted

1 tablespoon finely grated Parmesan cheese

1. Place a rack in the upper third of your oven and preheat the oven to 350 degrees F.

2. Make the stew: Heat a large Dutch oven or similar large, heavy-bottomed pot over medium-high heat. Add the oil. Once the oil is hot but not yet smoking, add the mushrooms and cook for 8 minutes, or until they are beginning to brown, stirring occasionally. Add the celery, garlic powder, salt, thyme, sage, and pepper. Cook until the mushrooms have browned more deeply and the celery begins to soften, about 3 additional minutes.

3. Sprinkle the flour over the top of the vegetables and cook for 1 minute, stirring

recipe continues

so that the flour turns golden and all of the white disappears. The pot will seem dry. Grab a whisk and slowly pour in the almond milk and broth, adding a few splashes at a time and whisking constantly to keep the mixture from becoming lumpy.

4. Add the potatoes. Partially cover the pot and bring to a low simmer. Let cook for 10 minutes, then add the frozen mixed vegetables. Continue to simmer, partially covered, until the vegetables are hot, the potatoes are tender, and the stew has thickened, about 15 additional minutes. Adjust the heat as needed so that the stew simmers but does not bubble aggressively. Once the stew has thickened, stir in the chicken. Taste and adjust the seasoning as desired.

5. While the stew simmers, prepare the croutons: Place the bread cubes in the center of an ungreased baking sheet. Sprinkle with the salt and garlic powder, then drizzle with the butter. Toss to coat the cubes, then spread them into an even layer. Bake for 5 minutes, then remove the pan from the oven and lightly toss. Spread the cubes back into a single layer and sprinkle the Parmesan over the top. Return the pan to the oven and continue baking until the cubes are golden brown, about 10 additional minutes. Set aside to cool on the baking sheet (the croutons will continue to crisp as they cool).

6. Ladle the stew into bowls and top generously with the croutons. Enjoy hot.

STORAGE TIPS:
Refrigerate the stew for up to 4 days or freeze for up to 3 months. Let thaw overnight in the refrigerator, then reheat gently on the stove top or in the microwave, with a splash of milk or broth if the stew becomes too thick.

Store leftover croutons in an airtight container at room temperature for up to 4 days.

NEXT LEVEL:

- For an extra boost of protein, top with shredded or diced cooked chicken (see page 161).

- For an extra serving of veggies: Once the soup is blended, stir 2 cups finely chopped stemmed kale into the slow cooker with the soup. Turn the slow cooker to high. Cover and let cook until the kale is tender, about 10 minutes.

Slow Cooker Sweet Potato Peanut Soup

ACTIVE TIME: 30 minutes · **TOTAL TIME:** 3 hours (on high); 6 hours (on low)
YIELD: Serves 6 (about 11 cups)

Sweet potato peanut soup kept me alive all fifty-two weeks of my first post-college year. I made a batch almost every week for one main reason (it was dirt cheap), two supplemental reasons (it was healthy and yielded an enormous amount), and a final, morale-saving reason (it was so rich and delicious, I never grew weary of it).

More than a decade later, I still adore this soup. It's healthy and will stretch your dollar, and despite its outward humility, it tastes surprisingly complex. The peanut butter brings richness; the sweet potatoes, body and satisfying heft; and the spices, a sophisticated warmth. This quiet soup will leave you talking.

1 tablespoon extra virgin olive oil

1 small yellow onion, chopped (about 1 cup)

3 cloves garlic, minced (about 1 tablespoon)

1 tablespoon minced fresh ginger

2 teaspoons ground allspice

1 teaspoon kosher salt

¼ teaspoon ground cinnamon

¼ teaspoon cayenne pepper, plus additional to taste

4 medium-large sweet potatoes (about 3 pounds), peeled and cut into ¾-inch cubes (about 9 cups)

4 cups low sodium vegetable broth or low sodium chicken broth, plus additional as needed

1 (15-ounce) can no-salt-added tomato sauce

½ cup creamy peanut butter

For serving: chopped fresh cilantro and chopped dry-roasted, unsalted peanuts

1. Heat the oil in a large skillet over medium heat. Add the onion and cook until beginning to soften, about 4 minutes. Add the garlic, ginger, allspice, salt, cinnamon, and cayenne and cook until very fragrant, about 30 seconds. Transfer to a 6-quart or larger slow cooker.

2. To the slow cooker, add the sweet potatoes, broth, tomato sauce, and peanut butter. Stir to combine. Cover and cook on low for 5 to 6 hours or on high for 2½ to 3½ hours, until the sweet potatoes pierce easily with a fork.

3. With an immersion blender, puree the soup until smooth, adding water or additional broth as needed if it is thicker than you would like. If you do not have an immersion blender, carefully transfer the soup to a blender and puree until smooth (be careful and do not fill the blender more than about a third of the way—it will sputter when hot!). Taste and season with additional salt as needed (the amount will vary based on the saltiness of your particular broth and peanut butter). If you'd like a bit more heat, add a pinch or two of extra cayenne. Serve warm, generously sprinkled with fresh cilantro and chopped peanuts.

STORAGE TIPS:
Refrigerate leftovers for up to 5 days or freeze for up to 3 months. Reheat gently in the microwave or on the stove top, adding a bit more water or broth to thin the soup if needed.

Slow Cooker Golden Coconut Lentil Soup

ACTIVE TIME: 30 minutes · **TOTAL TIME:** 4 hours (on high); 8 hours (on low)
YIELD: Serves 4 to 6 (10 cups)

Few ingredients capture me with their earnestness like lentils. Packed with nutrients, inexpensive, and amenable to a colorful array of flavors, the humble lentil has no pretense. My favorite way to eat them is deeply spiced with golden turmeric and ginger, preferably in a soup, where their creamy texture and fill-you-up prowess is maximized. Though hearty, this soup is surprisingly light and refreshing. Eating a bowl of it makes me feel like I spent a day at the spa, wrinkly fingers and cucumbers not required. I'm revitalized and relaxed, ready to return to real life with a calm, positive attitude and a blissfully satisfied appetite.

1 tablespoon extra virgin olive oil

1 large yellow onion, chopped (about 2 cups)

2 cloves garlic, minced (about 2 teaspoons)

2 teaspoons ground cumin

1 teaspoon kosher salt

¾ teaspoon ground turmeric

½ teaspoon ground ginger

⅛ teaspoon cayenne pepper

2 cups uncooked brown or green lentils, rinsed and drained

1 pound carrots, peeled and finely chopped into a ¼- to ½-inch dice (about 3 cups or 6 medium)

1 (15-ounce) can no-salt-added diced tomatoes in their juices

4 cups low sodium vegetable broth or low sodium chicken broth

1 (14-ounce) can light coconut milk

¼ cup freshly squeezed lemon juice (from about 1 medium lemon)

5 ounces baby spinach (about 5 lightly packed cups)

1. In a large nonstick skillet, heat the oil over medium heat. Add the onion and sauté for 4 to 5 minutes, until beginning to soften. Stir in the garlic, cumin, salt, turmeric, ginger, and cayenne. Transfer to a 6-quart or larger slow cooker.

2. To the slow cooker, add the lentils, carrots, tomatoes, and broth. Stir to combine. Cover and cook on high for 3 to 4 hours or low for 6 to 8 hours, until the lentils are tender and retain a slight amount of pleasant chew but are not mushy.

3. Stir in the coconut milk and lemon juice. Stir in the spinach a few handfuls at a time, allowing the heat of the soup to wilt it a bit as you go. Cover the slow cooker and turn the heat to high. Let cook until the spinach is completely tender and wilted, about 5 additional minutes. Taste and adjust the salt or other spices as desired. Enjoy hot.

STORAGE TIPS:
Refrigerate leftover soup for up to 5 days or freeze for up to 3 months. Let thaw overnight in the refrigerator, then reheat gently on the stove top or in the microwave, with a splash of broth or water to thin as needed.

STORAGE TIPS:
Refrigerate leftovers for up to 5 days or freeze for up to 3 months. Let thaw overnight in the refrigerator. Rewarm gently in the microwave or on the stove top.

PRO TIP:
Whatever you do, do not skip the freshly shredded Parmesan. It's the final note that the soup needs to go from "I'm into this" to "I CANNOT WAIT to come home to my leftovers!"

Instant Pot Pasta e Fajioli

ACTIVE TIME: 45 minutes · **TOTAL TIME:** 1 hour 10 minutes · **YIELD:** Serves 6 (about 12 cups)

Despite what my DNA-test results suggest, I see no reason not to pour myself a glass of wine, make this *pasta e fajioli* ("pasta and bean") soup, and pretend to be Italian. An Italian recipe by origin, this soup embodies what I adore about Italian cuisine. The ingredients are startlingly, almost insolently, straightforward, yet the results are spectacular. The Instant Pot cooks the soup in a jiffy, and the leftovers only improve as the week goes on. The finishing handful of freshly shredded Parmesan is essential, and if you'd like to take it to the next level, here's a pro tip from my (actually) Italian nonna-in-law: Freeze your Parmesan rinds in a ziptop bag whenever you have them, then add one to your soup as it cooks.

2 teaspoons extra virgin olive oil

1 pound uncooked Italian turkey or chicken sausage, either ground sausage or sausage links in casings

1 pound carrots, peeled and cut into ¼-inch dice (about 3 cups or 6 medium)

1 small yellow onion, diced (about 1 cup)

1 teaspoon kosher salt

3 cloves garlic, minced (about 1 tablespoon)

4 cups low sodium chicken broth, divided

1 (15-ounce) can no-salt-added tomato sauce

1 (15-ounce) can fire roasted diced tomatoes in their juices

1 (15-ounce) can reduced sodium light or dark red kidney beans, rinsed and drained

1 (15-ounce) can reduced sodium great Northern, cannellini, or navy beans, rinsed and drained

1 cup dry whole wheat miniature pasta, such as ditalini, small shells, or elbow macaroni (about 4 ounces)

2 teaspoons Italian seasoning

¼ teaspoon ground black pepper

¼ teaspoon red pepper flakes

1 (3-inch) Parmesan rind (optional; see headnote)

1 tablespoon red wine vinegar

Freshly shredded Parmesan cheese, for serving

Chopped fresh basil or parsley, for serving

1. Add the oil to a 6-quart or larger Instant Pot and select sauté. Once the oil is hot, add the sausage (if it is in casings, you can squeeze the meat from the casings directly into the Instant Pot, then discard the casings). Cook, breaking the meat into small pieces, until no pink remains, 5 to 7 minutes.

2. Add the carrots, onion, and salt. Cook for 4 minutes, stirring frequently, until the onion begins to soften and turn translucent. Add the garlic and cook until fragrant, about 1 minute. Carefully splash in about ½ cup of the broth. Scrape a spoon or spatula along the bottom of the pot and remove any stuck-on bits.

3. Add the remaining broth, tomato sauce, diced tomatoes, kidney beans, great Northern beans, pasta, Italian seasoning, black pepper, red pepper flakes, and Parmesan rind (if using). Stir to combine.

4. Close and seal the Instant Pot. Cook on high (manual) pressure for 3 minutes. Allow the pressure to release naturally for 10 minutes, then immediately vent to remove any remaining pressure. Carefully open the lid. Remove the Parmesan rind. Stir in the vinegar. Taste and adjust the seasoning as desired. Serve hot, sprinkled with Parmesan and fresh basil.

Instant Pot
Confetti
Rice and Beans,
page 258

Second-Helpings Sides

Tostones (Crispy Baked Plantain Chips) · Rosemary Cheddar Cornbread

Brown Butter Mashed Sweet Potatoes

Lemony Sautéed Summer Squash and Chickpeas

Kung Pao Vegetable Stir-Fry · Garlicky Sautéed Kale with Almonds

Instant Pot Confetti Rice and Beans · Golden Carrots and Farro

Every-Night Roasted Vegetables (5 Ways! + How to Use Them)

Classic Salt and Pepper · Spicy Curry · Soy Ginger · Maple Balsamic · Parmesan and Herb

Every-Night Roasted Vegetable Guide

•———————•

Meet a stellar collection of sides, each gunning to be the star of the plate! They offer unique flavors and approachable prep, whether you need a fast vegetable to serve with dinner, a steaming slice of cornbread to pair with your soup, or a more elevated dish for a special occasion. To these recipes—memorable, nutritious, and worthy of extra helpings—the phrase "on the side" almost doesn't apply.

Tostones (Crispy Baked Plantain Chips)

ACTIVE TIME: 20 minutes · **TOTAL TIME:** 45 minutes · **SERVES:** 2 to 4 (about 36 tostones)

Ben's idea of preparing me to visit him in the Dominican Republic, where he was serving a two-year stint with the US Peace Corps, was to 1) ask me to bring him a giant bag of Peanut M&M's and 2) inform me that I was going to *love* tostones. He could not have been more right. A staple in Caribbean cuisine, tostones are green, underripe plantains that are sliced into coins, fried, smashed thin, then fried a second time. They're crunchy, salty, and downright addictive.

This skinny version of tostones has the same alluring texture and taste as their fried counterparts, but they're oven baked. Think of them as a potato chip's cousin (the fun cousin) and serve them alongside sandwiches, soups, and rice-and-bean-based dishes. They also make a fun and surprising party app, though to be honest, they rarely make it onto the plate. You'll devour them straight from the pan faster than you can serve them. *Buen provecho!*

2 very large or 3 medium green, unripe plantains (about 1¾ pounds)	1 tablespoon extra virgin olive oil ½ teaspoon kosher salt, plus additional for serving	¼ teaspoon garlic powder

1. Place a rack in the center of your oven and preheat the oven to 425 degrees F. Generously coat a large rimmed baking sheet with nonstick spray.

2. Trim the ends off of each plantain. With a sharp knife, carefully cut slits all the way along the lengths of the plantains, cutting deep enough to penetrate all the way through the skins but not so deep that you cut the flesh of the plantain themselves. Make 3 of these slits total around each plantain's circumference, placing them along the natural ridges that run lengthwise down the plaintains' peels.

3. Place the plantains on a microwave-safe plate and microwave on high until they are very soft, 8 to 10 minutes, depending upon the size of your plantains and the power of your microwave. The peels will turn black and the plantains will be very hot. Let cool until you can easily handle them, then pull away the

peels. If any of the peels are stubborn and stick, use a paring knife to carefully cut them away.

If you do not have a microwave: Peel the plantains without heating them; the peels will be trickier to remove but will still come away from the surface of the plantain. Working lengthwise, remove a strip of the plantain by pulling up the end with your fingers. Use the knife to help work it loose, and keep pulling up until the whole strip comes away from the fruit. Continue removing the remaining strips of peel the same way.

4. Cut the peeled plantains crosswise into ½-inch-thick coins. Pile the slices in the center of the prepared baking sheet. Drizzle with the oil and sprinkle with the salt and garlic powder. Toss gently to coat the pieces evenly, then spread the plantains into a single layer, leaving some space around each slice.

5. Bake the plantains until beginning to turn golden on the bottom, about 10 minutes. With

quick fingers or a thin spatula, carefully flip them over. With the bottom of a sturdy drinking glass, slowly and firmly press on the plantains to flatten them into a ¼-inch thickness. Wiggle the glass back and forth and around as you press so that the plantains spread evenly.

6. Return the pan to the oven and continue to bake until the plantains are golden and crisp, about 8 additional minutes. Remove from the oven and immediately season with a generous pinch of additional salt. Transfer to a serving plate and enjoy immediately . . . or just eat them right off of the pan.

STORAGE TIPS:
While these are best enjoyed shortly after being made, you can refrigerate the leftovers for 1 additional day. Reheat in a 400-degree-F oven for 4 to 5 minutes, until warmed through. Season with a pinch of salt and serve immediately.

PRO TIP:
Although plantains look similar to bananas, they are two distinct fruits. Plantains behave more like a potato than a banana. They are starchier, lower in sugar, and should be cooked prior to eating.

Rosemary Cheddar Cornbread

ACTIVE TIME: 20 minutes · **TOTAL TIME:** 45 minutes · **YIELD:** One 8×8-inch pan (9 to 16 squares)

This cornbread recipe will likely evict me from every state south of the Mason-Dixon line, but I'm willing to risk breaking the rules. You see, once you eat your cornbread with melted pockets of cheddar cheese, flecks of rosemary, and gentle, lightly caramelized notes of honey, you won't want it any other way. Add the unique textural twist of coarser-ground cornmeal, and happily declare yourself a cornbread renegade.

Cornbread is a breeze to bake from scratch and well worth the extra few minutes. Most cornbread recipes call for buttermilk. Since it's not an ingredient I regularly keep on hand, I swapped it for a DIY buttermilk substitute of milk and white vinegar. That said, if you happen to have a carton of buttermilk at the ready, feel free to use 1 cup of it in place of the milk and vinegar.

In addition to making stellar company to a bowl of Blue Ribbon Chili (page 228), this cornbread's tasty possibilities extend well beyond the side of the plate. Try it toasted at breakfast, or better yet, in one of the Leftover Love suggestions on page 249.

1 cup nonfat milk or milk of choice, at room temperature

1 tablespoon white vinegar or lemon juice

4 tablespoons unsalted butter, plus additional softened butter for serving

1 cup medium- or coarse-grind yellow cornmeal (regular yellow cornmeal works too)

1 cup white whole wheat flour

2 teaspoons baking powder

¼ teaspoon baking soda

¾ teaspoon kosher salt

1 tablespoon chopped fresh rosemary leaves, from about 2 (6-inch) rosemary stems

¼ cup honey, plus additional for serving

2 large eggs, at room temperature

¾ cup shredded sharp cheddar cheese (about 3 ounces), divided

1. Stir the milk and vinegar together in a medium bowl or very large liquid measuring cup. Let sit 5 to 10 minutes, until the milk is slightly thickened and curdled.

2. Place a rack in the center of your oven and preheat the oven to 425 degrees F. Lightly coat an 8×8-inch baking pan with nonstick spray. Line with parchment paper so that the paper overhangs two opposite sides like handles. Lightly coat the paper with nonstick spray and set aside.

3. Cut the butter into 4 pieces and place in a small microwave-safe bowl. Microwave

for 30 seconds, then continue microwaving in 15-second bursts, stopping as soon as the butter melts. (Alternatively, you can melt the butter in a small saucepan over medium heat.) Set aside and let cool to room temperature.

4. In a large mixing bowl, whisk together the cornmeal, flour, baking powder, baking soda, and salt until combined. Stir in the rosemary.

5. To the bowl with the rested milk and vinegar, add the honey, eggs, and melted butter. Whisk together until smooth. If the butter resolidifies, warm the bowl in the

recipe continues

microwave in 10-second bursts, until it liquefies. If you do not have a microwave or your bowl is not microwave-safe, warm the bowl over a saucepan of simmering water on the stove over medium heat.

6. Make a well in the center of the dry ingredients and slowly pour the wet ingredients into it. By hand with a spatula or wooden spoon, stir gently just until combined. Fold in ½ cup of the cheese.

7. Pour the batter into the prepared pan and smooth the top. Sprinkle on the remaining ¼ cup cheese. Bake for 16 to 20 minutes, until the cornbread is light golden brown, a slightly deeper gold at the edges, and a toothpick inserted into the center comes out clean. Let cool for 5 minutes in the pan, then with the parchment paper handles, lift the cornbread out of the pan and onto a cooling rack to finish cooling, or place it on a cutting board for immediate serving. Slice and enjoy warm with additional butter and honey as desired.

STORAGE TIPS:
Store leftovers at room temperature for up to 3 days or freeze for up to 3 months.

TO BAKE AS MUFFINS:
Lightly coat 10 wells of a standard 12-cup muffin pan with nonstick spray or line with paper liners. Scoop the batter into the prepared muffin wells. Bake at 425 degrees F for 10 to 13 minutes, until a toothpick inserted into the center of a muffin comes out clean.

NEXT LEVEL:
- *For Bacon Cheddar Cornbread:* Fold 3 slices of cooked, crumbled bacon into the batter with the cheese.

- *For Italian-ish Cornbread:* Use shredded mozzarella or fontina cheese in place of the cheddar. Place ⅓ cup chopped dry-packed sun-dried tomatoes in a small bowl and cover with very hot water. Let sit for a few minutes to rehydrate. Drain and pat dry, then fold into the batter with the cheese.

MARKET SWAPS:
Play around with different combinations of herbs and cheeses. Stick with gooey, melty cheeses. I also recommend fresh herbs for the brightest flavor.

A few of my favorite combinations:

- ¼ cup chopped fresh basil and fontina

- 1 tablespoon chopped fresh thyme and gouda

- ¼ cup chopped green onions and pepper Jack

LEFTOVER LOVE:
- *Open-Faced Breakfast Sandwich:* Split and lightly toast a generous square of leftover cornbread. Top with a bit of butter and your choice of cooked bacon, crispy ham, or a chicken or turkey sausage breakfast patty. Add a fried egg and a sprinkle of extra cheese if you are feeling so inclined. Sprinkle with salt and pepper and enjoy immediately.

- *Leftover Thanksgiving Turkey Supreme:* Make a double (or triple!) batch of this herby cornbread at Thanksgiving, then use leftovers to make open-faced leftover-turkey sandwiches, with warmed cranberry sauce, sliced turkey, and a drizzle of gravy.

Brown Butter Mashed Sweet Potatoes

ACTIVE TIME: 20 minutes · **TOTAL TIME:** 45 minutes · **YIELD:** Serves 4 to 6

One of the annual traditions my friends look forward to most is Friendsgiving, a raucous, Thanksgiving-themed potluck. I host it every year, which by the unwritten rules of Friendsgiving means that I am in charge of the turkey. (Or rather, the *two* turkeys; word apparently has escaped that Thanksgiving with friends is particularly fun, and our numbers have grown.) My friends bring the sides and desserts, with one very important exception: I, and I alone, make the sweet potatoes. Why? I am *picky*. Sweet potatoes are my favorite of all the side dishes, and I simply can't allow them to be ruined by marshmallows, gobs of brown sugar, and whatever other nonsense threatens to disrespect a perfectly delicious, naturally sweet vegetable.

However you feel about the "m" word in your sweet potatoes, give this recipe a try. It combines the best of a traditional sweet potato casserole and fluffy classic mashed potatoes to exceed them both. Despite the lighter ingredient list, the sweet potatoes still taste gloriously indulgent thanks to brown butter. Browning butter is an easy process that toasts the butter's milk solids, and it infuses the sweet potatoes with an intense, nutty flavor that's so magnificent, Mr. Turkey (and every other side at the table) will feel upstaged.

---

3 pounds sweet potatoes, peeled and cut into 1-inch chunks (about 4 medium-large or 9 cups)

4 tablespoons unsalted butter

¼ cup nonfat milk (use 2% or whole milk for a little extra decadence), plus additional as needed

3 tablespoons pure maple syrup

1 teaspoon kosher salt

¼ teaspoon ground black pepper

---

1. Place the sweet potatoes in a large, heavy-bottomed pot. Cover them with water, then bring the pot to a boil over medium-high heat. Reduce the heat and simmer, uncovered, until the potatoes are fork tender, 10 to 12 minutes. Drain the potatoes and return them to the pot.

2. While the potatoes are boiling, melt the butter in a small, light-colored saucepan over medium-low heat. This will take several minutes. Continue to heat, swirling the pan periodically, until the butter melts completely, foams and crackles, turns clear golden (the crackling will stop), then turns toasty brown. This entire process will take 3 to 5 minutes, depending upon your pan. Once the butter begins to smell lightly nutty, whisk it constantly, scraping up any browned bits from the bottom. Watch the pan carefully in the last few minutes to ensure that the butter does not burn. As soon as the bits of butter in the bottom of the pan turn the color of a pecan, remove the pan from the heat and pour the butter into the pot with the sweet potatoes, or if your potatoes are not yet done cooking, a separate bowl to stop the butter's browning.

3. To the pot with the sweet potatoes and browned butter, add the milk, maple syrup, salt, and pepper. With an electric mixer, beat the sweet potatoes on medium-low speed, leaving them as chunky or as smooth as you like, adding a bit of additional milk if the potatoes seem too thick. Taste for seasoning and add salt and pepper as desired. Transfer to a serving bowl and serve warm.

MAKE-AHEAD & STORAGE TIPS:
The mashed sweet potatoes can be made up to 4 days in advance and stored in the refrigerator. To rewarm before serving, place the potatoes in a heatproof bowl set over a pan of simmering water. Stir the potatoes occasionally to ensure that they heat evenly. Taste and adjust the seasoning as needed.

Lemony Sautéed Summer Squash and Chickpeas

ACTIVE TIME: 35 minutes · **TOTAL TIME:** 35 minutes · **YIELD:** Serves 4

Every summer, I reach a point when my freezer becomes a zucchini-muffin storage locker, I've zucchini-boated enough dinners to qualify for a captain's license, and the word "zoodles" gives me the heebie jeebies. That's when I make this Lemony Sautéed Summer Squash and Chickpeas. It's a restorative reminder of how delicious zucchini and yellow squash can be if we resist the urge to fuss with them. No matter how many summer squash recipes I try, I never tire of this one. It's easy to pull together and is exactly the kind of light, bright dish I crave all season long. Serve it for a stellar side, or for a suggestion to transform it into a vegetarian main that doubles as an easy-to-pack lunch, check out Next Level on the following page.

1 (15-ounce) can reduced sodium chickpeas, rinsed and drained

1½ pounds mixed zucchini and yellow summer squash (about 4 small-medium)

2½ tablespoons extra virgin olive oil, divided

¼ cup raw sliced almonds

¾ teaspoon kosher salt, divided

¼ teaspoon ground black pepper

Zest and juice of 1 medium lemon (about 1 teaspoon zest and ¼ cup juice)

¼ cup shredded Parmesan cheese (about 1 ounce)

1. Spread the chickpeas onto a double layer of paper towels, and with a second layer of towels, pat dry. Allow to continue air-drying while you prepare the vegetables.

2. Trim off the ends of the zucchini and summer squash. Cut them in half lengthwise, then cut each half in half lengthwise again so that you have 4 long batons per squash. Slice the batons crosswise into thin, ⅛-inch-thick slices (you will have about 6 cups of sliced zucchini and squash total).

3. Heat 1 tablespoon of the oil in a large, deep cast-iron skillet or similar heavy-bottomed skillet over medium-high heat. Swirl the oil and ensure it coats the bottom of the pan. When the oil is hot but not yet smoking, add the almonds and cook, stirring very often, until they are deep golden brown. Do not walk away! This will take 1 to 2 minutes. The almonds should be very fragrant and toasty. Remove the almonds to a plate and set aside.

4. Return the skillet to medium-high heat. Add 1 tablespoon of the oil. Swirl to coat the pan again, then add the chickpeas and ¼ teaspoon of the salt. Let cook, stirring occasionally, until the chickpeas begin to turn golden, about 6 minutes. Stand back a little—the chickpeas will pop. Remove the chickpeas to the plate with the almonds.

5. Return the skillet to medium-high heat once more. Add the final ½ tablespoon of oil and the sliced zucchini and squash. Cook just until warm and beginning to glisten, about 1 minute. Add the lemon zest, lemon juice, remaining ½ teaspoon of salt, the pepper, and the reserved chickpeas and almonds. Toss to evenly combine, then transfer immediately to a serving plate. Sprinkle with the Parmesan and enjoy!

STORAGE TIPS:
Served warm, this recipe is best enjoyed the day it is made, as the vegetables will soften and let off more liquid once reheated. However, it can last 2 to 3 days in the refrigerator and is delicious enjoyed cold or at room temperature, without reheating.

NEXT LEVEL:
To transform this stellar side into a heartier vegetarian main, toss it with 8 ounces of cooked whole wheat orzo pasta, adding additional olive oil and lemon juice to make a quick dressing. Season with additional salt and pepper to taste.

Kung Pao Vegetable Stir-Fry

ACTIVE TIME: 40 minutes · **TOTAL TIME:** 40 minutes · **YIELD:** Serves 2 to 4

This is the side that doesn't know it's a side. Its sticky, *I-want-this-on-everything* takeout-style sauce, colorful collection of veggies, and crunchy, roasted peanuts make it a clear, confident flaunter that's ready to be the highlight of your plate. Its spotlight flavor is ideal alongside simply prepared proteins like grilled chicken, shrimp, or fish. You can also embrace its audacity and turn it into a stir-fry-style main. Make a little extra sauce, stir the veggies together with diced and sautéed chicken or tofu, then serve it over brown rice or quinoa.

For the Sauce:

3 tablespoons low sodium soy sauce

2 tablespoons balsamic vinegar

1½ tablespoons honey

1 tablespoon creamy peanut butter

2 teaspoons toasted sesame oil

2 teaspoons cornstarch

2 cloves garlic, minced (about 2 teaspoons)

2 teaspoons sambal oelek (fresh chili paste) or Sriracha

For the Stir Fry:

1 pound green beans, trimmed (about 3 cups trimmed)

¼ cup water

1 tablespoon extra virgin olive oil

2 medium red bell peppers, cut into ¼-inch-thick strips (about 2¼ cups)

1 small bunch green onions (about 6), chopped, with dark green parts divided from the white and light green parts (about 1 cup total)

½ cup dry-roasted, unsalted peanuts

1. Prepare the sauce: In a small mixing bowl or liquid measuring cup, whisk together the soy sauce, vinegar, honey, peanut butter, sesame oil, cornstarch, garlic, and sambal oelek until well blended. Set aside.

2. Make the stir-fry: To a large nonstick skillet with a tight-fitting lid or wok, add the green beans and water. Bring to a boil over high heat, then cover, reduce to medium-high heat, and cook until the beans are crisp-tender, 4 to 5 minutes.

3. Uncover and add the olive oil and bell peppers. Stir and cook, uncovered, until the peppers are crisp-tender, about 7 minutes more. Add the white and light green parts of the green onions and cook until fragrant, about 30 seconds.

4. Pour in the sauce, stir to coat the vegetables, then add the peanuts. Cook until the sauce is slightly thickened, about 2 minutes. Remove from the heat and sprinkle with the dark green onion tops. Enjoy hot.

STORAGE TIPS:
Refrigerate leftovers for up to 5 days. Reheat gently in the microwave or on the stove top with a splash of water as needed to thin the sauce.

MARKET SWAPS:
Feel free to swap the vegetables in this recipe for any you love or have on hand. In the spring, I love to use thinly sliced carrots and asparagus.

Garlicky Sautéed Kale with Almonds

ACTIVE TIME: 20 minutes · **TOTAL TIME:** 25 minutes · **SERVES:** 2 to 4

This is the side you make when you don't know which side to make. It won't take up any space in your oven, requires minimal prep, and will have you standing at the stove, impatiently nibbling bits of hot kale straight from the skillet in an *I-can't-even-wait-to-sit-down, this-is-so-good* kind of way that you didn't believe applied to vegetables. It's tender and nutty, salty and cheesy, and packs just enough heat to keep you coming back for more. The next time you need to round out your plate with something green, try this recipe.

¼ cup raw sliced almonds

1 tablespoon extra virgin olive oil

1 large bunch curly kale (about 12 ounces or 8 stems) or 2 medium bunches lacinato (dinosaur) kale (about 16 ounces or 18 stems), stems removed and roughly chopped

3 cloves garlic, minced (about 1 tablespoon)

½ teaspoon kosher salt

1 cup water

¼ teaspoon red pepper flakes

3 tablespoons finely grated Parmesan cheese

1. Heat a large, heavy-bottomed skillet with a tight-fitting lid or Dutch oven over medium heat. Once the skillet is hot, add the almonds to the dry skillet and cook, stirring frequently, until fragrant and toasted, 4 to 5 minutes. Do not walk away. Nuts have a tendency to burn the second you leave them to their own devices. Transfer the nuts to a plate and set aside. With a paper towel, carefully wipe out and discard any remaining bits of nuts that are left in the skillet.

2. Return the skillet to the heat and increase the heat to medium high. Add the oil. Once the oil is hot and shimmering, add the kale by large handfuls, stirring constantly to allow the kale to wilt. Be careful, as the oil may splatter a bit at first. Continue to add the kale by handfuls until it all fits in the skillet and begins to wilt a bit more, 2 to 3 minutes. Stir in the garlic and salt and cook, until the garlic is fragrant, about 30 seconds. Add the water and immediately cover the pan. Reduce the heat to medium.

3. Cook, covered, until the kale is completely wilted, fairly tender, and turns a more vibrant green, about 4 minutes, stirring every minute or two. Uncover and add the red pepper flakes. Increase the heat to medium high. Sauté, uncovered, until most of the liquid cooks off and the kale is pleasantly tender but not mushy, about 2 additional minutes. If the pan is dry before the greens are as tender as you like, add a little more water to prevent them from sticking. Remove from the heat and stir in the Parmesan and almonds. Enjoy hot.

Instant Pot Confetti Rice and Beans

ACTIVE TIME: 20 minutes · **TOTAL TIME:** 55 minutes · **YIELD:** Serves 6

If the word "confetti" instantly prompted you to think of a party, then you've mastered the concept of this recipe. It's a colorful rice-and-beans side, fit for a fiesta! Red bell pepper, yellow corn, bright baby spinach, and fire roasted tomatoes add welcome servings of veggies, cumin provides warmth, and brown rice and black beans make it filling and nutritious. To save you from standing at the stove, I've adapted this recipe for the Instant Pot, which has become my favorite way to cook rice. It's hands free and the texture turns out perfectly every time.

Serve this recipe with any of your favorite Southwest or Mexican dishes; top it off with avocado, cheese, and an over-easy egg to make it a main event; or try it in any of the Leftover Love suggestions on the following page.

1 tablespoon extra virgin olive oil

1 small yellow onion, chopped (about 1 cup)

1 medium red bell pepper, cut into 1-inch pieces (about 1¼ cups)

2 teaspoons garlic powder

1 teaspoon ground cumin

½ teaspoon kosher salt

¼ teaspoon ground black pepper

½ cup water or low sodium vegetable broth or low sodium chicken broth

1 cup uncooked long grain brown rice (do not use short grain or instant, as they will become mushy)

1 (15-ounce) can fire roasted diced tomatoes in their juices

1 (15-ounce) can reduced sodium black beans, rinsed and drained

1 cup corn kernels, cut fresh from the cob, canned and drained, or frozen (no need to thaw)

3 cups baby spinach (about 3 ounces), roughly chopped

Optional toppings: Green Enchilada Sauce (page 176), shredded cheddar, Monterey Jack, or pepper Jack cheese; nonfat plain Greek yogurt; sliced avocado; chopped fresh cilantro

1. Set a 6-quart or larger Instant Pot to sauté. Add the oil. Once the oil is hot but not yet smoking, add the onion and cook until it begins to soften, about 3 minutes, stirring occasionally.

2. Add the bell pepper, garlic powder, cumin, salt, and black pepper. Let cook for 1 minute, or until fragrant. Turn off the Instant Pot, then add the water. Stir, scraping up any bits of food that have stuck to the bottom of the pot. Rinse and drain the rice, then add it to the Instant Pot. Add the tomatoes then stir to combine.

3. Cover and seal the Instant Pot. Cook on high (manual) pressure for 22 minutes, then let the pressure release naturally for 10 minutes. After 10 minutes, vent to release any remaining pressure.

4. Carefully open the lid. Turn the Instant Pot to sauté. Stir in the beans and corn. Add the spinach a few handfuls at a time, stirring until it wilts, 1 to 2 additional minutes. Serve hot with your toppings of choice.

STORAGE TIPS:
Refrigerate leftovers for up to 5 days. Reheat gently in the microwave or on the stove top with a splash of water or broth to thin as needed. You can also freeze leftovers for up to 3 months, in individual portions or even a freezer-grade ziptop bag (let the rice cool completely, transfer it to the bag, then lay the bag flat and freeze until the rice hardens).

LEFTOVER LOVE:
• *Breakfast Burritos:* Heat leftovers in a skillet over medium heat, then pour in a few lightly beaten eggs. Cook and stir until the eggs are scrambled and cooked through. Wrap inside a warm whole wheat tortilla, with cheese, sliced avocado, and salsa.

• *Mexican Hash:* Mix leftovers with sautéed ground chorizo then top with a sunny-side-up egg.

• *Taco Salad:* Let leftovers come to room temperature. Serve over chopped romaine with sliced fresh tomatoes, optional grilled chicken (see Santa Fe Grilled Chicken, page 91, for a yummy way to grill it), and a small handful of shredded cheese. Drizzle with Zesty Ranch Dressing (page 90).

NEXT LEVEL:
For a spicier version, add ¼ teaspoon cayenne pepper with the spices in step 2. You can also top your rice with several good shakes of hot sauce.

Golden Carrots and Farro

ACTIVE TIME: 30 minutes · **TOTAL TIME:** 1 hour · **YIELD:** Serves 4 to 6

Perhaps more than any other recipe in this book, this is the one that taught (and retaught) me the essential kitchen lesson that successful cooking involves purchasing quality ingredients, then staying out of their way. I reinvented this dish a dozen different ways, each more complicated and muddied than the last. Many versions were good, but it wasn't until I identified and focused on the star, the carrots, that I created a recipe that was truly exceptional. This is that recipe. It's bright, filling, complex, and every single ingredient has a purpose. These are the best-tasting carrots (and one of the best side dishes) I've ever eaten. Each bite captivates more than the one before. Prepare to experience a same-old veggie in an entirely new way.

2 pounds carrots, scrubbed and cut into ½-inch-thick diagonal slices (about 6 cups or 12 medium carrots)

1 large yellow onion, cut into ¼-inch-thick slices (about 3 cups)

3 cloves garlic, minced (about 1 tablespoon)

3 tablespoons extra virgin olive oil, divided

2 tablespoons honey

2 teaspoons ground cumin

1½ teaspoons kosher salt, divided

¼ teaspoon ground turmeric

¼ teaspoon cayenne pepper

1 cup uncooked semi-pearled farro, rinsed and drained

Zest (about 1 tablespoon) and 2 tablespoons juice of 1 medium orange

⅓ cup toasted sliced or slivered almonds

¼ cup chopped fresh parsley

1. Place racks in the upper and lower thirds of your oven and preheat the oven to 400 degrees F. Coat two large rimmed baking sheets with nonstick spray. Place the carrots, onion, and garlic in a large bowl. Drizzle with 2 tablespoons of the oil and the honey, then sprinkle with the cumin, 1 teaspoon of the salt, the turmeric, and cayenne. Toss to evenly coat, then divide between the two prepared baking sheets. Spread the vegetables into a single layer, ensuring that they do not crowd one another. Roast for 25 to 35 minutes, turning twice throughout, until the vegetables are tender and lightly browned in spots.

2. While the vegetables roast, cook the farro according to the package instructions, until it is tender but still maintains a bit of chew. Transfer to a large mixing bowl. Stir in the orange zest, orange juice, remaining

1 tablespoon oil, and the remaining ½ teaspoon salt. Once the vegetables are roasted, add them to the mixing bowl, along with any cooking liquid that has collected on the pans. Stir in the almonds and parsley. Enjoy warm or at room temperature.

NEXT LEVEL:
• For a subtle but delicious variation, swap the almonds for toasted pistachios.

• For a sweet pop, stir in ⅓ cup golden raisins with the almonds and parsley.

LEFTOVER LOVE:
Golden Green Salad: Gently rewarm leftovers and toss with arugula. Top with Go-to Citrus Dressing, made with orange juice (page 89).

Every-Night Roasted Vegetables (5 Ways! + How to Use Them)

ACTIVE TIME: About 15 minutes, depending upon vegetables selected
TOTAL TIME: 30 to 45 minutes, depending upon vegetables selected
YIELD: Serves 2 to 4

Roasted veggies are my secret to consistently landing a vegetable on our plates at dinner, keeping prepped vegetables on hand for easy lunches, and convincing skeptics that yes, vegetables really and truly can be delicious. Make it a habit to pop a pan of vegetables into the oven while you cook the rest of the meal. By the time dinner is ready, they'll be gloriously golden and crisp on the outside, tender and sweet on the inside, with a deep, caramelized flavor. Don't be surprised when you find yourself munching these tasty morsels straight off the baking sheet like candy!

While classic salt and pepper is the seasoning I add to our vegetables most often—it's clean, simple, and lets the intrinsic flavor of the vegetables shine—it is by no means the only tasty option. Below, you'll find that plus four more fabulous ways to season a pan of vegetables and make your weeknight more exciting. To help you make the most of these recipes, I've included a few of my favorite vegetables to pair with each version, general cooking tips to prepare and roast any vegetable with success, and ideas for new vegetables to try. I'm so confident you'll want to make roasted vegetables in great big batches, I have creative ways to use up the leftovers too! Before you know it, you'll be in a roasted-veggie rhythm, and they'll be a rewarding, indispensable part of your healthy routine.

CLASSIC SALT AND PEPPER MASTER RECIPE:

1½ pounds vegetables of choice, cut appropriately (see Pro Tips on page 267)

1 tablespoon plus 1 teaspoon extra virgin olive oil

½ teaspoon kosher salt

¼ teaspoon ground black pepper

1. Place a rack in the upper third of your oven (or the upper and lower thirds if you have a large batch and will have two baking sheets). Preheat the oven to 400 degrees F.

2. Place the vegetables in the center of a large rimmed baking sheet. Drizzle with the oil and sprinkle with the salt and pepper. Gently mix until the vegetables are evenly coated, then spread them into a single layer on the baking sheet. For even better crisping, flip the vegetables so that the sides with the largest flat surface area (such as the cut sides of brussels sprouts) are facing down.

3. Bake until the vegetables are caramelized on the outside and tender on the inside, 20 to 30 minutes, turning once halfway through.

Maple Balsamic

Parmesan and Herb

Spicy Curry

Soy Ginger

The cooking time will vary depending upon your vegetables and the size they are cut. Thin, delicate vegetables such as thin asparagus may be done in as little as 15 minutes, while harder vegetables like sweet potatoes may need up to 30 minutes. Don't be afraid to check often as you get the hang of it, and watch carefully towards the end of the baking time. Season with additional salt and pepper to taste. Enjoy immediately, but be sure to also check out the ten ideas for leftover roasted veggies on page 266.

4. Once you've mastered this recipe, it's time to vary it up! Swap the olive oil, salt, and pepper for the mix of ingredients I've suggested in the following variations.

Spicy Curry

Try this warm, spicy blend with any combination of cauliflower, carrots, Brussels sprouts, and winter squash, such as butternut.

1½ pounds prepared vegetables

2 tablespoons extra virgin olive oil

1½ tablespoons curry powder

¾ teaspoon kosher salt

¼ teaspoon chili powder

⅛ teaspoon ground cinnamon

Place the vegetables in the center of a large rimmed baking sheet. Top with the oil, curry powder, salt, chili powder, and cinnamon. Toss to coat, then spread into a single layer. Roast according to the master recipe instructions, step 3.

NEXT LEVEL:
Top the roasted vegetables with chopped fresh cilantro or mint.

Soy Ginger

I love this surprising blend of flavors on almost any vegetable, but it's especially delicious with classic stir-fry veggies, like broccoli, red bell peppers, and carrots. Cauliflower and Brussels sprouts are excellent with it too.

1½ pounds prepared vegetables

1 tablespoon plus 1 teaspoon extra virgin olive oil

2 tablespoons low sodium soy sauce

1 tablespoon minced fresh ginger

2 teaspoons honey

For easy cleanup (honey is yummy but sticky), line a large rimmed baking sheet with aluminum foil or parchment paper. Place the vegetables in the center. Top with the oil, soy sauce, ginger, and honey. Toss to coat, then spread into a single layer. Roast according to the master recipe instructions, step 3.

NEXT LEVEL:
Top the roasted vegetables with toasted sesame seeds or chopped dry-roasted, unsalted peanuts.

Maple Balsamic

Wonderful with any combination of root vegetables, such as sweet potatoes, carrots, and parsnips. Try adding a red onion to the pan for a fabulous blend of sweet and savory flavors.

1½ pounds prepared vegetables

2 tablespoons pure maple syrup

1 tablespoon balsamic vinegar

1½ tablespoons extra virgin olive oil

¾ teaspoon kosher salt

¼ teaspoon ground black pepper

For easy cleanup, since maple syrup makes the vegetables deliciously sticky, line your baking sheet with aluminum foil or parchment paper. Place the vegetables in the center. Top with the maple syrup, vinegar, oil, salt, and pepper. Toss to coat, then spread into a single layer. Roast according to the master recipe instructions, step 3.

NEXT LEVEL:
Top the roasted vegetables with a generous handful of chopped toasted walnuts and crumbled feta cheese.

Parmesan and Herb

You can't go wrong using this combo for just about any vegetable. I especially love it with potatoes, butternut squash, and spring vegetables like broccoli and asparagus.

1½ pounds prepared vegetables

1 tablespoon plus 1 teaspoon extra virgin olive oil

1 teaspoon dried rosemary or thyme

½ teaspoon dried oregano

½ teaspoon kosher salt

¼ teaspoon black pepper

2 tablespoons finely grated Parmesan cheese

Place the vegetables in the center of a large rimmed baking sheet. Top with the oil, rosemary, oregano, salt, and pepper. Toss to coat, then spread into a single layer. Roast according to the master recipe instructions, step 3. Remove from the oven and toss with the Parmesan.

NEXT LEVEL:
Top the roasted vegetables with a squeeze of fresh lemon juice.

Every-Night Roasted Vegetable Guide

Vegetables You Might Not Have Roasted But Should:

- Fennel
- Parsnips
- Red or yellow onions
- Zucchini or summer squash
- Green beans
- Kale
- Mushrooms
- Cherry or grape tomatoes (delicious, even in winter)
- Eggplant

More Ways to Gussy Up a Pan of Roasted Veggies:

- Grate lemon or orange zest over the top, then finish with a squeeze of the juice.
- Freshly grated Parmesan, a handful of crumbled feta . . . or let's be real— just about any cheese.
- Chopped, toasted nuts.
- Toss breadcrumbs with melted butter or olive oil. Sprinkle over the veggies during the last 5 minutes of their roasting time and bake until golden.
- A handful of fresh herbs.
- Dip with Skinny Tzatziki Sauce (page 209).
- Dollop with Creamy Basil Pesto (page 100).

How to Store and Reheat Leftover Roasted Veggies:

- Refrigerate leftover roasted vegetables for up to 4 days, then use for any of the tasty spins below.
- To reheat: Line a baking sheet with aluminum foil and lightly coat the foil with nonstick spray (if you prefer not to use foil, leave the pan unlined). Spread the vegetables into a single layer and bake at 400 degrees F until heated through, 4 to 6 minutes.

10 Ways to Use Leftover Roasted Veggies:

1. On top of salads.
2. Mixed into omelets.
3. Underneath an egg as a hash.
4. On top of creamy vegetable soups (such as Cozy Roasted Parsnip Apple Soup, page 231, and Slow Cooker Sweet Potato Peanut Soup, page 237).
5. On top of pizzas (add shortly before the pizza is finished or place under the cheese to keep them from overcooking).
6. As a filling for Grown-Up Grilled Cheese (page 222).
7. Mixed into pasta.
8. Stuffed inside a baked sweet potato (page 199).
9. Turned into a quesadilla.
10. All on their own! I often reheat them for a superfast side.

PRO TIPS:

- For every 1½ pounds of veggies, use ½ teaspoon kosher salt, ¼ teaspoon ground black pepper, and enough olive oil to ensure the vegetables have a light coating on all sides. You can adjust the salt and pepper to fit with your other seasoning, though you'll almost always want at least one generous pinch of salt (or another salty element like soy sauce) to ensure your vegetables have great flavor.

- Don't crowd the pan! Vegetables need room for the hot air to circulate, or they will steam instead of caramelize. When in doubt, divide them between two pans.

- Cut larger, harder vegetables like sweet potatoes, carrots, and beets into ½- to ¾-inch chunks, and broccoli and cauliflower into ¾-inch florets. Leave softer, more "bendy" vegetables like asparagus and green beans whole, with any hard ends or stems trimmed.

- Cut big "bulb" veggies like onions and fennel into wedges that are about ½ inch inch thick.

- Trim off the tough stem ends of Brussels sprouts, remove any outer brown leaves, and cut them in half lengthwise from top to stem end.

- Veggies that are similarly "hard" will roast in the same amount of time (e.g., asparagus will roast more quickly than beets, potatoes, or other root vegetables).

- If you are roasting together vegetables with different cook times, you can either add the hard veggies first so that they have a head start or cut them into smaller pieces than the softer vegetables so that everything cooks in about the same amount of time.

- Scale away! Feel free to multiply the recipes by as many baking sheets and oven racks as you have, provided the vegetables do not overcrowd the pan. If you are baking multiple pans, to promote even browning switch their positions on the upper and lower racks halfway through.

Don't-Skip Desserts

Vanilla Ricotta Cheesecake
with Breezy Berry Sauce, page 303

Double Trouble Fudge Cookies · The Very Best Oatmeal Chocolate Chip Cookies

Sweet Summer Fruit Crumble Bars · Chocolate-Covered Strawberry Brownies

Any Way You Like It Lemon Yogurt Pound Cake · Zucchini Snack Cake

Chocolate Chip Coconut Banana Bread Pudding

Kitchen Sink Carrot Cake · *Greek Yogurt Cream Cheese Frosting*

Everyone's Invited Apple Crisp

Daddy's German Chocolate Cake · Dreamy Chocolate Mousse

Vanilla Ricotta Cheesecake with Breezy Berry Sauce · *Breezy Berry Sauce*

The core culinary principle that has united my family since childhood: Life is too short to skip dessert. Thankfully with this chapter's selection of more-wholesome goodies, you never need to miss a treat!

My love of dessert traces back to childhood, when my grammy would bake my sisters and me any dessert of our choosing for our birthdays. And I mean *any*. On my tenth birthday, I went so far as to request baked Alaska, one of the most labor-intensive desserts of all time. I'm surprised my grammy didn't revoke the birthday-dessert privileges right then and there.

When I look back across the desserts of my lifetime, of which there have been *many*, the ones that stand out to me most aren't the fancy, tiered layer cakes adorned with sugared flowers, or delicately rolled sponge cakes piped elaborately with buttercream.

The desserts that rule my heart are too homey and messy to put behind a glass case: the bubbly crisps, the gooey puddings, the brownies so fudgy they melt in your mouth.

The desserts in this chapter satisfy a deeper part of us that longs for comfort and familiarity. Want the proof? Serve a warm-from-the-oven pan of Chocolate Chip Coconut Banana Bread Pudding (page 287) with scoops of vanilla ice cream at your next dinner party and watch the reaction. I have yet to witness even the most elegantly torched meringue elicit the same level of enthusiasm as the cozy treats you'll find in this chapter.

As with the rest of this book, I've lightened up each of these recipes without sacrificing flavor. You'll find whole grains, more-natural sweeteners, nuts, fresh and dried fruits, and of course, chocolate. Enjoy every bite!

Double Trouble Fudge Cookies

ACTIVE TIME: 20 minutes · **TOTAL TIME:** 35 minutes · **YIELD:** 24 cookies

Deeply chocolatey with craggy edges and decadently tender centers, these flamboyantly rich yet not-too-sweet cookies are a magnificent cross between a brownie, a chocolate crinkle cookie, and a flourless chocolate cake. The two tricks to their supreme texture are avocado and replacing all of the flour with cocoa powder. You can't taste the avocado, but its good fat makes the cookies fantastically moist and gives them a wholesome touch. The abundance of cocoa powder ensures they are extraordinarily chocolatey and melt in your mouth. The real trouble here? You won't be able to stop eating them!

½ medium ripe avocado

4 tablespoons unsalted butter, at room temperature

½ cup packed light or dark brown sugar

¼ cup granulated sugar

1 large egg, at room temperature

1 teaspoon pure vanilla extract

½ teaspoon baking soda

¼ teaspoon kosher salt

1¼ cups unsweetened cocoa powder

4 ounces good-quality dark (65% to 72%) chocolate, chopped (about a heaping ¾ cup)

1. Place a rack in the center of your oven and preheat the oven to 350 degrees F. Line a baking sheet with parchment paper or a silicone baking mat.

2. In the bowl of a stand mixer fitted with the paddle attachment or a large mixing bowl, mash the avocado. Double-check that you have about ⅓ cup. (Reserve any extra for snacking, or just eat it right on the spot.) Add the butter, brown sugar, and granulated sugar. Beat on medium speed until the mixture is creamy and smooth, about 2 full minutes. Beat in the egg and vanilla extract until combined.

3. Sprinkle the baking soda and salt over the top. Add the cocoa powder, sifting it into the bowl if it is lumpy. By hand with a wooden spoon or rubber spatula, stir the ingredients just until the cocoa powder disappears. Fold in the chopped chocolate. The batter will be wet and sticky.

4. With a cookie scoop or spoon, portion the batter into mounds that are 1½ to 2 tablespoons each. Place them on the prepared baking sheet, leaving about 1 inch between mounds (their shapes will be irregular, but they will bake up deliciously). Bake for 10 to 12 minutes, until the cookies are barely dry to the touch at the edges, the tops still seem underbaked, and the centers appear fairly molten. Let cool on the baking sheet for 2 minutes, then with a spatula, gently transfer the cookies to a cooling rack to finish cooling completely . . . or for as long as you can handle the suspense.

STORAGE TIPS:
Store leftovers at room temperature for up to 5 days or freeze for up to 3 months.

NEXT LEVEL:

- For an even more intense chocolate flavor (because how can that be a bad thing?), add 1 teaspoon instant espresso powder to the batter along with the baking soda and salt.

- For a salty-sweet sensation, prior to baking, sprinkle the cookie dough mounds with a pinch of good-quality flaky sea salt, such as fleur de sel or Maldon Sea Salt Flakes.

The Very Best Oatmeal Chocolate Chip Cookies

ACTIVE TIME: 30 minutes · **TOTAL TIME:** 1 hour 50 minutes · **YIELD:** 18 cookies

I spent the better part of an excellent year baking every chocolate chip cookie recipe I could find: the ones from famous chefs, the ones with the most impressive online reviews, the ones from the back of the chocolate chip bag, the ones from my cookbooks—I tried them all. Then, I applied my "research" to create a recipe for the superlative chocolate chip cookies of my fantasy. These cookies have lightly crisp edges, dreamy soft and thick middles, and generous melting puddles of chocolate that permeate every bite. Another victory: Their ingredient list is wholesome enough to justify baking them on a regular basis.

For the best taste and texture, be sure to refrigerate the dough as directed (I promise it will be worth the wait!), use quick-cooking oats, and don't skip the cinnamon or the generous pour of pure vanilla extract. The elements work together to deepen the cookies' flavor and make them worthy of their title, The Very Best Oatmeal Chocolate Chip Cookies!

½ cup raw walnut or pecan halves (see Pro Tips)

¾ cup quick-cooking oats (not instant oatmeal; see Pro Tips)

¾ cup white whole wheat flour

¾ teaspoon baking soda

½ teaspoon kosher salt

¼ teaspoon ground cinnamon

½ cup unsalted butter

6 tablespoons packed coconut sugar or light brown sugar

¼ cup granulated sugar

1 tablespoon pure vanilla extract

¼ teaspoon apple cider vinegar or lemon juice

1 large egg, at room temperature

¾ cup dark chocolate chips

---

1. Toast the nuts: Place a rack in the center of your oven and preheat the oven to 350 degrees F. Spread the nuts in a single layer on an ungreased baking sheet. Bake until the nuts are toasted and fragrant, 8 to 10 minutes, shaking the pan once halfway through. Do not walk away from the nuts towards the end of their baking time to ensure that they do not burn (it happens fast!). Immediately transfer the nuts to a cutting board and let cool. Turn off the oven.

2. In a medium mixing bowl, whisk together the oats, flour, baking soda, salt, and cinnamon.

3. Cut the butter into a few pieces and place it in a large microwave-safe bowl. Microwave for 30 seconds. Continue to microwave in 15-second bursts, just until melted. (Alternatively, you can melt the butter in a large saucepan over medium heat. Remove the pan from the heat as soon as the butter is melted.) Stir in the coconut sugar and granulated sugar until smooth. Stir in the vanilla, vinegar, and egg until well combined.

4. Add the dry ingredients to the butter mixture. With a rubber spatula or wooden spoon, stir until combined. The batter will seem loose and wet. Roughly chop the nuts,

recipe continues

then add them to the bowl. Add the chocolate chips, then fold to combine. Cover the bowl with plastic wrap, pressing the wrap against the surface of the dough. Refrigerate for at least 1 hour, or up to 3 days.

5. When ready to bake, remove the dough from the refrigerator. Place a rack in the center of your oven and preheat the oven to 350 degrees F. Line a baking sheet with parchment paper or a silicone baking mat (for the best texture and most even baking, do not leave the sheet unlined). With a medium cookie scoop or spoon, portion the dough by 1½ tablespoonfuls, then roll into balls that are approximately 1½ inches wide. Arrange the balls on the baking sheet, leaving 1½ inches between each (you will have about 18 cookies total). With your fingers, lightly flatten the tops of the cookies. Bake for 10 to 13 minutes, until the cookies are golden brown and just set at the edges and on top.

6. Place the baking sheet on a cooling rack. Let the cookies cool on the sheet for 5 minutes, then gently transfer them to the rack to finish cooling completely. If the cookies are still too soft to lift with a spatula, slide the sheet of parchment paper or silicone mat, with the cookies still on it, off of the baking sheet and onto the cooling rack, leaving the cookies in place. Let the cookies rest a few additional minutes, then enjoy.

MAKE-AHEAD & STORAGE TIPS:

Store leftover baked cookies at room temperature for up to 1 week or freeze, tightly wrapped, for up to 3 months.

To freeze unbaked cookie dough: Scoop and shape cookie dough as directed. Arrange the unbaked cookies in a single layer on a parchment-lined baking sheet, then place the baking sheet in the freezer. Once the cookies have hardened, transfer them to a ziptop bag and freeze for up to 3 months. Bake individual cookies directly from frozen, adding a few additional minutes to the baking time as needed.

PRO TIPS:

• Not nuts about nuts? You can swap the ½ cup nuts called for in the recipe for an additional ¼ cup chocolate chips. The cookies will spread more during baking, so leave them a little extra space on the baking sheet. I also recommend chilling the dough for at least 4 hours, ideally overnight.

• No quick-cooking oats on hand? Make them yourself by pulsing regular old-fashioned oats 1 or 2 times in a food processor, until they are lightly broken up (do not pulse them completely into a flour). Measure the oats after you have run them through the food processor to ensure you have the correct amount.

Sweet Summer Fruit Crumble Bars

ACTIVE TIME: 35 to 55 minutes, depending upon fruit selected
TOTAL TIME: 2 hours · **YIELD:** One 8×8-inch pan (about 16 bars)

Summer, precious summer! The season when life dares to slow down, flip-flops are standard-issue attire, and the sun stays up late to play. If ever there were a dessert to match the sublimity of these special months, it is these fruit crumble bars. Like summer itself, these bars are easy going and fuss free. The buttery bottom crust and crumble top are made using the same base dough, and the fruit filling works well with any stone fruit or berry. For the best flavor, pick the sweetest and ripest fruit you can find. You'll taste sweet summer in every bite.

For the Crust and Topping:

½ cup white whole wheat flour

½ cup all-purpose flour

¼ cup packed coconut sugar or light brown sugar

¼ cup granulated sugar

¼ teaspoon ground cinnamon

¼ teaspoon kosher salt

4 tablespoons unsalted butter, very cold, cut into cubes

3 tablespoons nonfat plain Greek yogurt

½ cup raw pecan halves

For the Fruit Filling:

⅓ cup honey

2 tablespoons cornstarch

Zest (about ¾ teaspoon) and 1 tablespoon juice from 1 small lemon

1½ teaspoons pure vanilla extract

½ teaspoon ground cinnamon

⅛ teaspoon ground nutmeg

2 cups peeled and thinly sliced ripe peaches (about 1 pound or 3 medium)

1 cup fresh berries of choice: whole raspberries, blueberries, or blackberries; hulled and chopped strawberries; pitted and halved cherries; or additional sliced peaches

For Serving:

Vanilla ice cream or frozen yogurt, or nonfat plain or vanilla Greek yogurt

1. Place a rack in the center of your oven and preheat the oven to 375 degrees F. Line an 8×8-inch baking pan with parchment paper, leaving an overhang on two opposite sides like handles. Lightly coat with nonstick spray. Set aside.

2. Prepare the crust: In a large bowl, whisk together the white whole wheat flour, all-purpose flour, coconut sugar, granulated sugar, cinnamon, and salt until combined. With a pastry cutter or fork, cut in the butter and Greek yogurt until the mixture is moistened and crumbly and the largest bits are the size of small peas. Some crumbs will be small and fine and others larger. Place the

mixing bowl in the refrigerator while you prepare the filling.

3. Prepare the filling: In a medium bowl, stir together the honey, cornstarch, lemon zest, lemon juice, vanilla, cinnamon, and nutmeg. Gently stir in the peaches and berries.

4. Remove the bowl with the crust mixture from the refrigerator. Scatter a generous two-thirds of it into the bottom of the prepared pan, then press into an even layer. Spoon the fruit filling and any juices that have collected at the bottom of the bowl over the

recipe continues

crust, scattering the fruit so that it is evenly distributed.

5. Roughly chop the pecans, then add them to the bowl with the remaining crust mixture. Lightly toss to combine, then scatter the mixture evenly over the top of the fruit filling. You may have some fruit peeking through.

6. Bake for 35 to 45 minutes, until the crumbs and pecans are golden and the filling is hot and bubbly. There will be some juiciness to the filling, but it should not appear watery. Check the bars periodically beginning at the 25-minute mark. If at any point the topping starts to brown more quickly than you would like, loosely tent the pan with aluminum foil and continue baking as directed. Place the pan on a cooling rack and let the bars cool completely.

7. Using the parchment paper handles, lift the cooled bars onto a cutting board. If any of the sides of the bars stick to the pan, use a small knife to loosen them. With a large, sturdy knife, slice the bars into pieces of your desired size. Serve at room temperature, or warm in the microwave. Top with ice cream, frozen yogurt, Greek yogurt, or Simple Vanilla Glaze (see Next Level) as desired.

STORAGE TIPS:
Refrigerate leftovers for up to 4 days or freeze for up to 3 months.

PRO TIPS:
• This recipe also works beautifully with frozen fruit, especially blueberries and raspberries. If using frozen peaches, strawberries, or other stone fruit, be sure the fruit was picked and frozen at the peak of its ripeness. No need to thaw it first. Simply place the fruit in a mesh sieve or colander, then lightly rinse it to break up any stuck-together pieces and remove bits of frost. Add the fruit to the recipe as directed and extend the baking time of the bars by a few minutes, until the filling is hot, bubbly, and mostly set.

• To quickly peel fresh peaches: Fill a very large pot with enough water to cover the peaches, and bring to a steady boil. Prepare an ice bath by placing several generous handfuls of ice cubes in a large bowl and then fill the bowl with cold water. With a small, sharp knife, score the bottom of the peaches with an *X*. With a slotted spoon, gently lower the peaches, as many as will fit, into the boiling water. Poach for 2 minutes (start timing as soon as the peaches are in). With the slotted spoon, remove the peaches and plunge them into the ice bath to stop their cooking. Let cool in the water 1 minute. The skins should easily slip off with your fingers. Every now and then, you'll get a stubborn peach that still won't peel and you'll have to use a paring knife to finish the job, in which case you deserve an extra crumble bar!

NEXT LEVEL:
Simple Vanilla Glaze: In a small bowl, whisk together ½ cup powdered sugar, ½ teaspoon pure vanilla extract, and 1 tablespoon milk until smoothly combined. Drizzle over the top of the cooled bars.

MARKET SWAPS:
Let these bars be your summer fruit playground. You can use any combination of stone fruit (plums, apricots, cherries) and berries (blueberries, blackberries, raspberries) you love. If using a fruit that is less sweet, such as blackberries, strawberries, or raspberries, add a little more honey to the filling.

Chocolate-Covered Strawberry Brownies

ACTIVE TIME: 30 minutes · **TOTAL TIME:** 1 hour 45 minutes

YIELD: One 8×8-inch pan (16 moderate, very fudgy brownies; or 9 larger, more dangerous brownies)

You need an outstanding brownie recipe. A foolproof, unapologetically fudgy, make-anytime, take-everywhere brownie recipe. Here it is! Shiny-topped, impressively chocolatey, and melt-in-your-mouth tender, these brownies will be your go-to. The batter comes together in just one bowl, they are ready for the oven in 15 minutes, and they will have your friends and family fighting for the final crumbs. These beauties are spectacular just as they are, without additional toppings, but when I want something extra special that will make my guests gush, I layer on thinly sliced strawberries and a glossy drizzle of dark chocolate.

For the Brownies:

6 tablespoons unsalted butter

¾ cup packed coconut sugar or light brown sugar

½ cup honey

⅔ cup unsweetened cocoa powder

½ teaspoon kosher salt

¼ teaspoon baking powder

⅛ teaspoon baking soda

2 teaspoons pure vanilla extract

⅓ cup unsweetened applesauce

2 large eggs

¼ cup white whole wheat flour

1 cup dark chocolate chips

For the Topping:

1 cup thinly sliced strawberries (about 6 ounces)

2 ounces dark chocolate, chopped, or ⅓ cup dark chocolate chips

1 teaspoon coconut oil

1. Place a rack in the lower third of your oven and preheat the oven to 350 degrees F. Lightly coat an 8×8-inch baking pan with nonstick spray. Line with parchment so that the parchment overhangs two opposite sides like handles. Coat with nonstick spray.

2. Make the brownies: In a medium saucepan (one that's large enough to hold all of the ingredients), melt together the butter and coconut sugar over low heat. Whisk to combine. The butter and sugar will be separate at first, then come together and resemble caramel as you continue to stir. Once smooth and combined, remove the pan from the heat and whisk in the honey. Return to the heat, increase the heat to medium, and continue to warm the mixture until it is smooth, 30 seconds to 1 minute. Do not let the mixture boil.

3. Remove the pan from the heat. By hand with a spatula or wooden spoon, stir in the cocoa powder, salt, baking powder, and baking soda until incorporated. Stir in the vanilla and applesauce. Add the first egg, then stir until it completely disappears. Add the second egg, then stir again until the batter is very smooth and shiny.

4. Sprinkle the flour over the top of the batter and stir until it disappears. Once the flour disappears, continue stirring for about 40 additional turns of the spatula. The batter should be glossy and smell absolutely intoxicating. Fold in the chocolate chips, then pour the batter into the prepared pan. Smooth the top.

recipe continues

5. Bake for 22 to 25 minutes, until a toothpick inserted into the center comes out mostly clean, with only a few moist crumbs (but not liquidy batter) clinging to it. Set the pan on a cooling rack and let cool completely.

6. Prepare the topping: Arrange the strawberry slices over the top of the cooled brownies. In a small microwave-safe bowl, place the chocolate chips and coconut oil. Microwave for 30 seconds. Continue to microwave in 15-second bursts, stirring often. (Alternatively, you can melt the chocolate in a small saucepan over low heat.) Stop heating the chocolate as soon as you are left with only a few small solid bits. Stir until the chocolate is smooth, letting the residual heat melt the remaining chocolate bits the rest of the way.

7. Drizzle the melted chocolate over the top of the strawberries. Let sit at room temperature while the chocolate sets, about 30 minutes, or pop the brownies into the refrigerator for quicker cooling. Using the parchment paper handles, lift the brownies onto a cutting board. Slice and enjoy!

STORAGE TIPS:
If the brownies are topped with strawberries, refrigerate leftovers for up to 3 days. If untopped, store them at room temperature for up to 1 week or freeze for up to 3 months. Thaw overnight in the refrigerator and bring to room temperature prior to serving.

NEXT LEVEL:
- *Nutty:* Fold up to ¾ cup chopped toasted walnuts or pecans into the batter with the chocolate chips.
- *Extra Fancy:* Add a drizzle of melted white chocolate over the top of the drizzled dark chocolate.
- *Intensely Chocolatey:* Add ¾ teaspoon instant espresso powder to the batter with the baking soda in step 3.

MARKET SWAPS:
- *Razzle Dazzle Brownies:* Swap the fresh strawberries for whole fresh raspberries.
- *Sea-Salt Caramel Brownies:* Omit the strawberry and melted chocolate topping. Instead, top with a generous drizzle of good-quality caramel sauce and sprinkle with flaky sea salt.

Any Way You Like It
Lemon Yogurt Pound Cake

ACTIVE TIME: 25 minutes · **TOTAL TIME:** 1 hour 35 minutes · **YIELD:** One 4½×8 ½-inch loaf (8 to 10 slices)

Effortless to make and yet undeniably chic, this easy-breezy lemon cake's strength is its understatement. With its moist texture, sturdy crumb, and subtle sweetness, it's a cake confident in its own appeal. The lemon is sunshiny without being overt, the honey is welcoming and floral, and the final drizzle of glaze will have you running your fingers across your plate to catch every last morsel.

This cake is a versatile canvas, so pull out your brush and paint it with your favorite flavor combinations. I've listed ideas for you under Market Swaps, but don't be afraid to try your own. Simple lemon is sublime, and I know you'll love it with berries, different citrus juices, and even fresh herbs, if you're feeling adventurous.

For the Lemon Cake:

½ cup coconut oil

1½ cups white whole wheat flour

2 teaspoons baking powder

½ teaspoon kosher salt

½ cup granulated sugar

2 teaspoons lemon zest (from about 2 medium lemons)

3 large eggs, at room temperature

½ cup nonfat plain Greek yogurt, at room temperature

⅓ cup honey

¼ cup freshly squeezed lemon juice (from about 1 medium lemon)

½ teaspoon pure vanilla extract

⅛ teaspoon pure almond extract

For the Glaze:

¾ cup powdered sugar, plus additional as needed

1½ tablespoons freshly squeezed lemon juice, plus additional as needed

1½ tablespoons nonfat plain Greek yogurt

¼ teaspoon pure vanilla extract

1. Make the cake: Place a rack in the center of your oven and preheat the oven to 325 degrees F. Lightly coat a 4½×8 ½-inch loaf pan with nonstick spray. In a small microwave-safe bowl, microwave the coconut oil for 30 seconds. Continue to microwave in 15-second bursts, just until melted. (Alternatively, you can melt the coconut oil in a small saucepan over medium heat.) Set aside and let cool to room temperature.

2. In a medium mixing bowl, whisk together the flour, baking powder, and salt. In a large bowl, place the sugar and lemon zest (I like to zest the lemons directly over the bowl with the sugar to capture the wonderful oils in the zest). With your fingers, rub the sugar and zest together until fragrant and the sugar is moist.

3. To the sugar mixture, add the eggs, Greek yogurt, honey, lemon juice, vanilla extract, almond extract, and melted coconut oil. Whisk until the mixture is very well blended. If the coconut oil resolidifies, microwave in 10-second bursts, just until it liquifies. If you do not have a microwave or your bowl is not microwave safe, warm the bowl over a saucepan of simmering water on the stove over medium heat. Slowly add the dry ingredients

recipe continues

PRO TIPS:
Looking to add berries? You can use fresh or frozen! If using frozen, do not thaw them first; simply break up any that have stuck together and remove large bits of frost. Frozen berries may extend the baking time by a few minutes, so don't be afraid to leave the cake in the oven for longer as needed.

to the wet ingredients, stirring very gently with a whisk or rubber spatula. As soon as the flour disappears, stop stirring.

4. Scrape the batter into the prepared pan and smooth the top. Bake for 50 to 60 minutes, until the cake is golden at the edges and a toothpick inserted into the center comes out clean. It may sink a bit at the very center, which is fine; it will still have a fabulous texture. Check on the cake a few times starting at the 30-minute mark. If at any point it starts browning more quickly than you would like (this is the honey caramelizing as it bakes), loosely tent the pan with aluminum foil and continue baking as directed.

5. Remove the cake from the oven and place the pan on a cooling rack. Let cool in the pan for 5 minutes, then run a dull knife around the edges of the cake to loosen it. Unmold the cake and place it on the rack to cool completely.

6. While the cake cools, prepare the glaze: In a small bowl, whisk together the powdered sugar, lemon juice, Greek yogurt, and vanilla. Add more powdered sugar, 1 tablespoon at a time, if you'd like the glaze thicker; or add lemon juice, 1 teaspoon at a time, if you'd like it thinner. Transfer the cooled cake to a serving plate and drizzle the glaze over the top. Let set a few minutes, then slice and enjoy.

STORAGE TIPS:
Store leftovers at room temperature for up to 5 days, or in the refrigerator for 1 week. Tightly wrap and freeze for up to 3 months. Let thaw overnight in the refrigerator. Do not thaw at room temperature or the cake may become soggy.

NEXT LEVEL:
Top individual slices with Breezy Berry Sauce (page 307), fresh berries, and whipped cream.

MARKET SWAPS:
This cake is a blank canvas for your citrusy creations! You can change out the lemon zest and juice for the same amount of a different citrus fruit to create new, fun flavor pairings. For more variety, add berries, nuts, and even herbs. Here are a few of my favorite combinations:

Lemon with:
- Chopped unsalted, raw pistachios or sliced raw almonds; sprinkle the nuts over the batter prior to baking
- 1 cup blueberries or raspberries; toss the berries with 1 tablespoon all-purpose flour, then gently fold into the batter, leaving any excess flour at the bottom of the bowl

Orange with:
- ½ cup dried cranberries; fold gently into the batter
- ⅔ cup dark chocolate chips or chunks; fold gently into the batter

Grapefruit or Lemon with:
- 3 tablespoons poppy seeds; fold gently into the batter
- 1½ teaspoons finely chopped fresh rosemary or 1 tablespoon chopped fresh mint; rub the herbs into the sugar with the citrus zest

Lime with:
- 1 cup blackberries or chopped sweet cherries; toss the fruit with 1 tablespoon all-purpose flour, then gently fold into the batter, leaving any excess flour at the bottom of the bowl
- 1 cup sweetened shredded coconut; fold gently into the batter

Zucchini Snack Cake

ACTIVE TIME: 45 minutes · **TOTAL TIME:** 1 hour 45 minutes
YIELD: One 9×13-inch sheet cake (18 to 20 slices)

Isn't "snack cake" the most wonderful term? It suggests something wholesome enough to munch for a 3-p.m. pick-me-up yet sweet enough to satisfy a late-night craving. This simple sheet cake is gratifyingly moist, lightly springy, and delicately spiced. The velvety cream cheese frosting, while not altogether mandatory, has yet to be met with anything other than unbridled enthusiasm. This cake is sturdy enough to pick up with your fingers, making it a superb choice for picnics . . . or any time you need a slice of cake in a hurry.

1 cup raw walnut or pecan halves, plus additional for topping the cake

½ cup coconut oil

2 cups shredded zucchini (no need to peel; from about 2 small–medium or 14 ounces)

2 cups white whole wheat flour

2 teaspoons baking soda

¼ teaspoon baking powder

1 teaspoon kosher salt

1 tablespoon ground cinnamon

½ teaspoon ground nutmeg

¼ teaspoon ground ginger

3 large eggs, at room temperature

⅔ cup honey

½ cup mashed ripe banana (about 1 extra large banana)

⅓ cup packed coconut sugar or light brown sugar

1 tablespoon pure vanilla extract

1 batch Greek Yogurt Cream Cheese Frosting (page 293), optional

1. Place a rack in the center of your oven and preheat the oven to 325 degrees F. Lightly coat a 9×13-inch baking pan with nonstick spray. Spread the nuts on an ungreased rimmed baking sheet and place in the oven for 8 to 12 minutes, until toasted and fragrant, tossing the nuts once halfway through. Keep a close eye on them to ensure they do not burn. Immediately transfer to a cutting board. Let cool, then roughly chop and set aside. Leave the oven heated.

2. In a small microwave-safe bowl, microwave the coconut oil for 30 seconds. Continue to microwave in 15-second bursts, just until melted. (Alternatively, you can melt the coconut oil in a small saucepan over medium heat.) Set aside and let cool to room temperature.

3. Squeeze the zucchini between several layers of paper towels or clean kitchen towels to remove as much water as possible, changing the towels as needed. Set aside.

4. In a large mixing bowl, stir together the flour, baking soda, baking powder, salt, cinnamon, nutmeg, and ginger until evenly combined. In a separate, medium bowl, whisk the eggs, honey, banana, coconut sugar, vanilla, and coconut oil. If the coconut oil resolidifies, microwave in 10-second bursts, just until it liquifies. If you do not have a microwave or your bowl is not microwave safe, warm the bowl over a saucepan of simmering water on the stove over medium heat. Stir in the shredded zucchini.

recipe continues

5. Slowly pour the zucchini mixture into the bowl with the flour mixture. By hand with a rubber spatula, fold just until the ingredients are combined and the flour disappears. The batter will seem thick and dry at first but will come together as you continue to fold. Fold in ¾ cup of the chopped nuts.

6. Pour the batter into the prepared pan and smooth the top. Bake until a toothpick inserted into the center comes out with just a few moist crumbs clinging to it, 26 to 28 minutes. Let cool in the pan completely. Spread with the cream cheese frosting, if using, and sprinkle decoratively with the additional nuts.

STORAGE TIPS:
Store leftovers in the refrigerator for 5 to 7 days or freeze (frosted or unfrosted) for up to 3 months. Let thaw overnight in the refrigerator. Serve at room temperature.

PRO TIP:
If you are using very large, later-season zucchini: Prior to grating, split the zucchini in half lengthwise and with the tip of a small spoon, scrape out the seeds.

NEXT LEVEL:
If you love an extra kick of cinnamon (me!), try blending ¼ teaspoon ground cinnamon into the cream cheese frosting prior to frosting the cake.

Chocolate Chip Coconut
Banana Bread Pudding

ACTIVE TIME: 30 minutes · **TOTAL TIME:** 1 hour 35 minutes · **YIELD:** One 8×8-inch pan (serves 6)

On the last night of our trip to Kauai, Hawaii, we stopped for dinner at a charming café where almost every table has an ocean view. It's the kind of place where, before the meal has ended, you seriously contemplate selling everything you own and moving to Hawaii, if for no other reason than to eat the restaurant's coconut banana bread pudding twice a week. When I spotted it on the menu, I nearly ordered it for an appetizer, and should you choose to make this recipe (my adaptation) for any reason, including breakfast, I support you. Sweet mashed banana and coconut milk make the interior custardy rich, the top is toasty and golden, and coconut flakes give the pudding a tropical flair. The melty chocolate chips both inside and on top of the bread pudding are my personal addition. Every bite is a taste of paradise.

1 French baguette or small, round loaf of similar artisan bread, cut into 1-inch cubes (about 12 ounces, or 8 loosely packed cups)

2 medium very ripe bananas (about 8 ounces each), plus additional banana slices for serving

1 (14-ounce) can light coconut milk

⅔ cup granulated sugar

¼ teaspoon kosher salt

6 large eggs

1 teaspoon pure vanilla extract

¾ cup sweetened shredded coconut, divided

½ cup semi-sweet or dark chocolate chips, divided

For serving: vanilla frozen yogurt or ice cream, whipped cream, or nonfat plain or vanilla Greek yogurt

1. Place a rack in the center of your oven and preheat the oven to 350 degrees F. Lightly coat an 8×8-inch baking dish or similar 2-quart casserole dish with nonstick spray and set aside.

2. If your bread is fresh and soft: Spread the bread cubes in a single layer on an ungreased rimmed baking sheet. Bake in the oven for 5 minutes, then remove from the oven and gently toss the cubes. Return the pan to the oven and continue baking until the cubes are lightly dry and slightly toasty, about 3 additional minutes. If your baguette is a day or so old and already dry, you can skip this step. Leave the oven heated.

3. In a large mixing bowl, mash the bananas (you should have a scant 1 cup). Whisk in the coconut milk, sugar, salt, eggs, and vanilla. Add the bread cubes and stir to combine. Lightly press the bread into the coconut milk mixture, then let stand 10 minutes to allow the liquid to absorb. Press the bread down once more.

4. Fold ½ cup of the shredded coconut into the bread mixture, then with the help of a large spoon, pour half of the mixture into the prepared baking pan. Prod it into an even layer, then scatter ¼ cup of the chocolate chips over the top (this will keep the chips from sinking to the bottom). Add the remaining

recipe continues

bread mixture, prodding it into an even layer once more. Scatter the remaining ¼ cup shredded coconut and ¼ cup chocolate chips over the top.

5. Bake for 35 minutes, then loosely tent the pan with aluminum foil to keep the bread from browning too quickly. Continue baking for 20 to 30 additional minutes, until the bread pudding is puffed, the top and edges are nicely golden, the coconut top is toasted, and the center is still very moist and tender but not raw or overly liquidy. Let rest 10 minutes. Slice and serve warm, topped with additional banana slices and frozen yogurt or ice cream, whipped cream, or Greek yogurt as desired.

MAKE-AHEAD & STORAGE TIPS:

To skip toasting the bread cubes in step 2, you can use bread that is already dry, or slice the bread 1 day in advance and leave the cubes sitting out overnight to dry.

Prepare through step 4 up to 1 day in advance. Cover the assembled dish tightly with plastic wrap and refrigerate. When ready to bake, let the pan stand at room temperature for 15 minutes, uncover, then bake as directed.

Store leftovers in the refrigerator for up to 4 days. Reheat gently in the microwave or place in a baking dish, cover with aluminum foil, and rewarm in a 300-degree-F oven.

NEXT LEVEL:

Scatter ½ cup toasted and chopped macadamia nuts or pecans over the first layer of bread cubes in step 4.

PRO TIP:
For an old-fashioned, homey look, trim only the bottom layer and leave the top layer's risen dome facing upward. For a more professional-looking flat top, trim both layers.

Kitchen Sink Carrot Cake

ACTIVE TIME: 45 minutes · **TOTAL TIME:** 2 hours 30 minutes
YIELD: One 9-inch, 2-layer cake (12 to 16 slices)

This carrot cake is just the right amount of everything. It has the old-timey tradition and Grandma's-house nostalgia that make carrot cake a beloved stalwart, but the varied spices, marvelous mix-ins, and wholesome additions like white whole wheat flour and Greek yogurt give it an edge you didn't realize a dessert as steadfast as carrot cake needed. It's moist without being mushy, brimming but not cluttered, and tastes like you've been slaving away on it all day, even though the batter is so forgiving you don't need the help of a mixer.

I'm of the school of carrot cake–thought that more mix-ins are merrier. You'll find this one handsomely loaded with toasted nuts, golden raisins, and cheery coconut. Each of the elements blends together to create one cohesive, perfect carrot cake experience, yet each individual bite will surprise you. In the unlikely event the cake itself doesn't keep you going back for slice after slice, the cream cheese frosting most certainly will!

2 cups raw walnut or pecan halves

⅓ cup coconut oil

2 cups white whole wheat flour

2 teaspoons baking soda

2 teaspoons ground cinnamon

½ teaspoon ground ginger

¼ teaspoon ground cloves

¼ teaspoon kosher salt

3 cups peeled and freshly shredded carrots (about 1 pound or 6 medium)

½ cup unsweetened shredded coconut

¼ cup golden raisins

4 large eggs, at room temperature

¾ cup plus 2 tablespoons nonfat plain Greek yogurt, at room temperature

¾ cup pure maple syrup

¾ cup packed coconut sugar or light brown sugar

2 teaspoons pure vanilla extract

1 to 1½ batches Greek Yogurt Cream Cheese Frosting (page 293)

1. Place a rack in the center of your oven and preheat the oven to 350 degrees F. Lightly coat two 9-inch round cake pans with nonstick spray. Spread the nuts on an ungreased rimmed baking sheet and place in the oven for 8 to 12 minutes, until toasted and fragrant, tossing the nuts once halfway through. Keep a close eye on them towards the end of their baking time to ensure they do not burn. Immediately transfer to a cutting board. Let cool, then roughly chop and set aside. Leave the oven heated.

2. In a small microwave-safe bowl, microwave the coconut oil for 30 seconds. Continue to microwave in 15-second bursts, just until melted. (Alternatively, you can melt the coconut oil in a small saucepan over medium heat.) Set aside and let cool to room temperature. In a large mixing bowl, stir together the flour, baking soda, cinnamon, ginger, cloves, and salt. Fold in the carrots, coconut, raisins, and ½ cup of the chopped nuts. Further chop the remaining nuts until they are fairly fine, and reserve them for decorating the finished cake.

3. In a second, larger mixing bowl, briskly whisk together the eggs, Greek yogurt, maple syrup, coconut sugar, vanilla, and coconut

recipe continues

oil until very smooth and no lumps remain. If the coconut oil resolidifies, microwave in 10-second bursts, just until it liquifies. If you do not have a microwave or your bowl is not microwave safe, warm the bowl over a saucepan of simmering water on the stove over medium heat.

4. Slowly and carefully add the dry ingredients to the bowl with the wet ingredients. By hand with a wooden spoon or rubber spatula, gently stir to combine, stopping as soon as the flour disappears. The batter will be very thick.

5. Pour the batter into the prepared pans, dividing the batter evenly between them. With the back of a rubber spatula or an offset spatula, smooth the tops. Bake for 24 to 28 minutes, until a toothpick inserted into the center of the layers comes out clean with just a few moist crumbs clinging to it, and the tops of the cakes spring back lightly when touched. Place the pans on a cooling rack. Let the cakes cool in the pans for 15 minutes, then unmold and place the cakes on the racks to cool completely.

6. With a large serrated knife, trim the domed portion off the top of one of the cake layers to create a flat surface. Place the cake layer on your cake plate or stand, with the trimmed side facing down. Tuck wax or parchment paper strips underneath the edges of the cake to protect the plate. If you'd like the finished cake to be flat on top, trim the second layer too.

7. Evenly cover the top of the first layer with cream cheese frosting. Place the second cake layer on top, either cut-side down (if the layer is trimmed) or domed-side up (if the layer is

not trimmed). Spread more frosting on the top, then gently spread the frosting over and down around the sides of the cake. Spread the frosting as evenly as you can and don't stress if it isn't perfect.

8. Gently press the remaining chopped nuts onto the sides of the cake. Slice generously.

MAKE-AHEAD & STORAGE TIPS:
The cake layers can be baked 1 day in advance—cool completely, then wrap tightly with plastic and store at room temperature. Frosted (or unfrosted) cake layers can be frozen for up to 2 months. Thaw overnight in the refrigerator and bring to room temperature before serving. Do not thaw at room temperature, as the cake may become soggy.

Refrigerate leftover baked, frosted cake for up to 5 days. Let stand at room temperature for at least 15 minutes prior to serving.

TO BAKE A SHEET CAKE:
Prepare the batter as directed and pour into a 9×13-inch cake pan that is lightly coated with nonstick spray. Bake at 350 degrees F for 40 to 45 minutes, until the edges of the cake are beginning to pull away from the sides of the pan, the center springs back lightly when touched (it will feel moist but shouldn't feel excessively damp or loose underneath), and a toothpick inserted into the center comes out clean. Set the pan on a cooling rack to cool completely. Spread the cream cheese frosting generously over the top and decorate with the remaining chopped nuts.

Greek Yogurt Cream Cheese Frosting

ACTIVE TIME: 15 minutes · **TOTAL TIME:** 15 minutes
YIELD: 2⅓ cups: enough to generously frost a 9×13-inch cake or 18 cupcakes; and to moderately (but adequately) frost an 8- or 9-inch 2-layer cake or 24 cupcakes

Meet the place where cake becomes a vehicle to eat frosting, no apologies or complaints. Rich, creamy, and lightly tangy, this frosting is velvety smooth and impossible to resist devouring directly from the bowl. Greek yogurt stands in for a portion of the butter, keeping this recipe lighter than its traditional counterparts. The more powdered sugar you add, the sweeter and thicker the frosting will become, so feel free to add more or less to suit your desired taste and texture. If you prefer a more heavily frosted layer cake, make one and a half times the recipe.

8 ounces reduced fat cream cheese, at room temperature

4 tablespoons unsalted butter, at room temperature

2 tablespoons nonfat plain Greek yogurt, at room temperature

½ teaspoon pure vanilla extract

⅛ teaspoon pure almond extract

⅛ teaspoon kosher salt

3 to 4 cups powdered sugar, sifted if lumpy

1. In the bowl of a standing mixer fitted with the paddle attachment or a large mixing bowl, beat together the cream cheese and butter at medium speed for 2 minutes, or until very smooth and well combined. Beat in the Greek yogurt, vanilla extract, almond extract, and salt until evenly combined. Reduce the mixer speed to low and gradually add 3 cups of the powdered sugar, increasing the speed to medium as you go. Beat for 1 to 2 minutes, until well combined.

2. If you are using the frosting for a layer cake (which benefits from a stiffer, thicker frosting) or prefer a stiffer frosting in general, slowly add the remaining 1 cup powdered sugar until the frosting reaches your desired consistency. Frost away!

MAKE-AHEAD TIPS:
Prepare and refrigerate up to 1 day in advance. The frosting will stiffen in the refrigerator, so let it stand at room temperature until it becomes spreadable, then frost to your heart's content.

Everyone's Invited Apple Crisp

ACTIVE TIME: 30 minutes · **TOTAL TIME:** 1 hour 25 minutes · **YIELD:** One 9x9-inch dish (serves 6 to 8)

Every September, my girlfriends and I spend an afternoon apple picking and picnicking at a local orchard. It's become a treasured annual tradition, as has the apple crisp that I bake with my excessively large (though never regrettable) haul afterward. A number of my friends have dietary restrictions, so I wanted to create a special apple dessert that everyone could enjoy together. This cinnamon-scented, golden-topped, and tender apple-packed crisp is free of major allergens, including gluten, dairy, soy, peanuts, and tree nuts. It's naturally sweetened with maple syrup and tastes the very essence of autumn. A surprise element of dried cranberries gives it twinkle, and orange juice adds lightness and brightness. Whether or not you have a dietary restriction of your own, this wholesome twist on a fall classic is sure to be a cherished part of your tradition too.

For the Filling:

2 pounds (4 or 5 large) crisp apples, either entirely sweet-crisp (such as Honeycrisp) or a mix of sweet-crisp and tart (such as Granny Smith)

⅓ cup dried cranberries

3 tablespoons pure maple syrup

2 tablespoons freshly squeezed orange juice

1 teaspoon pure vanilla extract

1 tablespoon cornstarch

1 teaspoon ground cinnamon

For the Topping:

¼ cup coconut oil

1½ cups old-fashioned oats

½ cup oat flour (see Pro Tips to make your own)

½ cup unsweetened shredded coconut

½ cup pure maple syrup

½ teaspoon ground cinnamon

½ teaspoon kosher salt

¼ teaspoon ground nutmeg

For Serving:

Vanilla frozen yogurt or ice cream, or plain or vanilla nonfat Greek yogurt, optional (dairy free if needed)

1. Make the filling: Place a rack in the center of your oven and preheat the oven to 350 degrees F. Peel and core the apples, then cut them into ¼-inch-thick slices. Place in a large mixing bowl (you will have about 6 cups of sliced apples).

2. Add the remaining filling ingredients: cranberries, maple syrup, orange juice, vanilla, cornstarch, and cinnamon. With a large spoon, stir to combine. Transfer to an ungreased 9×9-inch baking dish, including any juices that collect in the bottom of the bowl.

3. In a medium microwave-safe bowl, prepare the topping: Place the coconut oil in the bowl and microwave for 30 seconds. Continue

to heat in 15-second bursts, until melted. (Alternatively, you can melt the coconut oil in a medium saucepan over medium heat.) Add the oats, oat flour, coconut, maple syrup, cinnamon, salt, and nutmeg. Stir until the dry ingredients are evenly moistened. It will be sticky and irresistible. Sprinkle over the apples, spreading it as evenly as you can.

4. Bake the crisp for 50 to 60 minutes, until the filling is bubbling and the top is golden. Check at the 30-minute mark—if the top starts browning too quickly, lightly tent it with aluminum foil, then continue baking as directed. Let rest for 5 to 10 minutes. Serve warm, with any desired toppings.

MAKE-AHEAD & STORAGE TIPS:

Unbaked apple crisp can be frozen too! For apple crisp on demand, prepare the recipe through step 3, tightly cover, and freeze for up to 3 months. Allow to thaw overnight in the refrigerator. Let come to room temperature, then bake as directed in step 4.

Refrigerate leftovers for 4 to 5 days or freeze for up to 3 months. Let thaw overnight in the refrigerator, then rewarm in a 350-degree-F oven.

PRO TIPS:

- *A few important allergy notes:* To ensure this crisp is gluten free, be sure to use certified gluten free oats. Also, some brands of dried fruit, coconut, and toppings like ice cream and yogurt (even dairy free options) are processed on equipment that also processes wheat, nuts, and soy, making them unsafe for persons with food allergies. Be sure to check labels to ensure the products you use are the right fit for your needs.

- *To make your own oat flour:* Blend old-fashioned or quick-cooking oats in a food processor or blender, until they are finely ground into a flour. You will need a slightly heaping ½ cup of oats to make the ½ cup of oat flour for the crisp topping. Measure the flour after it is blended, then add to the recipe as directed.

MARKET SWAPS:

- You can use this crisp topping for any of your favorite fruit crisp fillings. In the summer, I love fresh strawberries, blueberries, or a mix (if using berries, reduce the cinnamon in the filling to ¼ teaspoon, add 1 additional teaspoon pure vanilla extract, and begin checking for doneness at the 40-minute mark). In the fall, a mix of pears and apples is surprising and sublime.

- Feel free to play around with spices. When I'm using pears or strawberries, I love swapping the nutmeg for ground ginger.

- No nut allergy to worry about? For a warm, nutty, and extra-addictive crunch, replace ½ cup of the old-fashioned oats in the topping with the same amount of roughly chopped raw pecans.

Daddy's German Chocolate Cake

ACTIVE TIME: 1 hour · **TOTAL TIME:** 2 hours 30 minutes
YIELD: One 8-inch, 2-layer cake (12 to 16 slices)

German chocolate cake was my dad's favorite. I remember my grandma baking it for him on his birthday. I sometimes wonder if, like his daughter, he'd survey the cake after blowing out the candles, quietly seeking the biggest slice. I'll never know for certain. He let my sisters and me pick our pieces first.

My father was taken from us suddenly at the age of forty-five. I'll never stop missing him, especially on his birthday. He deserved to blow out the candles, to seek the biggest slice for many more years than he was given.

This German Chocolate Cake is a love letter to my dad, and if you bake it, it will be a love letter to whomever is lucky enough to snag a slice. This is a German chocolate cake for the most discerning of chocolate cake lovers. It's deep and chocolatey, the crumb is superiorly moist and maintains a nice amount of spring, and the frosting is rich, nutty, and caramelly without being overpowering.

Ironically, this recipe took more attempts to perfect than any other in this book. I'm not sure if my dad had a role in that; he loved a challenge almost as much as his daughter still does. I am, however, absolutely certain that after trying one bite, he would *insist* on the biggest slice.

For the Frosting:

1½ cups sweetened shredded coconut

1½ cups chopped raw pecans

1 (12-ounce) can 2% evaporated milk, well shaken

2 tablespoons cornstarch

⅔ cup granulated sugar

⅓ cup packed light or dark brown sugar

3 tablespoons unsalted butter, cut into pieces

¼ teaspoon kosher salt

2 large egg yolks, at room temperature

1½ teaspoons pure vanilla extract

For the Cake:

4 ounces bittersweet chocolate, chopped

½ cup hot coffee or hot water (coffee will yield a more intense chocolate flavor)

¾ cup plus 2 tablespoons nonfat milk, at room temperature

⅓ cup nonfat plain Greek yogurt, at room temperature

¾ cup pure maple syrup

½ cup unsalted butter, at room temperature

¾ cup granulated sugar

2 large egg whites and 4 whole large eggs, at room temperature

1 teaspoon pure vanilla extract

¾ cup white whole wheat flour

¾ cup all-purpose flour

½ cup unsweetened cocoa powder

¾ teaspoon baking soda

½ teaspoon kosher salt

1. Begin with the frosting: Place a rack in the center of your oven and preheat the oven to 350 degrees F. Spread the coconut and pecans onto an ungreased rimmed baking sheet. Bake until the pecans are deeply toasted and fragrant and the coconut is lightly golden in places and smells divine, 8 to 9 minutes, tossing once or twice throughout. Check a few minutes early and don't walk away from the oven towards the end of the baking time, to

recipe continues

ensure the coconut and pecans do not burn. Immediately transfer to a medium mixing bowl. Leave the oven heated.

2. In a medium saucepan, whisk together the evaporated milk and cornstarch until smooth. Add the granulated sugar, brown sugar, butter, salt, and egg yolks. Heat the mixture slowly over medium heat until the butter melts, the mixture comes to a simmer, and the mixture thickens enough to easily and completely coat the back of a spoon, 6 to 7 minutes. Whisk very frequently at first, then whisk constantly during the last several minutes to ensure the mixture does not burn. Don't shortcut the thickening in this step. It's key to ensuring you have a smooth, spreadable, and lusciously thick frosting.

3. Remove the pan from the heat and stir in the vanilla. Pour into the bowl with the coconut and pecans and fold to combine. Let the frosting cool completely to room temperature, about 1 hour. The mixture will continue to thicken as it cools and become spreadable.

4. Make the cake: Line the bottoms of two 8-inch round baking pans with parchment paper and coat with nonstick spray. Set aside.

5. Place the chocolate in a medium heatproof mixing bowl. Pour the hot coffee over the top. Let sit 1 minute, then whisk until the chocolate is smooth and melted. Whisk in the milk and Greek yogurt, then whisk in the maple syrup. Set aside.

6. In a large, separate mixing bowl or the bowl of a stand mixer fitted with the paddle attachment, beat together the butter and sugar on medium speed until it is light and fluffy, about 2 minutes. Add the egg whites and beat

until fully incorporated. Beat in the 4 whole eggs, one at a time, fully incorporating each egg before adding the next. Beat in the vanilla.

7. In a separate bowl (the last one!), whisk together the white whole wheat flour, all-purpose flour, cocoa powder, baking soda, and salt until evenly combined.

8. With the mixer on low speed, add one-third of the dry ingredients to the egg mixture. As soon as the dry ingredients disappear, add half of the liquid chocolate mixture and beat on low speed again, just until combined. Repeat, adding the next one-third of the dry ingredients, the remaining half of the chocolate mixture, then the final third of the dry ingredients. Make sure each addition is fully incorporated before adding the next, and stop to scrape down the bowl as needed. Stop the mixer as soon as the last of the dry ingredients disappears.

9. Divide the batter evenly between the two prepared pans and smooth the tops. Bake the layers for 27 to 30 minutes, until the tops spring back lightly when touched and a toothpick inserted into the center of each comes out without any wet batter clinging to it. Place the pans on a cooling rack and run a knife around the edges of the layers to loosen them from the pans. Let cool in the pans for 10 minutes, then invert the layers onto the wire rack to finish cooling completely.

10. If the layers are domed on top, use a serrated knife to trim the top off of one so that it is flat and even (leave the second layer untrimmed). Place the trimmed layer on a cake plate or stand, trimmed-side down. Scoop half of the frosting into the center and with a knife or offset spatula, gently spread it to the edges, leaving a scant ½-inch border unfrosted all the way around (the sides of the cake will be left bare). Place the second cake layer on top, with its domed side up. Spread the remaining frosting in an even layer on top. If it will be more than 1 hour before you serve the cake, place it in the refrigerator. Remove from the refrigerator 30 minutes to 1 hour prior to serving, to allow the cake to come to near room temperature. Slice and enjoy.

MAKE-AHEAD & STORAGE TIPS:
The frosting can be prepared and refrigerated up to 1 day in advance. It will become too stiff to spread, so before using, rewarm it very slowly and gently in the microwave (or in a heatproof bowl set over a pan of simmering water), stirring often, and stopping as soon as it is loose enough to spread easily.

The cake layers can be baked up to 1 day in advance. Once completely cool, wrap them tightly in plastic and refrigerate.

Refrigerate the frosted, assembled cake for up to 5 days.

Dreamy Chocolate Mousse

ACTIVE TIME: 15 minutes · **TOTAL TIME:** 1 hour 25 minutes · **YIELD:** 2 cups (serves 4)

Classic chocolate mousse is wonderful. It's also finicky, labor intensive, creates an apocalyptic mess, and its unabashedly indulgent ingredient list reserves it to special occasions. Since I'm as likely to crave chocolate mousse on a Tuesday as I am on a fancy night out, I created this Dreamy Chocolate Mousse that we can enjoy as often as we please. The entire recipe comes together in your blender, no delicate egg white–whipping or chocolate tempering required. Instead of heavy cream and butter, this mousse's fabulously rich, silky texture comes from tofu and chia seeds. I know it sounds odd, but by the time you've added melted chocolate and a lavish pour of vanilla extract, the only thing you'll be wondering is how to stop yourself from devouring the entire batch before it reaches the serving bowl.

¼ cup unsweetened almond milk or milk of choice

3 tablespoons chia seeds

8 ounces good-quality dark (55% to 65%) chocolate, roughly chopped

12 ounces silken or soft tofu (do not use firm, extra firm, or any other kind besides these two)

1 tablespoon unsweetened cocoa powder, plus additional to taste

2 teaspoons pure maple syrup, plus additional to taste

1 teaspoon pure vanilla extract

⅛ teaspoon kosher salt

For serving (optional): whipped cream or whipped coconut cream; sliced berries, sweet cherries, and/or banana slices; chocolate shavings or mini chocolate chips

1. In a small bowl or liquid measuring cup, stir together the almond milk and chia seeds. Set aside for 20 minutes to jell while you prepare the rest of the recipe.

2. Place the chocolate in a medium microwave-safe bowl. Microwave for 30 seconds. Stir, then continue melting in 15-second bursts, stirring in between. Stop when the chocolate is nearly melted but a few small bits remain. Remove from the microwave and stir, letting the residual heat melt the chocolate the rest of the way. Set aside to cool slightly. (Alternatively, you can melt the chocolate in a heatproof bowl set over a pan of gently simmering water. Do not let the water touch the bottom of the bowl.)

3. Place the tofu in a blender and puree until very smooth, stopping to scrape down the blender as needed. Add the cocoa powder, maple syrup, vanilla, and salt and blend again. Once the chia has jelled, add it to the blender, along with the melted chocolate. Blend until smooth and creamy, stopping to scrape down the blender as needed. This may take several minutes, depending upon your blender.

4. Taste the mousse. If you'd like a stronger chocolate flavor, add more cocoa powder, 1 teaspoon at a time (a little goes a long way). If you'd like it sweeter, add additional maple syrup, 1 teaspoon at a time. When it tastes to your liking, transfer the mousse to an airtight container or individual serving dishes. Chill

recipe continues

in the refrigerator for at least 1 hour prior to serving. At 1 hour, the mousse will have a thick, pudding-like consistency; at 2 hours or more, it will be firmer, similar to the center of a truffle. Enjoy cold, topped with whipped cream, fruit, and chocolate shavings as desired.

302

STORAGE TIPS:

Refrigerate leftovers, covered, for up to 4 days. If you'd like the mousse to have a softer, more pudding-like consistency after it has been refrigerated for longer than 2 hours, let it stand at room temperature prior to serving.

PRO TIPS:

• The quality of chocolate you buy truly makes this recipe shine. Use the best you can afford and enjoy every luscious bite.

• Silken tofu is often sold in shelf-stable packets. Look for it in the Asian food section of your grocery store or in the refrigerator section with other meat-alternative products.

NEXT LEVEL:

• *Chocolate Peanut Butter Banana Graham Parfaits:* Blend 1 to 2 tablespoons creamy peanut butter into the mousse with the melted chocolate. Layer with banana slices, crushed graham cracker crumbs, and whipped cream.

• *Mexican Chocolate Mousse:* Add ¼ teaspoon cinnamon and a pinch of cayenne pepper.

• *Somethin' Somethin' Chocolate Mousse:* Blend in a splash of Grand Marnier, Irish cream liqueur, Chambord (black raspberry liqueur), or whiskey.

• *Strawberry Pretzel Parfaits:* Layer the mousse with crushed pretzels and sliced fresh strawberries. Top with whipped cream.

• *Double Chocolate Raspberry Dream:* Layer the mousse with mini semi-sweet chocolate chips, white chocolate chips, and fresh raspberries. This is especially tasty with the Somethin' Somethin' Chocolate Mousse variation, made with Chambord.

Vanilla Ricotta Cheesecake
with Breezy Berry Sauce

ACTIVE TIME: 30 minutes · **TOTAL TIME:** 9 hours · **YIELD:** One 9-inch cheesecake (about 10 slices)

Don't let the angelic look of this cheesecake fool you—it's a rebel. It flies in the face of standard cheesecake recipes that demand meticulous attention to detail. Say good-bye to precise cream-cheese beating, multiple dirty mixing bowls, and the water bath. This entire recipe is made in your food processor, and the result is the most ethereally light, fluffy cheesecake you will ever taste.

In place of the bricks of cream cheese used in American cheesecakes, this recipe takes a note from the Italians and uses ricotta instead. The result is a smooth, balanced, and luscious cheesecake that pleases in every way. It's cloud-like yet creamy, delicately sweet but not cloying, and its soft kisses of lemon and almond make it anything but ho-hum. My final break with cheesecake tradition is to replace the standard butter-based crust with ground almonds. Rebellious? Maybe, but after you taste how spectacularly the nuts pair with the ricotta filling, you'll embrace the rule-bending too.

2 pounds part-skim ricotta cheese

1 cup raw whole almonds

1 cup plus 2 tablespoons granulated sugar, divided

⅓ cup all-purpose flour

¼ teaspoon kosher salt

6 large eggs, at room temperature

1 teaspoon lemon zest (from about 1 medium lemon)

1½ tablespoons pure vanilla extract

¼ teaspoon pure almond extract

For serving: Breezy Berry Sauce (page 307), fresh berries, whipped cream

1. Place the ricotta in a mesh sieve set over a large bowl. Let drain for 2 hours at room temperature or overnight in the refrigerator. If refrigerating overnight, remove the ricotta from the refrigerator at least 1 hour before you plan to bake, to allow it to come to room temperature.

2. Place a rack in the center of your oven and preheat the oven to 350 degrees F. Coat a 9-inch springform pan with nonstick spray. Spread the almonds in a single layer on an ungreased rimmed baking sheet and place in the oven for 8 to 12 minutes, until toasted and fragrant, tossing the nuts once halfway through. Keep a close eye on them towards the end of their baking time to ensure they do not burn. Immediately transfer the nuts to the bowl of a food processor fitted with a steel blade. Let cool a few minutes. Reduce the oven temperature to 325 degrees F.

3. Add 2 tablespoons of the sugar to the food processor with the almonds. Pulse in 5-second bursts, until the nuts are finely ground. Stop before the almonds grind all the way into nut butter. Scatter the mixture evenly over the bottom of the prepared pan. With the bottom of a drinking glass or a dry measuring cup, press the mixture firmly and evenly along the

recipe continues

bottom and ¼ inch up the sides of the pan to form a crust. Set aside.

4. With a damp towel, carefully wipe the food processor bowl and blade clean. Refit the bowl with the blade, then add the strained ricotta cheese. Pulse for 3 short bursts. Add the remaining 1 cup sugar. Blend until smooth, about 1 minute. Sprinkle the flour and salt over the top, then blend again just until the flour is incorporated. Add the eggs 1 at a time, blending between each and stopping the food processor as soon as the egg disappears. Add the lemon zest, vanilla extract, and almond extract, then blend again just until combined. Do not overmix.

5. Carefully pour the ricotta batter into the pan and smooth the top. Bake the cheesecake for 50 to 60 minutes, until it is clearly set at the edges but the center still has a slight jiggle. Turn off the oven and open the oven door halfway. Let the cheesecake cool in the oven for 30 minutes, then gently place the pan on a cooling rack and run a hot knife around the cheesecake edges to loosen it from the pan. Leave the pan on the rack and continue cooling completely to room temperature, about 1 additional hour. Cover the pan and refrigerate for at least 6 hours, or overnight. Slowly unmold the sides of the pan and lift them away from the cake, leaving the pan's bottom in place (slice and serve the cake from the pan's bottom). Top the entire cheesecake with sauce, berries, and whipped cream, or slice and then top the individual pieces, depending upon your preference. Congratulate yourself on your cheesecake prowess.

STORAGE TIPS:
Refrigerate leftover baked cheesecake for up to 3 days or freeze for up to 2 months. Let thaw overnight in the refrigerator.

PRO TIPS:
• Avoid the dreaded cheesecake crack: Make sure all of your ingredients are at room temperature before you begin, don't overmix the batter in the food processor, and above all, don't rush the cooling process.

• Try it all and your cheesecake STILL cracks? Fear not! It will taste just as delicious. If you are worried about the presentation, hide the crack with a lovely topping of fresh fruit or whipped cream.

NEXT LEVEL:
• For an elevated vanilla flavor, replace the vanilla extract with vanilla bean seeds scraped from 2 whole vanilla bean pods. Split the pods lengthwise and use a knife to scrape the seeds from the insides. As a bonus, the seeds add pretty speckles to the cheesecake too.

• *Cannoli Cheesecake:* Once the cheesecake has cooled to room temperature, sprinkle the top generously with mini chocolate chips, then refrigerate as directed.

Breezy Berry Sauce

ACTIVE TIME: 20 minutes · **TOTAL TIME:** 30 minutes · **YIELD:** 1 cup

Just the thing to top your cheesecake. And yogurt. And oatmeal. And eat out of the jar with a spoon when no one else is watching.

---

2 cups fresh or frozen mixed berries, any kind you like (I love a mix of blueberries, with blackberries or raspberries)

⅓ cup water

2 to 4 tablespoons honey

2 tablespoons freshly squeezed lemon juice (from about ½ medium lemon)

1 teaspoon pure vanilla extract

---

1. In a small saucepan over medium-low heat, combine the berries, water, 2 tablespoons of the honey, and the lemon juice. Bring to a gentle simmer. Let cook until the berries have softened, 5 to 10 minutes, depending upon if they are fresh or frozen.

2. Remove from the heat, stir in the vanilla extract, and let cool 10 minutes. Taste and add additional honey if you would like the sauce to be sweeter. If your sauce is chunky and you prefer it smooth, carefully transfer it to a blender. Puree until smooth, tasting again and adjusting the sweetness as desired. Strain the sauce through a fine-mesh sieve set over a bowl, using the back of a spoon to press it through if it is particularly seedy or stubborn. Use immediately or transfer to a small jar or similar airtight container and refrigerate.

STORAGE TIPS:
Refrigerate leftover sauce for up to 1 week or freeze for up to 3 months.

PRO TIP:
This sauce yields plenty to serve with the Vanilla Ricotta Cheesecake (page 303), but it's also easy to double. Feel free to multiply if you have a house of serious sauce lovers, a large supply of berries in need of a tasty purpose, or want extra to enjoy as you please.

MARKET SWAPS:
For a different citrus twist, swap the lemon juice for orange juice. To up the citrus factor, zest your desired amount of lemon or orange zest directly into the finished sauce, then stir to combine.

HELPFUL RECIPE LISTS

Great for Leftovers

Sweets 'n' Beets Hash with Avocado, *page 23*

Freezer Breakfast Sandwiches, *page 28*

Cheesy Southwest Breakfast Casserole, *page 32*

Clean Out the Pantry No-Bake Granola Bars, *page 48*

Santa Fe Grilled Chicken Salad, *page 91*

Summer Celebration Orzo Salad, *page 97*

Balsamic Farro Salad with Edamame and Cranberries, *page 103*

Modern Macaroni Salad, *page 104*

Picnic Slaw, *page 107*

Killer Kale Salad (3 Ways!), *page 112*

Shaved Brussels Sprouts Salad, *page 115*

Thai Peanut Chicken Stir-Fry, *page 122*

Kickin' Black Pepper Pork Stir-Fry, *page 125*

Instant Pot Jambalaya, *page 127*

Instant Pot Spring Green Farro Risotto, *page 137*

Italian Turkey Sausage Skillet with Farro, Greens, and Beans, *page 139*

One Pot Creamy Sun-Dried Tomato Orzo with Spinach, *page 145*

Asian Noodle Salad with Spicy Peanut Dressing, *page 155*

Lemon Chicken Pasta Salad with Tarragon and Grapes, *page 159*

Quick Chickpea Pasta, *page 163*

Butternut Squash, Chicken, and Wild Rice Casserole, *page 164*

Grammy's Green Chile Chicken Enchiladas, *page 173*

Ultimate Creamy Mac and Cheese (4 Ways!), *page 186*

Slow Cooker Hearty Turkey Bolognese, *page 192*

Spaghetti Pie, *page 194*

Portobello Philly Melts, *page 204*

On-Purpose Veggie Burgers with Roasted Red Pepper Sauce, *page 214*

Slow Cooker Crispy Pineapple Pork Carnitas, *page 217*

Asian Lettuce Wraps, *page 220*

All of the soups!, *starting on page 227*

Tex-Mex Fiesta

Cheesy Southwest Breakfast Casserole, *page 32*

Cowboy Caviar, *page 76*

Melon Margaritas, *page 63*

Taco Stuffed Mini Peppers, *page 79*

Santa Fe Grilled Chicken Salad, *page 91*

Baked Avocado Chicken Taquitos, *page 160*

Grammy's Green Chile Chicken Enchiladas, *page 173*

Steak Fajita 'Dillas, *page 207*

Slow Cooker Crispy Pineapple Pork Carnitas, *page 217*

Instant Pot Confetti Rice and Beans, *page 258*

Picnic and Potluck Favorites

Clean Out the Pantry No-Bake Granola Bars, *page 48*

Cowboy Caviar, *page 76*

Cocoa Loco Roasted Nuts, *page 73*

Summer Celebration Orzo Salad, *page 97*

Balsamic Farro Salad with Edamame and Cranberries, *page 103*

Modern Macaroni Salad, *page 104*

Picnic Slaw, *page 107*

Killer Kale Salad (3 Ways!), *page 112*

Shaved Brussels Sprouts Salad, *page 115*

Asian Noodle Salad with Spicy Peanut Dressing, *page 155*

Lemon Chicken Pasta Salad with Tarragon and Grapes, *page 159*

Rosemary Cheddar Cornbread, *page 246*

Lemony Sautéed Summer Squash and Chickpeas, *page 252*

Golden Carrots and Farro, *page 261*

The Very Best Oatmeal Chocolate Chip Cookies, *page 273*

Double Trouble Fudge Cookies, *page 270*

Sweet Summer Fruit Crumble Bars, *page 275*

Zucchini Snack Cake, *page 284*

30(ish)-Minute Dinners

One-Pan Meals

Meatless Mains

Slow Cooker and Instant Pot

SUGGESTED MENUS

Comfort Food Dinner

Ultimate Creamy Mac and Cheese (4 Ways!), *page 186*

Classic Salt and Pepper Every-Night Roasted Vegetables, *page 262*

Chocolate Chip Coconut Banana Bread Pudding, *page 287*

Back to School Dinner

Caprese Chicken Skillet, *page 133*

Parmesan and Herb Every-Night Roasted Vegetables, *page 265*

The Very Best Oatmeal Chocolate Chip Cookies, *page 273*

Birthday Bash

Warm Antipasti Dip, *page 65*

Slow Cooker Hearty Turkey Bolognese, *page 192*

Daddy's German Chocolate Cake, *page 297*

Dinner to Wow the Crowd

Honey Roasted Grape Crostini, *page 70*

Raymonde's Moroccan Lemon Chicken, *page 152*

Vanilla Ricotta Cheesecake
with Breezy Berry Sauce, *page 303*

Dinner with Friends

Caramelized Onion Bacon Dip, *page 68*

Slow Cooker Crispy Pineapple Pork Carnitas, *page 217*

Chocolate-Covered Strawberry Brownies, *page 279*

Marvelously Meatlesss

One Pot Creamy Sun-Dried Tomato Orzo with Spinach, *page 145*

Lemony Sautéed Summer Squash and Chickpeas, *page 252*

Kitchen Sink Carrot Cake, *page 291*

Summer BBQ

Picnic Slaw, *page 107*

Buffalo Chicken Burgers with Blue Cheese Sauce, *page 212*

Zucchini Snack Cake, *page 284*

Date Night In

Shaved Brussels Sprouts Salad, *page 115*

Almond-Crusted Trout with Lemon-Butter Caper Sauce, *page 167*

Dreamy Chocolate Mousse, *page 300*

Game Day

Rosemary Cheddar Cornbread, *page 246*

Blue Ribbon Chili, *page 228*

Double Trouble Fudge Cookies, *page 270*

Last-Minute Dinner Guests

5-Ingredient Maple Dijon Salmon, *page 148*

Garlicky Sautéed Kale with Almonds, *page 257*

Any Way You Like It Lemon Yogurt Pound Cake, *page 281*

Lazy Weekend Brunch

Girls' Night Sangria, *page 60*

Fruit and Honey Scones, *page 20*

Cheesy Southwest Breakfast Casserole, *page 32*

Holiday Soiree

Slow Cooker Apricot-Glazed Pork and Vegetables, *page 181*

Brown Butter Mashed Sweet Potatoes, *page 250*

Everyone's Invited Apple Crisp, *page 294*

ACKNOWLEDGMENTS

To my readers: Your enthusiasm and support for this book and my blog as a whole give my life richness and meaning. Because of you, my passion and my career are one in the same. This book is for you. I hope every page lights up your kitchen and makes your life easier too.

To Maggie Ensing, for standing beside me in the kitchen through countless hours of recipe testing. I am blessed to have you as a sounding board, sanity keeper, and shining example of what it means to be a friend. Your intuition (both in the kitchen and regarding my mental state at any given moment) is invaluable.

To Becky Hardin: Thank you for the passion, creativity, and calm energy you poured into this project (and for letting me take over your kitchen and home in the process). You made these recipes look more beautiful than I dared to dream. You are wildly talented, and I am blessed to call you a coworker and a friend.

To my editor, Lucia Watson, for loving this book from the beginning and for guiding it to become the rich, well-rounded resource I so passionately believed it to be. To my incredible team at Avery—Ashley Tucker, Suzy Swartz, Farin Schlussel, Megan Newman, Lindsay Gordon, Anne Kosmoski, Sara Johnson, Alyssa Adler, Carla Iannone, Erica Rose, and Justin Thrift: I'm so happy my book found a home with you.

To my agent, Janis Donnaud: You are simply the best. Choosing to work with you has been one of the best decisions of my career.

To my sisters, Elizabeth and Elaine, for tirelessly testing recipes, for supporting me while I lived and breathed this book for three years, and for being my cheerleaders and best friends.

To Susie Gall, Rachel Gurk, and Courtney Minor: Cooking fifty recipes per week with me every week that we photographed for this book was an exhausting task. Your nonstop energy, attention to detail, and upbeat attitude made this achievement both possible and fun.

To Meghan Larsen-Reidy, Erin Hunter and Bryan Bennett, Lindsay Johnson, Kathryn and Reed Parker, Amy Medlock, Heather and Tyler Cooksey, Aubrey and Dan Russo, Rachel Hochstetler, and all of the other wonderful friends and family who tested these recipes: This book is better because of you.

To Melissa Moody: Thank you for letting me invade your home with my many dishes and props. Erika Aldag, Emily Volz, and Maggie, thanks for joining the fun.

To Caitlin Fultz: Thank you for your constant encouragement throughout this process and for your innate sense of when I needed a reminder, an honest opinion, or a bar of chocolate.

To Taylor Teppen, for your unfailing positive attitude and for so enthusiastically supporting the launch of this book.

To Shannon Dickson, Laura Graff, and Elisabeth Sullivan: When I told you I was going to write a cookbook all those years ago, instead of telling me I was crazy, you told me you believed in me. Thank you for holding me in your hearts at every step.

To Kate and Conor Kelly and Mary and Garrett Mandeville, the vets of "Well Plated Tapas": Thank you for enduring my unending supply of leftovers, offering valuable feedback, and meaning it when you ask me how I'm doing.

To Grammy and Grandma: My love of the kitchen began in yours. I am forever grateful.

To Paul, Danielle, and Maria: Thank you for loving me like a daughter and a sister and for being living reminders of the value of hard work, honesty, and making time for the people you love.

To Mom and Daddy, I would not be who I am without your love. Thank you for supporting me even when you disagreed, for teaching me that no great achievement comes without great effort, and for ending every phone call with "I love you." Mom, thanks for telling every single person who will listen about my blog and book. Daddy, I miss you every day. It brings me immense comfort and tender happiness to think I am making you proud.

To Ben: My first and biggest fan. Your patience, sense of humor, practicality, infinite support, and inexhaustible dishwashing enabled me to dream, sweat, test, perfect, and ultimately bring not only this book into existence but also my blog as a whole. You now have my blessing to order the delivery pizza I know you've been craving instead of our (copious) leftovers. Love you more.

Index

Note: Page numbers in *italics* indicate photos separate from recipes.

ERIN CLARKE is the creator of the incredibly popular recipe blog *Well Plated by Erin*. She has established herself as *the* go-to resource for nourishing yet delicious meals that are fast and easy enough for any weeknight, special enough for a date night, and comforting enough to earn picky-eater approval. She is an active runner and a healthy-living enthusiast, and has a habit of showing up unannounced on friends' doorsteps with a pan of enchiladas in one hand and a pitcher of sangria in the other.

wellplated.com • **f** wellplated • **◯** wellplated • **�p** wellplated